The Crisis over

British Intervention

in the Civil War

UNION
IN PERIL

HOWARD JONES

University of Nebraska Press

Lincoln and London

© 1992 by the University of North Carolina Press
All rights reserved
Manufactured in the United States of America

⊗ The paper in this book meets the minimum requirements of American National Standard for Information Sciences—Permanence of Paper for Printed Library Materials, ANSI Z39.48-1984.

First Bison Books printing: 1997
Most recent printing indicated by the last digit below:
10 9 8 7 6 5 4 3 2 1

Library of Congress Cataloging-in-Publication Data
Jones, Howard, 1940–
Union in peril: the crisis over British intervention in the Civil War / Howard Jones.
p. cm.
Originally published: Chapel Hill: University of North Carolina Press, 1992.
Includes bibliographical references (p.   ) and index.
ISBN 0-8032-7597-8 (pbk.: alk. paper)
1. United States—Foreign relations—1861–1865. 2. Confederate States of America—Foreign relations. 3. United States—Foreign relations—Great Britain. 4. Great Britain—Foreign relations—United States. I. Title.
E469.J57 1997
973.7'21—dc21
96-49131 CIP

Reprinted from the original 1992 edition by the University of North Carolina Press, Chapel Hill.

FOR HOWIE AND TIMOTHY

CONTENTS

ILLUSTRATIONS

ACKNOWLEDGMENTS

Numerous friends and acquaintances have made this work a pleasurable experience. As has been the case several times, my friend and colleague Forrest McDonald read the manuscript first, offering many useful suggestions along with continuous encouragement throughout the course of this project. Lawrence F. Kohl gave the work a careful reading, sharply disagreeing with many of my conclusions and forcing me to rethink or bring more focus to my arguments. Longtime friend and candid critic Pete Maslowski again brought his skeptical eye to the manuscript, challenging me to reassess my ideas and clarify their expression. Constitutional specialist Maurice G. Baxter once more guided me through the legal labyrinth, making sure that my arguments were crisp and accurate. Robert E. May brought his deep knowledge of Southern history to the manuscript, giving it an intensive reading and making numerous recommendations for improvement while extending the warmest encouragement that can come only from a friend. Tony A. Freyer discussed many aspects of the work as it progressed, sharing his extensive knowledge of constitutional law and exhorting me always to place the story within the grand perspective of history.

Frank J. Merli, fellow wanderer in the maze of events that constitutes the diplomacy of the Civil War, joins me in believing that the international dimension of this period in history has not received its proper emphasis. For his encouraging and penetrating counsel, his willingness to share his broad and thorough knowledge of the sources, and his eagerness to give my manuscript a far more careful reading than anyone could expect, I express my sincere appreciation along with a fond hope that the final product meets the standards for scholarship set for both of us some years ago by our mentor and friend Robert H. Ferrell.

A special thanks goes to Kenneth Bourne of the London School of Economics and Political Science, who honored a commitment made over dinner in Tuscaloosa—to read my manuscript once completed. Thus the work received a careful assessment not only from the British perspective but from a renowned scholar of Anglo-American relations and the chief biographer of Lord

Palmerston. I hope this book exemplifies the fairness in judgment that he so fervently emphasized.

Others made vital contributions. The archivists and staffs of several research depositories proved enormously helpful: those of the Library of Congress and National Archives in Washington, D.C., and of the British Library and Public Record Office in England; C. M. Woolgar, archivist of the Library of the University of Southampton in England; Gwyn Jenkins, assistant keeper of the Department of Manuscripts and Records, the National Library of Wales in Aberystwyth; Guy R. Swanson of the Museum of the Confederacy; Chris Steele of the Massachusetts Historical Society; and those associated with the Interlibrary Loan Service of the University of Alabama. I also wish to thank the Trustees of the Broadlands Archives for permission to use the Palmerston Papers. In addition, the Earhart Foundation in Ann Arbor, Michigan, again demonstrated its commitment to research, this time twice awarding generous grants that permitted me to devote two summers of uninterrupted work to the project. Edward P. Crapol and Norman Ferris read the manuscript for the publisher and made valuable recommendations that found their way into the work. Trudie Calvert again provided excellent editorial advice during the final stages of the manuscript's preparation. All those associated with the University of North Carolina Press—particularly Lewis Bateman and Ron Maner—proved helpful, encouraging, and highly professional. Last, I want to thank Matthew Hodgson, director of the press, for expressing interest in the project during its early stages and encouraging me to publish with him again.

I was particularly fortunate that Gabor S. Boritt, Robert C. Fluhrer Professor of Civil War Studies at Gettysburg College, invited me to present my research to his class. What better place to explore ideas on this period than before a seminar in Civil War history at Gettysburg College?

A writer's family always contributes more to a book than can adequately be expressed. My parents remain close and interested supporters, always inquiring about the progress of my work while repeatedly asking about my next project. My daughters, Deborah and Shari, along with their husbands, Chuck and Tim, maintain a steady interest in my work even while pursuing their own concerns. Out of the continued growth of family has come my grandson Timothy, who has brought more excitement and inspiration into all our lives than he or his mother, Shari, can ever know. Finally, to my closest confidante and warmest friend, Mary Ann, I again extend my appreciation for doing everything possible to provide an atmosphere conducive to research and writing while making our marriage the source of everything good that has happened to me.

Any work, of course, must stand on its own, and every author must bear ultimate responsibility for the final verdict of readers. For any good qualities that this book might have, I readily share in attribution with all those included above. The errors or shortcomings are my own creation.

Tuscaloosa, Alabama   Howard Jones
Spring 1992

Union in Peril

*[England's recognition of the
Confederacy as belligerents] raised
them in regard to the prosecution of
an unlawful armed insurrection to
an equality with the United States.*

—William H. Seward, 1866

*Less than justice was rendered to the
Confederacy by "neutral" Europe.*

—Jefferson Davis, 1881

Introduction

In late 1862, the government of Great Britain debated the possibility of masterminding a European intervention in the American Civil War. Historians have not adequately explained why that intervention never occurred, though there is substantial agreement that a European involvement in the war would have had momentous consequences for the North, the South, and the European powers. American readers, in particular, have little understanding of the important international repercussions of Fort Sumter. Indeed, the focus on America's domestic problems after April 1861 has distorted the history of this era by diminishing the crucial role of diplomacy. The Lincoln administration's greatest fear in foreign affairs was that England would extend diplomatic recognition to the Confederacy. If the British announced recognition, the Union's minister in England was to suspend his functions as a diplomat, thereby setting the two Atlantic nations on a path that could lead to war. Though some writers have claimed

I

that the Union's fear was more imagined than real during the first eighteen months of the war, they cannot deny that by mid-1862 the Palmerston ministry in London had moved close to an intervention that doubtless would have led to recognition and a third Anglo-American war. The search for answers to why the British did not intervene in the Civil War provides the substance of this book.

THE AMERICAN CIVIL WAR not only caused profound domestic difficulties, but it also raised perplexing international issues that could not be resolved amicably. Though a great body of international law existed by the mid-nineteenth century, it included no effective guidelines for controlling events in America. International law remained amorphous, open to varying interpretations and enforceable only by the nation with the power to do so. The complexities of the Civil War ultimately led to its assuming a dual status in the minds of Union leaders. On one hand, most Northerners refused to call the conflict a war because that term suggested the South's existence as an entity dangerously close to the status of a nation. The conflict was therefore domestic—an insurrection or armed uprising led by traitors whose fate depended solely upon the constitutional right of the governing body in Washington to put it down. On the other hand, President Abraham Lincoln termed the conflict a rebellion, which suggested a more highly organized effort and, according to international law, bestowed belligerent status in the South and implied that it had resorted to war to win freedom from the parent state. Lincoln therefore intended to force the South into submission by using his military powers as commander in chief, which included the installation of a blockade. But a blockade implied the existence of war, which was public in nature and required other nations either to take sides or declare neutrality. When first England and then France chose the latter course, their justifiable and well-intentioned decisions aroused deep animosities within the Union. The explanation was simple: a declaration of neutrality automatically conferred legitimacy on the South as a belligerent, which the North regarded as the first step toward diplomatic recognition of Confederate independence.

The Union's chief concern in foreign affairs was to prevent

British recognition of the South that would encourage France and other nations on the Continent to follow suit. Recognition of the Confederacy would deal the Union cause a devastating moral blow, for by justifying secession it would undermine the Constitution. Southern morale would soar, for recognition would encourage financial investment at home as well as loans from abroad, assure foreign challenges to the Union blockade as neutrals tried to maintain trade with the South, and perhaps lead to a military alliance that would facilitate permanent disunion. Even though the Confederate government never seemed to understand the importance of tying foreign military assistance to its move for independence, its call for recognition as an act of justice shook the foundations of the American republic. The Lincoln administration had to block foreign intervention even at the risk of threatening war with England.[1]

The intent of English neutrality was to avoid war while continuing to trade with both North and South. England's strategic positions in Canada and the West Indies, along with its growing commercial interests in the Atlantic, assured trouble. From the beginning of the American conflict, the London government expressed concern over the Union's dissolution, regardless of the legality of secession. Lord Palmerston, England's pragmatic and realistic prime minister, expressed the sentiment of many in his country by insisting that Southern separation was a fait accompli and that the North should admit as much. Lord John Russell, England's diminutive but headstrong foreign secretary, agonized over the trial of the Union and its harmful economic effect on England and concluded that Southern independence was a fair price to pay for peace. But the North's rigid opposition to a breakup of the Union made England hesitant to do anything that might seem to condone secession. Initially, the British hoped that North and South would mend their differences short of war. After the fighting broke out at Fort Sumter, the British preferred that the Americans settle their differences on the battlefield. Throughout the ordeal, the ministry thought neutrality the only satisfactory course.[2]

Evidence demonstrates that Palmerston's government lacked a clear understanding of American events and that when it moved close to intervention, it could not devise a viable solution. British observers did not comprehend the principles that led to the war and the resolve that perpetuated it. Further confusion arose from the denial by both North and South that their conflict arose from slavery. Instead, the North declared its intention to maintain the Union and the South demanded independence from an oppressive North. Foreign intervention would have further complicated an already complicated set of events. Indeed, British intervention would probably have led to an Anglo-American war. Secretary of State William H. Seward repeatedly emphasized this danger, and more than a few times England's mercurial interest in intervention abated, especially as the Union bounced back after battlefield losses with greater resolve and ever-increasing military and naval strength. But the potential for intervention remained high until late 1862. From the Union's perspective, the explanation for the troubles with England was clear. The Palmerston ministry wrongfully assumed from the beginning of the conflict that North and South could never be reunited and based British policy on this assumption throughout the intervention crisis.

For humanitarian as well as economic reasons, Russell joined Chancellor of the Exchequer William E. Gladstone and others in declaring that the war had to end with Southern independence. Whether these British spokesmen believed their own humanitarian pronouncements is difficult to determine, but they lived in the Victorian Age in England, when expressions of concern for others—including Americans on both sides of the conflict—were not uncommon from all levels of British society. But, the American war inflicted great economic hardships on England, and it was in its self-interest for the fighting to end as quickly as possible. Whatever their priority, British observers of the war decided that their country would profit most from peace in America. But their most reasoned solution—a Southern separation—never became acceptable to the North.

Advocates of Southern independence as a solution to the war failed to take into account the North's determination to maintain the Union at all cost. The concept of the Union had taken on a mystical intensity in the North, causing ever more fervent resolution despite adversity on the battlefield. The British never grasped the magnitude of Northerners' devotion to the Union and could only define the fighting in America as a meaningless bloodbath—in the words of more than one English observer a "horrible war." Yet even though the British government never could formulate practical solutions to the American troubles, it had always been interested in mediating the dispute, particularly after a former American minister to London, Edward Everett, urged that it do so. In early February 1861, before the fighting broke out, Everett could not hide his despair when he presented the British minister in Washington, Lord Lyons, with a long petition from Boston calling for a joint mediation by England, France, and Russia. Surely, Everett surmised, these same European powers would offer mediation on the Continent if civil strife developed in a neighboring country. Lyons, however, pointed out two important differences: Europe was of the "same political family," and the United States had always opposed European interference in the New World. Would not foreign mediation enrage the American people, both North and South? He hesitated to recommend mediation "*unasked*." Nonplussed, Everett allowed that intervention would upset Americans, but he thought a Great Power declaration would deflate the South's hopes by undermining its chances for foreign assistance. He had already "hinted something of the kind" to Russia's minister in Washington, Baron Edouard de Stoeckl.[3]

Lyons doubted the feasibility of mediation—especially in view of the rigid stance taken by Seward. The mediating nation bore the awesome responsibility of suggesting terms of settlement, and a compromise seemed impossible. The British public, Lyons knew, could not satisfy Southerners because it would oppose any agreement safeguarding slavery; and it could not placate Northerners without opposing the spread of the institution. Seward was an additional and important consideration. He had warned Bremen's minister in Washington that if Europe interfered on behalf of South Carolina, he would "pitch into" the intruder, fully expecting the South to set aside its domestic differences with the North and align with fellow Americans against outside interference. Seward, Lyons had earlier moaned, was a "dangerous" foreign minister, who would seek popularity at home by stirring up violence abroad. To Seward, foreign affairs provided a "safe lever" in shaping American opinion.[4]

Abraham Lincoln,
president of the United States
(National Archives)

Seward's warning posed a threat—or so it seemed to British observers who believed that he had earned his reputation for Anglophobia. Indeed, threats of war with England became an integral part of Seward's diplomatic repertoire. And no one (most of all the British) could be sure what measures he would resort to in an effort to assure his leadership of an administration that he believed could survive only if he saved it from the new president. Would not Seward make an outstanding prime minister and Lincoln (with proper handling) a capable ceremonial head?

Seward had underestimated his superior, who soon placed restraints on his secretary's pugnacious diplomacy. Lincoln's quiet strength surprised most observers. His lean and gangly six-foot, four-inch frame suggested the image of a village rube who had put down the ax to take on state responsibilities too great for him to handle. Likable, humble, and harmless (unless he fell into the maneuvering hands of stronger and self-serving men around him), Lincoln epitomized, to critics, the weaknesses of democracy.

But looks and mannerisms were deceiving. Even though Seward had served on the Senate's Committee on Foreign Relations and was therefore more experienced than Lincoln in such matters, the president exerted his constitutional authority in making foreign policy. Internal problems, of course, dominated Lincoln's attention, but numerous references to the president in Seward's dispatches demonstrate that Lincoln never lost control over his secretary of state. Seward had expected to head the entire government, Secretary of the Navy Gideon Welles cynically confided to his diary. But when in April 1861 Seward seemed prepared to provoke a foreign war in hope of reuniting the American states, Lincoln killed the ill-advised plan and, in so doing, let Seward know who would be "chief."[5] The new president agreed with Seward that even though slavery was the root cause of the domestic crisis, the Union had to be preserved at any cost. Indeed, Lincoln believed, the issues of slavery and Union were inseparable. At the same time, he permitted his secretary of state to implement a threatening stance in foreign policy as an implied warning to London that intervention would lead to war.

As Seward at first underestimated his superior's wisdom, so did the British fail to give Seward the respect he would ultimately deserve as a diplomatist. Seward's dispatches to his minister in London, Charles Francis Adams, show how quickly the secretary matured as a diplomat and how fervently he upheld the principles of republican government underlying the Union. Seward repeatedly frustrated the British (and the French) by his iron-willed determination to outlast the Confederacy and restore the Union. In no small measure did he emerge as the chief defender of the faith. His dispatches (with Lincoln's counsel) developed into eloquent and philosophical statements of legal and moral rights as the war took on ever larger moral and philosophical dimensions. If Seward's combative diplomacy and rock-hard allegiance to the Union were not the most important reasons why the British decided against recognizing the Confederacy, he had at least forced them to examine and reexamine their own arguments.

This book offers several conclusions, some of which challenge conventional wisdom.[6] First, the chief proponents of British intervention were Russell and Gladstone, who, like so many Englishmen both inside and outside the government, were convinced that

Southern separation was a fait accompli (particularly after the first battle of Bull Run). For both idealistic and realistic reasons, they argued, England must end the Union's war of subjugation. Second, even though Adams in London was in many ways an astute diplomat, he never fully realized that it was *Russell*, and not Palmerston, who was the leading advocate of intervention. The prime minister recognized the advantages in separation but was hesitant to risk war with the Union to achieve them. Third, England's limited understanding of the war, which was fostered by sheer distance, by a predictable emphasis on the impact of American events on British interests, and by frequently erroneous and alarmist analyses by Lyons and his chargé d'affaires, William Stuart, led the Palmerston ministry to consider intervention. Regardless of the form such intervention took—mediation, armistice, or recognition—it would surely alienate the Union by conferring legitimacy on its challenger. Fourth, the battle of Antietam followed by the Emancipation Proclamation kept alive Russell's hopes for intervention by necessitating some bold measure to end a terrible war accentuated by a seemingly imminent servile insurrection and ultimate race war of national proportions. Fifth, the great majority of British interventionists were not malevolent persons who wanted the American republic to commit national suicide so they might further their own ends; they wanted to stop the war for the sake of humanity in general and British textile workers in particular. Admittedly, some Englishmen saw military, economic, and strategic advantages for England resulting from a dismembered United States. And, of course, British humanitarian concerns did not exist in a vacuum; peace in America would revive commerce as well as stop a war that threatened to destroy both antagonists and, in the process, involve outside nations.

The Palmerston ministry also had to consider the political dangers inherent in intervention. Not only did the prime minister (a Liberal) preside over a coalition cabinet, but he confronted a Parliament that was precariously balanced between Liberals and Conservatives (led by Lord Derby and Benjamin Disraeli). Further, Palmerston had to heed the growing economic plight of the mill workers in Lancashire, who had no members in Parliament but aroused widespread attention and sympathy.[7] The chief concern expressed in the highest circles of the London government (primarily by Gladstone, the third most powerful ministry figure behind Palmerston and Russell) was that the workers not resort to violence before intervention occurred, thereby giving the effort a predominantly economic and political cast rather than appearing to be a humanitarian attempt to end the war. Both public and private relief efforts (including assistance from private Americans in the North) helped to ease the workers' swelling discontent. Finally, the *Trent* affair during the winter of 1861–62 resulted in a diplomatic victory for England, providing the Palmerston ministry with political credibility at home and awarding it a virtual free hand in determining foreign policy throughout much of the intervention crisis.

One other conclusion deserves special attention: if the most formidable obstacle on the American side of the Atlantic to British intervention was the North, the most outspoken opponent on the British side was Secretary for War George Cornewall Lewis.[8] As the interventionists seemed to move toward the use of force to terminate the American war, Lewis emerged as the opposition leader in the cabinet, presenting the most convincing arguments against involvement. Widely respected by both British political parties as a fair and impassioned defender of their nation's responsibility to act in a just and wise manner, he became the voice of reason when Russell appeared willing to intervene in the blind faith that such action would somehow end the conflict without causing a third Anglo-American war. Palmerston could point to Lewis's arguments as incontrovertible evidence of the futility and danger of becoming involved in the American war. Lewis discerned that the monumental problem in resolving the fundamental issue in Anglo-American relations for the first eighteen months of the war was how to determine when the Southern people had established independence and therefore merited recognition as a nation. Regardless of British motives, he insisted, the government in London was unable to resolve the issues that had catapulted North and South into war. How could observers from three thousand miles away devise a solution to problems that Americans themselves had been unable to settle except by war?

1

Problems of
Recognition

For many reasons, the possible British recognition of the Confederacy constituted the most dangerous issue confronting the United States and England during the Civil War. If Southern independence were formally acknowledged, the Confederacy would acquire nationhood and win access to British ports and purses as well as the right to negotiate military and commercial treaties. From the Union's perspective, recognition would undermine its arguments about the sanctity of the Constitution. Indeed, England's granting of recognition might compel France and other European nations to do the same. Accompanied by military and commercial alliances, such action might guarantee the triumph of secession. Even an offer of mediation or a call for an armistice would raise Northern objections because either move implied the existence of a Southern entity, if not a nation. Any effort at intervention by England—including making its good offices available—would be especially unwelcome because of the widespread feeling in the North that the British regarded a divided republic as presenting an opportunity to rearrange the North American balance of power. Were they not already strategically situated to the north in Canada and to the south in the West Indies? Would they not seek to expand their maritime power at the expense of a United States torn apart by war? When England declared neutrality during the Civil War and thereby extended belligerent status to both antagonists, the Union's leaders suspected that formal recognition of Southern independence was at hand.[1] So perilous did this prospect seem that the Lincoln administration warned England of war if it took that step.

SHORTLY AFTER assuming his duties as secretary of state, Seward expressed some of his concerns to Lyons. The Union, Seward confidently declared, intended to avoid the use of force against the rebels. Warding off the crisis at home for three months would foster a "counter-revolution" of Union sentiment that would probably begin in Texas and spread throughout the South. The North would facilitate this trend by interrupting the South's trade with England and other countries. Seward and Lyons were a classic study in contrasts. The secretary of state could be calm and gracious, but most contemporaries knew him as brash and outspoken, explosive in temperament, impulsive in action, and so anti-British that, as one contemporary put it, he appeared to be "an ogre fully resolved to eat all Englishmen raw." Lyons was cool and aloof, almost distant, and convinced that Americans were unable to refrain from violent behavior if the opportunity arose. The British must not buckle under to America's customary displays of aggressive behavior or the Union's demands for concessions would have no limits. The British would do nothing to prolong a war or prevent reunion, but they could not be held responsible for the outcome, he declared to Seward, if the Union interfered with British commerce. Some Englishmen might be placated by cotton secured overland through Northern ports, but others would not. If British ships were barred from Southern ports, the London government would undergo great pressure to open them as a matter of legal right—perhaps even by war. The British would act within international law, and on this point, Lyons wrote Russell

William H. Seward,
U.S. secretary of state
(National Archives)

in London, "it certainly appeared that the most simple, if not the only way, would be to recognize the Southern Confederacy." [2]

On the evening following their meeting of that day, March 25, Seward's attitude abruptly stiffened into the behavior Lyons had come to expect—an outgrowth, he thought, of the secretary's discussions that afternoon with hard-line members of Lincoln's cabinet. At a dinner party attended by Lyons along with several of Lincoln's advisers, French minister Henri Mercier, and Russian minister Edouard de Stoeckl, Seward became engaged in an animated discussion with Mercier and Stoeckl and waved Lyons to join the small circle. All three ministers gathered around Seward and assured him that in the event of North-South hostilities they would make every effort to protect the trade of their own nations. The secretary responded with a stern warning: "If one of your ships comes out of a Southern Port, without the Papers required by the laws of the United States, and is seized by one of our Cruisers and carried into New York and confiscated, we shall not make any compensation." Stoeckl, according to Lyons, argued "good-humouredly" against this position by insisting that for a blockade to be legal it must be effective. Seward rejoined that this maritime action did not constitute a blockade. The Union's problem was domestic in nature, and its cruisers would act under municipal law in lying off the Southern coast to collect duties and enforce customs laws. Lyons thought the measure a thinly disguised paper blockade and warned that the attempt to enforce revenue laws would place outside nations in the dilemma of either extending recognition to the South or submitting to violations of their commerce. At that point Seward, half hidden by his own cigar smoke, launched into a tirade against foreign nations and uttered statements that Lyons said would have been "more convenient for me not to have heard."[3]

Alarmed by Seward's threat against British trade, Lyons urged Russell to maintain a flexible position toward the impending American conflict, while attempting to restrain Seward by establishing some form of cooperative arrangement with France. Such an understanding, Lyons had earlier argued, might discourage Seward from taking some rash action, particularly if the decisions reached by the governments in London and Paris were firm and judicious. Commercial interference by the Union might be prevented by fear that it would produce recognition of the South. But,

Lord Lyons, British minister to the United States (Lord Newton, Lord Lyons: A Record of British Diplomacy, *2 vols. [London: Edward Arnold, 1913], 1:frontis.)*

Washington's diplomatic corps. Secretary of State Seward entertaining dignitaries at Trenton Falls, New York. Seated, left to right: Molena, Nicaraguan minister; Seward; Baron Edouard de Stoeckl, Russian minister; Sheffield, British legation attaché. Standing, left to right: Donaldson of the State Department; unidentified; Secretary Bodesco of the Russian legation; Swedish minister Count Piper; Italian minister Bertenattie; Hanseatic minister Schleider; French minister Henri Mercier; Lord Lyons, British minister. (National Archives)

Lyons added, "I am afraid we must be prepared for it." It seemed advisable to leave British policy in doubt. He became convinced over the next few months that Seward sought political gains by threatening Europe. A foreign war would not reunite North and South, Lyons assured Russell. The minister intended to avoid antagonism while making Seward see that his conduct would achieve nothing. If war broke out, the British and French must be neutral. Lyons informed Russell that Mercier was receptive to a joint policy but wanted to go farther: perhaps both the British and French ministers should have "a discretionary power to recognise the South?" Lyons thought the outcome in America too uncertain to risk such a step. The imminence of recognition could bring war with the United States. Anglo-French cooperation offered the best preventative.[4]

Seward played out his strategy, even though it was, albeit unknowingly, pushing England and France together on the common ground of recognition of the South. The best response to the threat of foreign intervention, he thought, was a threat of his own. If he could convince Southerners that the danger from outside was greater than that posed by the North, all Americans might rally around the flag and resolve the sectional crisis. Further, such a show of national unity might ward off any attempts by European powers to exploit the American problem by renewing their expansionist efforts in the hemisphere. On April 1 Seward presented Lincoln with a memorandum containing striking proposals: the United States should demand that France and Spain explain their recent interventionist activities in Mexico and Santo Domingo, and if these explanations were not satisfactory, Congress should declare war on both European nations. Seward immodestly added, "I neither seek to evade nor assume responsibility."[5]

This outlandish idea deserved the ill treatment it received. One can imagine the president's reaction. Already confronting internal problems that could develop into external problems of unparalleled danger to the republic, he now had to deter his chief cabinet adviser from hurrying the process. Lincoln knew that Seward regarded himself as guarantor of the Union. When invited into the cabinet, Seward had expected to emerge as its leader. Now, Lincoln suspected, the secretary's ill-advised plan to end the war constituted an attempt to dominate the cabinet and perhaps the administration itself. The president ignored Seward's recommendations and made clear that if such actions must be taken he would do them. War with the Confederacy was less risky than war with Europe.[6]

With that matter settled, the Lincoln administration turned to another difficult assignment: it had to convince Europe that the internal troubles stemming primarily from slavery were not about slavery after all. For domestic reasons, Seward's instructions to the new minister-select to London, Charles Francis Adams, avoided naming slavery as the issue underlying the American conflict. Had not Lincoln affirmed his opposition to intervention in slavery where it existed and sought to preserve the Union? Seward likewise opposed slavery without being an abolitionist, for he feared that a sudden end to slavery would disrupt the Southern economy and thereby undermine the entire republic. The South, Seward believed, needed the time afforded by gradual emancipation to adjust to a free labor economy. Both Lincoln and Seward also understood the dangerous domestic political ramifications of focusing on slavery as the source of the problem. Most Northerners did not like blacks and had no inclination to fight for them, and even larger numbers had no sympathy for abolition. An antislavery crusade might also alienate Unionists in the South as well as drive the border states of Maryland, Delaware, Kentucky, and Missouri out of the Union.[7]

The British never understood the important relationship between American domestic politics and slavery, and Lincoln's effort to dismiss slavery as the chief national issue had the unforeseen result of allowing them to focus on commerce rather than conscience. By bowing to domestic pressure and steering around the slavery issue, Lincoln relieved the British from having to make a decision between their moral commitment to antislavery and their economic interests in Southern cotton. With moral questions cast aside, economic considerations became paramount. Despite "all our virulent abuse of slavery and slave-owners," one Englishman wrote, "we are just as anxious for, and as much interested in, the prosperity of the slavery interest in the Southern States as the Carolinan and Georgian planters themselves, and all Lancashire would deplore a successful insurrection of the slaves, if such a thing were possible." The focus on commercial issues in Anglo-American discussions, in turn, increased the possibility of recognition of Southern independence.[8]

In reality, the Lincoln administration considered slavery the central cause of the crisis and counted on England to recognize the obvious. Both the president and his Republican party had taken a firm stand against the spread of slavery into new territories, thus pointing to its ultimate demise. Even though Lincoln placed the highest priority on preserving the Union, he considered the issues of slavery and Union to be inseparable. In this regard, he expounded a near mystical faith in American nationalism as opposed to sectionalism and states' rights. For over seventy years the character of American democracy and republican government had hinged on the question of the nature of the union the Founding Fathers had established. Lincoln's Inaugural Address had made his position clear: an abiding faith in the permanence and predominance of the Union necessitated the resolution of any issue that threatened its welfare. Though the president opposed slavery, he realized that the law protected its existence and sought, instead, to kill the institution by blocking its expansion. Southerners recognized this danger. Not by coincidence had the most explosive confrontations between North and South throughout the antebellum period related to slavery.

By the time war seemed certain, the two sections of the country had assumed the appearance of being distinctly different—one slave, one free. Slavery had become so much a part of the national debate that to many Northerners it easily became the chief stake in the war. Southern victory might prolong slavery's existence for a time, but Northern conquest would force the liberation of nearly 4 million slaves in a bitter process that would raise the specter of race war. Among more than a few American observers, Seward joined Attorney General Edward Bates and Lincoln's secretary John Hay in harboring such fears. If the British realized how deeply slavery had penetrated the American consciousness, they had little understanding of its inseparability from the question of the American Union. In a statement revealing his failure to grasp the relationship between slavery and union, Russell commented in late December 1860 that he could not see how the North could allow slavery to exist. Russell was not alone in this belief; many Americans had demonstrated no more than a superficial understanding of the interrelated issues. At a White House dinner in late March of the following year, American dignitaries declared that the North was preparing to lead a war for emancipation and confidently agreed that England's antislavery views would prevent it from helping the South build a nation based on slavery.[9]

Slavery was the great issue standing before the three principals—Union, Confederacy, and England—and yet no one seemed willing to address it. Although slavery was integrally connected to almost every issue leading to the Civil War, many Americans from both North and South sidestepped the peculiar institution and insisted that other matters were more decisive. Even for those who opposed slavery, the possibility of emancipation ultimately leading to racial equality proved too much to accept. Lincoln himself despised black bondage but never denounced white supremacy. In his Inaugural Address he had spoken for his party by declaring that he had no legal right to interfere with slavery where it already existed. Northerners and Southerners alike maintained that they sought to restore liberty—but the word had taken on so many qualifications and exceptions that neither side accepted the other's definition. Charles Francis Adams believed that the Union failure to call for emancipation gave the British a convenient excuse for choosing not to see slavery's relation to the quarrel in America.[10]

With slavery out of the official picture, several long-standing Anglo-American differences began to surface, forcing Seward to harden his stance against any British involvement in American affairs that might provide a pretext for recognizing the Confederacy. The division in America had domestic origins, Seward insisted, and the Union would entertain no outside recommendations for compromise. Any effort by England to deal with the Confederates would terminate its friendship with America. In Northern eyes, he warned, British recognition of Southern independence would constitute an alliance with the republic's enemies and a virtual declaration of war. Seward instructed Adams not to engage in any debate over moral principles supposedly lying behind the American controversy. Outsiders had no right to cast judgments on the American problem. The South had unfairly accused the Union of oppression and would appeal to England on the bases of making false charges and granting unrealistic commercial concessions. British recognition of the Confederacy, Seward declared, would lead to endless trouble between North and South over expansion on the North American continent. "Permanent dismemberment of the American Union in consequence of that intervention would be perpetual war—civil war."[11]

Union apprehensions regarding recognition appeared justified. The prime minister, Lord Palmerston, was a perennial arch-critic of America. Now seventy-six years of age, he remained an impressive figure despite thinning white hair, failing eyesight, and a faint stoop in his walk that belied his height and still sharp mind. He had been foreign secretary during the 1840s, when England threatened war with America over the Alexander McLeod affair. Both in and out of office during the years afterward, Palmerston had been conspicuous on the international scene, never failing to promote British interests by exploiting the weaknesses of rivals. He disliked Americans in general and Seward in particular; nor

Lord Palmerston, British prime minister
(Massachusetts Historical Society)

did he approve either of American republican government or of its outspokenly Anglophobic Irish-American journalists. In foreign affairs he believed that the only way to undermine America's claim to manifest destiny was to make bold displays of British strength. The unfounded though popular belief among Americans was that Palmerston's ministry, along with the opposition Conservative party, would welcome the South into the family of nations as a strategic move designed to divide America and permit England to expand both above and below the republic. Only the vulnerability of Canada would restrain the British—or so it seemed in Washington.[12]

Unknown to Americans, Palmerston had already toyed with the possibility of extending recognition to the South. Less than two weeks after South Carolina announced secession in December 1860, he considered a complicated arrangement that involved the offer of recognition and the use of his longtime opposition to the slave trade as a lever to prevent the South from reopening the practice. To Russell, the prime minister wrote that "we might make some engagement against [the] slave trade the condition of acknowledgment." Concern over French activities in Europe soon led Palmerston to expand his proposition into a farfetched plan designed to confine slavery to the South. According to the plan, England would recognize the Confederacy in exchange for a treaty agreeing not to reopen the slave trade, and the North and French emperor Napoleon III would persuade Mexico to prohibit the entry of slaves from the South. Palmerston did not abandon the plan until the summer of 1861.[13]

Northern suspicions of British intentions were reinforced by discussions at the Foreign Office between Russell and the outgoing American minister, George Dallas. Russell was small and frail, but appearances were deceiving: he would tolerate no disrespect for his country. To Queen Victoria, he had once declared that the "golden rule" governed all his official actions. England must not "infringe the rules of justice," and those same rules must not be "infringed against her." Now, to Dallas, Russell brought to bear his knowledge of international law based on personal study and frequent reliance on the advice of the crown's law officers. He declared opposition to separation and offered assurances of England's reluctance to encourage the South. But at that point the

Lord John Russell,
British foreign secretary
(Massachusetts Historical
Society)

foreign secretary abruptly changed course and remarked that he could not bind Her Majesty's government to any policy. England did not seek advantages from America's domestic troubles and, in fact, wanted the Union restored. But it must wait to see if circumstances necessitated British action.[14]

No matter how realistic from England's standpoint, Russell's policy could prove damaging to the Union. In truth, he probably had wrestled with the problem of secession. A Whig in philosophy and a Liberal in party, he thought that a people had a natural right to rebel against an established authority if it became oppressive, and he seemed to place credence in the South's claim to independence over an imperial North, which itself denied that slavery was a cause of the war. Russell exemplified the outlook of many Englishmen in never coming to understand the North's reverence for the Union. During the Italian crisis in October 1860, he had cited the Swiss theorist on international law Emmerich de Vattel in arguing that the rebellious peoples in Naples and the Roman states were the best qualified to handle their own affairs. Although the foreign secretary insisted that he would not attempt to judge the question of secession in America, he failed to convince Dallas that England's motives were pure. Russell, it seemed, reflected his people's opinion that peaceful disunion would benefit both North and South and, by the way, the rest of the world as well. The British did not grasp the dangers of disunion, Dallas surmised. Russell's reply also seemed purposeful. In less than a week, an outspoken Southern sympathizer in Parliament, William Gregory, intended to present a motion in the House of Commons calling for recognition of the Confederacy.[15]

The government in Washington was justifiably concerned about the British attitude toward events in America. News had arrived in England of the South's bombardment of Fort Sumter in Charleston Harbor and the evacuation of Union forces two days later on April 14. Emotional exchanges had escalated to exchanges of firepower in a showdown that graphically demonstrated the futility of compromise. Within a week the Confederate president, Jefferson Davis, announced the licensing of privateers by letters of marque; President Lincoln answered on April 19 by proclaiming his intention to install a blockade off the Southern coast and by threatening to hang privateers as pirates; and Virginia joined the Confederacy, to be followed in early June by three more states to make a total of eleven. Surely, British observers concluded, the North could not subdue so many people, close so many miles of coastline, and invade and occupy so much territory. Southern separation seemed irrevocable. Palmerston and Russell thought so even before the Confederacy had reached full size. The prime minister had told

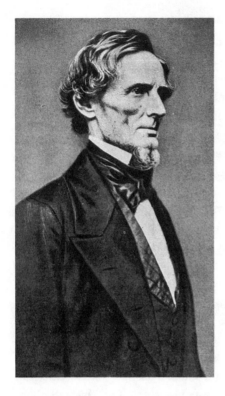

Jefferson Davis,
president of the Confederacy
(National Archives)

Queen Victoria on New Year's Day of 1861 that the Union was virtually dissolved. And despite Russell's claimed refusal to judge American affairs, he had decided as early as January that the Union should acknowledge the legal right of secession and permit the separation: "One Republic to be constituted on the principle of freedom & personal liberty—the other on the principle of slavery & the mutual surrender of fugitives." By the time of Lincoln's inauguration, Russell thought that only a slave rebellion could undermine the Southern position.[16]

The foreign secretary's view received support from the *Times* of London's special correspondent in America, William H. Russell. Internationally known after his exemplary coverage of the Crimean War, he provided the ministry in London (and countless readers of the *Times*) with unbiased, realistic, and generally accurate firsthand information about his travels through North and South. During that time he met many important Union and Confederate leaders and in one instance was allowed by Seward to read a stormy dispatch headed for Adams pertaining to the widespread belief that England preferred a divided United States. Russell reached New York in March 1861 and noted little support for the federal government, and then, at the time of Sumter's fall, began touring the South, where he found (contrary to Seward's expectations) no Union sentiment and, instead, fierce loyalty to the Confederacy. Seward nonetheless felt contempt for those who thought secession would work. "Why," he declared, "I myself, my brothers and sisters have been all secessionists—we seceded from home when we were young, but we all went back to it sooner or later. These States will all come back in the same way." Russell did not agree. The North might defeat the South, but the effort would destroy the Union. A Georgian personified the Southern spirit of invincibility when he proudly assured Russell, "They can't conquer us, Sir!"[17]

Considering Southern separation a strong likelihood, the Palmerston ministry had to prepare for the possibility of dealing with two American nations. Lord John Russell faced the immense task of maintaining communication with both North and South while solidifying his own country's relations with France to make sure that his chief European rival did not exploit Anglo-American troubles and expand its interests elsewhere. On May 1 the foreign secretary invited Dallas to his home and announced that three representatives of the Confederacy were in England, requesting an interview. Dallas was stunned. Russell declared his intent to see the Confederates on an unofficial basis. Then, following Lyons's recommendation, the foreign secretary explained that England and France had agreed to adopt the same wait-and-see policy regarding recognition. Russell's support for an Anglo-French concert suggested to anxious Union officials that the two European nations were in league to encourage a breakup of the United States that would permit them to expand their interests in the Western Hemisphere.[18]

The Union's concern about intervention in 1861 was largely unwarranted, for British interests lay in staying out of America's problems and in making sure that France did the same. Besides, the Palmerston ministry had no terms to suggest for a reconciliation of North and South. An intervention could land the British in war with either the North or South—or both. With these concerns in mind, Palmerston recommended confidential communications

William H. Russell, Times *of London correspondent in the United States*
(John Bigelow, Retrospections of an Active Life, *5 vols. [New York:*
Baker and Taylor, 1909–13], 1:opposite 342)

with both American antagonists as a means for taking any step toward mediation if deemed wise. At the moment, the prime minister insisted to a member of Parliament, both North and South must satisfy their desire for conflict before they might listen to reason. Yet the Palmerston ministry could not ignore American events. In early May Russell assured Parliament that the government had stationed vessels in the Gulf of Mexico to protect the nation's shipping and property. Regrettably, he added, the task would not be easy. The Confederacy had authorized privateers to prey on commerce and the North intended to blockade Southern ports. In the House of Commons Russell proclaimed the ministry's intention to avoid involvement in American affairs, but he qualified that statement by insisting that the government would protect British interests. Regarding the war in the United States, Russell drew cheers by declaring that "for God's sake, let us if possible keep out of it!" [19]

England's objective of nonintervention grew increasingly elusive, primarily because the conflict in America had the capacity to force the London government to take sides and thereby sever the ties that had been growing between the Atlantic nations since their last war in 1812. The British had too much at stake in the struggle to be mere onlookers. The transatlantic connection ran both ways, tightening an interdependence built on social, political, economic, and diplomatic considerations. The reform movements of preceding decades had found allies on both sides of the Atlantic, and commercial groups had become dependent on mutual investments and trade. American wheat and cotton provided the bases of an Atlantic community that, since the midcentury rapprochement promoted by the Webster-Ashburton Treaty, Oregon settlement, and recent resolution of several Central American issues, had overcome numerous problems to remain intact in the prewar decade. The British government had to formulate a policy that would steer the nation between the American antagonists and protect its interests without allowing its own people to involve themselves and their nation in these events. Russell considered the Lincoln administration wrong in dismissing Southern discontent as a mere rebellion that deserved no attention from the outside. The American events constituted a civil war that directly threatened British interests. The South had a civil government,

PUNCH, OR THE LONDON CHARIVARI.—July 6, 1861.

NAUGHTY JONATHAN.

" YOU **SHAN'T** INTERFERE, MOTHER—AND YOU OUGHT TO BE ON MY SIDE—AND IT'S A GREAT SHAME—AND I DON'T CARE—AND YOU **SHALL** INTERFERE—AND I WON'T HAVE IT."

"Naughty Jonathan" (London Punch, *July 6, 1861)*

Russell insisted, and deserved the status of belligerent. To avoid confusion, he instructed Lyons to inform Seward immediately of the British position.[20] But before Lyons could make these views known to Seward, the sheer timing of events in London greatly enhanced the Union's suspicion of British designs.

ON MAY 13—the day that Adams arrived in England and the day before he reached his post in London—the queen infuriated the Union government by issuing a proclamation of neutrality that automatically granted belligerent status to the South. The chairman of the Senate Foreign Relations Committee in Washington, Charles Sumner, angrily called it "the most hateful act of English history since the time of Charles 2nd." When France followed with a similar declaration of neutrality in June, Seward warned both nations of the possibility of war.[21]

England's decision to adopt a neutral stance had resulted, at least in part, from a misreading of Lincoln's blockade declaration and had not come as easily as Americans thought. From the vantage point of London, a sense of emergency dictated a declaration of neutrality that would place the nation in conformity with international and municipal law. A careful reading of Lincoln's statement ("I have deemed it advisable to set on foot a blockade") suggests that he intended to establish a blockade but had not yet done so. Lyons realized this and accepted Seward's note on the matter as "an announcement of an intention to set on foot a blockade, not as a notification of the actual commencement of one." Yet the government in London interpreted Lincoln's words to mean that the process of setting up the blockade was under way. The ministry sought to keep its subjects from dragging the nation into the war by warning that if they broke either the law of nations or British law, they did so at their own risk. In accordance with the law of nations, the British believed that a civil war had developed in America that involved two antagonists and, in that regard, shared the same characteristics as a war between nations. Other countries directly affected by the American war had the right to declare neutrality and thus bring into play an entire system of rules of conduct. England intended to follow a strict impartiality toward the belligerents.[22]

The neutrality proclamation, in conjunction with the British Foreign Enlistment Act of 1819, prohibited British subjects from enlisting or engaging in foreign service and from "fitting out or equipping" vessels in British dominions for warlike purposes without government approval. British subjects were not to join the military or naval service or violate the lawful blockade of any nation at peace with England. Subjects engaging in these activities would receive no protection from the government. Thus, as the British would emphasize, they were adhering to the precedent established by President George Washington in 1793, when he announced neutrality during the Anglo-French war.[23]

Union officials did not reason out the advantages of British neutrality and mistakenly regarded the decision as purposefully partial toward the South, if not in motive then surely in consequence. Logically, a declaration of neutrality assured that with no special advantages granted to either side, the North would benefit from its superiority in resources, people, and seagoing vessels. Further, according to international law, recognition of belligerency in a civil war relieved the parent government (the Union) of responsibility for the insurgents' actions; permitted cruisers of that government (along with the Confederacy, which had no ships) to search foreign merchant vessels for contraband and submit confiscated goods to prize courts; allowed the parent state to establish a blockade that foreign states must respect; and barred insurgents from hostile preparations within the jurisdiction of a neutral state. But the Lincoln administration ignored or overlooked these points. On one hand, it denied the existence of a war and labeled secession treason and Confederate maritime raids piracy. On the other hand, it expected to seize contraband heading for the South, thereby implying a state of war.[24]

Despite these admitted advantages to the Union, the administration complained that British neutrality awarded stature and credibility to the Confederacy. The South (as well as the Union) would have the right to borrow money and purchase war matériel from England, to enter its ports with prizes resulting from privateering (still condoned by international law), to enlist men for every activity short of violating neutrality laws, to commission vessels from British shipbuilders, and, as long as the actual equipping and fitting for wartime purposes did not take place in England, to incorporate the new vessels into a fledgling Confederate navy.[25] To both North and South, the granting of belligerent rights seemed to be the first step in a process leading to recognition of Southern independence.

Northerners were wrong in considering the neutrality proclamation a calculated British affront. One of the Union's strongest defenders in the House of Commons, William E. Forster, joined his colleagues in believing a blockade to be in force and supported neutrality because he thought the policy would help the Union, not hinder it. The president's blockade proclamation, according to international law (upheld by the U.S. Supreme Court in the *Prize Cases* of 1863), constituted an act of war that implied the existence of belligerents and gave added impetus to the British adoption of neutrality.[26] Further, Lincoln's threat to hang privateers as pirates put more pressure on England to declare neutrality. After the Crimean War, England and other maritime nations in 1856 had drawn up the Declaration of Paris which, among other provisions, outlawed privateering. The United States had refused to accept the pact and therefore had no legal right to expect other nations to declare Confederate privateering to be piracy. Russell realized that British treatment of Southern privateers as pirates would benefit the Union by undermining the ministry's claims to neutrality and effectively closing the door to recognition. Though Lincoln soon retreated from his warning, Russell had seen enough to confirm his inclination to stay out of the struggle.

Adams compounded the problems stemming from Lincoln's pronouncements by failing to reach London as quickly as possible to counter the ministry's worst expectations. By 1861 he felt secure as Republican leader in the House of Representatives and had entertained thoughts of the presidency. Indeed, he had not welcomed the appointment to London, and neither had his wife and family. One son recorded in his diary that his mother cried when the news "fell on our breakfast-table like a veritable bombshell, scattering confusion and dismay." But the elder Adams gave in to Seward's persuasions. Despite the immediacy of issues with England, Adams had delayed his departure from Boston until May 1 to attend his son John's wedding. Seward would remark offhandedly one day in 1863 to the minister's son Charles Francis, Jr., that the "greatest misfortune that ever happened to the United States was that the marriage of your brother occurred on the 29th of April, 1861." Charles Francis, Jr., later termed the delay "inexplicable" and "inexcusable" and declared that his father should have left immediately after receiving the appointment. Seward, the younger Adams added, had consented to the delay because he "was still dwelling in his 'Southern Unionist' dream-land" and had no grasp of the critical nature of events in Europe and at home. In fairness to the senior Adams, he could have done nothing to dissuade the British from neutrality; an earlier arrival would have required his protest against the proclamation and further inflamed emotions. But even though his presence might not have made a difference in easing British apprehensions, his tardy arrival allowed these apprehensions to grow. By the time he arrived in England, the Southern commissioners were in London and, according to his son's account, had already "scored the apparently great success of a recognition of belligerency."[27]

Initially, the British position enraged the new minister. Both his father, John Quincy, and grandfather, John, had served in the London legation, and neither had lived a day without experiencing suspicions about British motives. Charles Francis Adams was bald-headed, cultured, and studious, perhaps even stodgy, and

Charles Francis Adams,
Union minister to England
(Massachusetts Historical
Society)

should have fitted in well with British society. And, despite his lack of personal charm, at times he did. Russell perhaps saw many of his own qualities in Adams and regarded him as a "calm & judicious man" of "discretion & firmness." The foreign secretary admitted that at first they did not understand each other. Adams was reserved and cautious, often choosing to temper the bellicosity of Seward's dispatches before expressing their contents to Russell. The apparent design of British actions continually reminded him of his family's prior experiences in London. Even after the Civil War, Adams remained convinced that in establishing policy, the British cabinet made up its mind in advance of facts and, as he wrote Russell, anticipated "their occurrence as a justification." He did not accept the argument that the British had announced neutrality in an effort to encourage Confederate independence, but he was tempted to follow the family inclination in believing that British leaders (not the people at large) would seize any opportunity to undermine the republic. He already had acquired a measure of evidence in the declaration of neutrality and its implications.[28]

Adams's first impressions soon gave way to uncertainty. He had received a friendly reception in England but noted considerable anxiety among its people about American affairs, especially the availability of cotton. He knew about South Carolinian James H. Hammond's emotional exaggeration of cotton's supreme power. If cut off from supplies of the staple, Hammond had dramatically declared, "England would topple headlong and carry the whole civilized world with her, save the South. No, you dare not make war on cotton. No power on earth dares make war upon it. Cotton is King." Adams also learned that Confederate commissioners led by Alabama firebrand William L. Yancey were in London seeking diplomatic recognition and assistance and that Parliament was uncertain about what policy to follow toward America. Adams preferred to hold judgment on the ministry. Perhaps its language had not been "sufficiently guarded."[29]

Seward, however, had made up his mind that America's relations with England were in crisis. About the Confederate commissioners, he shouted to Sumner: "God damn them, I'll give them hell."[30] The president managed to tone down his secretary's warning to England but also believed that Dallas should have protested Russell's decision to meet with the Southern emissaries. Seward directed Adams to refrain from all discussions with England as long as its government continued to deal with the Union's enemies. On Russell's statement of Anglo-French harmony regarding recognition, Seward sarcastically noted that this so-called revelation came only after the agreement was known. Russell had not told the Union government that England and France had informed other European nations of the agreement and expected them to follow England's lead. On recognition, Adams was not to enter into any discussion touching upon a "technical definition." Recognition, Seward told Adams, would constitute an announced acknowledgment of Confederate sovereignty and independence, followed by acceptance of the new nation's representatives on an official basis. But British policy, as it already stood, carried dangerous implications: "A concession of belligerent rights is liable to be construed as a recognition of them." As he perhaps knew, the *Richmond Whig* defiantly called the neutrality proclamation "a long and firm [step] in exactly the direction which the people of the Southern States expected." The Confederacy had never won a field or taken a port, Seward complained, and yet it called upon the British "to intervene and give it body and independence by resisting our measures of suppression." The only purpose of British recognition would be to destroy the republic.[31]

Despite fears in Washington, any interest that the British might have had in the Confederacy was at least momentarily stalled by the question of slavery. As the White House, for domestic reasons, had to veer around slavery in its diplomatic dealings with England, so did the South, for purposes of foreign policy, consider it expedient to duck the issue and rely on the British need for cotton and on what Yancey called the "justice of the cause."[32] Adams could not have known, but by the time Yancey and his two Confederate colleagues, Pierre A. Rost and Ambrose D. Mann, met unofficially with Russell twice in early May, they had attributed secession to Northern economic and political oppression, not slavery, and, despite Yancey's well-known interest in reopening the African slave trade, offered assurances against its revival.[33] The emissaries' cool reception did not surprise Jefferson Davis; in a meeting with William H. Russell, the Confederate president expressed concern that England's views on slavery might interfere with the South's war aims. A cabinet member, Judah P. Benjamin, was confident that England's dependence on Southern cotton would remove "this coyness about acknowledging a slave power."[34] If so, that time had not yet arrived. Yancey reported to his superiors that the British public opposed the Confederacy because of slavery.[35]

Adams and Russell aired their differences in a meeting of more than an hour at the latter's country home outside London on May 18. The American minister felt more concern about British behavior than his dispatch of the day before had revealed. He had arranged a meeting with Russell on May 14, before the Privy Council had taken final action on the queen's proclamation of neutrality and before the document appeared in the press. But the meeting was canceled because Russell had been called to his brother's sickbed early that morning, just hours before his death that same day. Adams's first impression of Russell did little to dispel his apprehensions. Of short stature, like Adams himself, the British foreign secretary received his visitor kindly even though his face betrayed deep inner feelings of worry rather than resolution. Further, his countenance suggested a desire to maintain a healthy distance from his fellow diplomat and the country he represented. The British sympathized with the North, Russell declared, but they were not pleased with the Union's blockade, the high Morrill Tariff, and the designation of Southern privateers as pirates. Adams tried in vain to alleviate these concerns. He insisted that the blockade would become effective in view of the small number of harbors along the Southern coast, that the United States intended the tariff to raise revenue and not to impose protection, and that the Union would exercise "forbearance and humanity" toward privateers.[36]

British goodwill, Adams noted afterward, did not seem as "unequivocally manifested as I had hoped." Perhaps, he thought, England's formal but initially favorable disposition toward the North had changed because of the Lincoln administration's insistence that the war did not stem from slavery. As the two sides labored to make slavery a nonissue, the South's arguments for states' rights and free trade emerged as principles that British citizens could support. England seemed determined to pursue a policy that would, even if inadvertently, endanger relations with the United States.[37]

To Adams's chagrin, Russell still refused to guarantee that recognition would not occur. The proclamation of neutrality was not "precipitate," Russell declared. His government had to define its position regarding American events so as to warn British subjects of the liabilities of becoming involved in those events. The crown's law officers had concluded that, in fact, a state of war existed in the United States. At least seven states were in open resistance, with others threatening to join them, and adherence to international law along with the importance of British commerce made it impossible to deny belligerent rights. But this allowance "implied no recognition, nor allowed any other than an intermediate position on the part of the Southern States." If the British government ever considered recognition, he would first notify Adams and allow him to present the Union's case. The British sympathized with the North, Russell candidly declared. In reply,

Adams stated that the Union would put down the insurrection but insisted that the queen's proclamation had made the task more difficult by unjustly awarding the Southerners belligerent status and encouraging their friends in England. The lord chancellor himself, Adams pointed out, had recently referred to the South as "a belligerent State" engaged in a "*justum bellum*" or a "war of two sides."[38]

If the South deserved belligerent status, the time might be opportune for a mediation offer that both sides would accept in lieu of all-out war—or so it seemed in London. Russell had been supportive of mediation, if invited, even before the guns had been fired at Fort Sumter. A civil war would be so vicious that neither North nor South would recover for more than a generation. Other British observers dreaded the nearly certain outbreak of servile war; not only would such an event disrupt the cotton economy for years, but a racial upheaval would rock the South and perhaps the entire republic once the chains of bondage were broken. Still others believed that the United States had become so much a part of the international economy that the North-South conflict would disrupt trade with all Europe and cause widespread political unrest. European peoples had divided into different nation-states; Americans could do the same.[39]

Lyons's observations from Washington substantiated the ministry's view that the South should be considered a belligerent. Surely the North realized the impossibility of forcing the South back into the Union and resisted secession only out of "wounded pride." Northerners, Lyons believed, might "be more easily induced to sacrifice their pride, and desist from an attempt to crush a rebellion, than the South be forced into a submission which they believe to be incompatible not only with their freedom and their fortunes, but even with their safety in the midst of their slave population."[40]

Intervention offered England the opportunity to play a historic role in ending this calamitous event before it had international repercussions. The Palmerston ministry could engage in a humanitarian enterprise that had the additional economic attraction of reopening the cotton trade, and it could be instrumental in averting the destructive pattern often associated with civil wars of the belligerents' dragging in outside observers and setting off a larger, all-encompassing war. In accordance with international law, Russell instructed Lyons to use his good offices, either by himself or with others, in seeking a reconciliation of North and South—but only in the admittedly unlikely event that Americans asked him to do so.[41]

Russell's doubt was justified, for Lyons had just notified London of a development that temporarily dispelled the hope of mediation. In late April a group of private residents of Washington, D.C., had presented Prussian minister Baron Frederick C. J. von Gerolt with a proposal that members of the diplomatic corps jointly offer mediation in an effort to secure an armistice until Congress could meet in July. The following day the newspapers printed a letter from Seward to the governor of Maryland stoutly rejecting any European involvement.[42]

THE LINCOLN ADMINISTRATION'S aggressive diplomacy had greatly strained Anglo-American relations, but it had succeeded in demonstrating a steel-like determination to resolve the crisis without foreign involvement. Intervention in any form, the president and his advisers believed, would imply the existence of two states and lead, as a matter of course, to recognition. Mediation, however innocent and high-minded, would undermine the Union's reasons for the war and furnish respectability to the South's claim to self-government. The *Times* of London compared the struggle with that of the American colonists of the late eighteenth century. In an intriguing use of history, the paper defended the American revolutionists for trying to free themselves from crown oppression.[43] The Union's spokesmen refused to enter any debates with England over moral issues and fair play; the English did not understand the deeper issues and could only see a majority of Americans imposing their will on a minority. Lincoln's insistence on preserving the Union could become dangerous, for more than a few English observers preferred the establishment of two American nations over the extensive damage that both sides would sustain in a lengthy civil war.

The Union's rigid diplomatic stance had a built-in danger, however, for the Lincoln administration made itself vulnerable to charges of inhumanity and vindictiveness. The *Economist* of London reprimanded the North for seeking to subjugate the South and warned that the outcome would be a long and bitter war of conquest, followed by a long and bitter period of military rule. In that journal's view secession was a fait accompli. "Even if the North were sure of an easy and complete victory . . . the war which was to end in such a victory would still be . . . an objectless and unprofitable folly."[44] Since neither North nor South had avowed slavery as a cause of the war, the British surmised that no other issue could be worth the price of blood. The Union, they dourly concluded, sought a war for vengeance.

2

British Neutrality and the Rules of Modern Civilized Warfare

The Palmerston ministry planned to stay out of the Civil War by maintaining neutrality and adhering to international law. Russell referred to the law of nations and relied on advice from the crown's law officers, making certain that England followed accepted rules of behavior in foreign affairs. At least four great legal theorists—Emmerich de Vattel, Henry Wheaton, John Austin, and Hugo Grotius—had earlier examined and expounded upon nearly every issue that troubled Anglo-American relations during the Civil War. Available to Russell were volumes of information pertaining to insurrections, rebellions, and civil wars; neutrality and the nature of belligerent status; intervention and mediation; privateering, wartime commerce, and blockades; the meaning, timing, and implications of diplomatic recognition. The works of these writers were masterful analyses of international problems, brilliantly codified and extensively footnoted to historical and judicial records, in sum suggesting finality in wisdom and scholarship. But this comfortable feeling was deceptive. International law remained amorphous and slippery, shaped and reshaped in accordance with constantly shifting power structures in the world community. Indeed, interpretations of legal precepts varied depending on each nation's vital interests. And therein lay the rub: no stand taken on any major issue in a war could be acceptable to all parties involved. In the American conflict, England's insistence upon neutrality was not satisfactory to either antagonist—and particularly to the Union. And, most galling to both North and South, England not only declared itself neutral, but it made every effort to remain so throughout the contest. The numerous problems that arose from British neutrality during the Civil War continued to aggravate Anglo-American relations for decades afterward.[1]

WITH WAR in America a certainty, the British intended to comply with the maritime principles contained in the Declaration of Paris and to formalize their position as neutral between the belligerents. Signatories of the pact—Austria, England, France, Prussia, Russia, Sardinia, and Turkey—had agreed to the following provisions: neutral and belligerent flags protected all cargo except contraband; blockades must effectively prevent access to a coast; and privateering was abolished. Eventually more than forty other nations approved the pact, a membership roll that comprised nearly all Europe and South America. But the United States had not been party to the declaration because of the prohibition against privateering. Further, the declaration's failure to exempt from seizure all private property at sea caused problems. Moreover, the declaration bound only participating nations and did not affect international law. The Union view toward neutrals and belligerents in the present conflict was certain to cause difficulties. In an effort to mesh the pact with the law of nations, the signatories had agreed not to enter a treaty with nonsignatory nations relating to any of the pact's provisions unless those nonsignatories approved all parts of the declaration. Russell thought that if the Union complied with the declaration, the British might inform the Confederacy that they would term its acceptance a "sine qua non of our friendship—I will not say of our neutrality." Thus the foreign secretary hoped to persuade both North and South to follow the rules, thereby increasing the chances of England's staying out of the struggle.[2]

The chief obstacle to Russell's strategy was the United States's refusal to accept the Paris declaration's outlawing of privateering. Historically, privateering had provided a means for nations with small navies to license privately owned vessels for raiding commerce (whether or not contraband) and taking captured goods into prize courts—including those in neutral countries—for adjudication. Russell suspected that the United States wanted to maintain privateers for potential future use against England. To deal with the present difficulty, he considered a proposition prohibiting the entrance of prizes into British ports. But he knew that such a move could constitute an unneutral act that furthered the Union cause. The North had a navy that it could supplement with privateers; the South did not. And without the attraction of lucrative awards in British prize courts, the South would lose a major impetus for privateering.

Russell realized that the Union was on solid legal ground, and he could only hope that privateering might not pose a problem. Any commander carrying a letter of marque was supposed to follow the law of nations during wartime. Otherwise, the government issuing the letter became responsible for losses stemming from privateering. The assurance of reparations might smooth over wartime difficulties and provide the next best thing to American compliance with the terms of Paris.[3]

Lyons was not optimistic. The Lincoln administration had offered to adhere to the abolition of privateering but at what Lyons perceived to be a heavy price to European nations. Because Lincoln considered the Union indissoluble, the South's attempt to use privateers would automatically make it guilty of piracy. All signatories of the Paris pact would therefore bear the burden of monitoring the South. Lyons would have none of that. Terming the American proposal "rather amusing," he dismissed it as a transparent attempt to trick the Paris signatories into aiding the

North in the war. It would be "very convenient," he wryly remarked, if European navies enforced the ban on privateering and freed the U.S. Navy to implement the blockade against European commercial vessels. Russell saw the point. If he needed further reason for a hurried declaration of neutrality in mid-May, he received it from the Union's poorly concealed attempt to push the British (and French) into policing the seas against Southern privateers. The ministry would not accept a Union renunciation of privateering on the implicit condition that England would enforce that prohibition against the South.[4]

In late May the Lincoln administration made another attempt to resolve the privateering issue. Administration leaders recognized the value in reserving the right of privateering for future purposes; but they also realized that in the present conflict only the South would gain from an extralegal navy. England had opposed the Union's efforts to brand privateers as pirates. Perhaps France would see the Union's position. If so, the Union would gain a virtual ally against the South while driving a wedge between the European countries. In Paris the Union minister, William Dayton, made two proposals to French foreign secretary Edouard Thouvenel. He asked that Southern privateers be treated as pirates and, in exchange for U.S. acceptance of the entire Declaration of Paris, to the provision against privateering a section be added exempting from seizure all noncontraband private property. The second proposal was not new. The United States had presented it as early as 1856 when, because of the abolition of privateering (which would hurt the United States, a small-navy nation), Secretary of State William Marcy tried to safeguard all privately owned noncontraband matériel from confiscation—including that of the enemy. England and France had shown no interest in the Marcy amendment. Perhaps now, the Union government apparently reasoned, the French wanted its acquiescence in the declaration so badly that they would strike the deal. If the British went along as well, so much the better.[5]

But neither England nor France expressed interest and the European concert remained intact. Thouvenel consulted Russell, who opposed both American proposals. Compliance on either count, he warned, would constitute a hostile action against the South and thereby violate Anglo-French neutrality. The amendment on privateering would reduce the wartime powers of big-navy and commercial nations by making it virtually impossible to distinguish between ships carrying noncontraband goods and those fitted out for war but disguised as merchant vessels. After a long delay, the French rejected both proposals.[6]

The privateering issue was inseparable from the recognition question and soon became the most immediate source of Anglo-American discord. Because the United States had not approved the Declaration of Paris, Russell thought that the South (as belligerent) was acting in accordance with international law in licensing privateers as long as the commanders followed the rules of warfare in raiding Union shipping and taking their prizes to admiralty courts for adjudication. That view, of course, raised further suspicion in the North that England was partial to the South. In practical terms, a privateer was no different from a naval vessel, and the North understandably regarded British approval of Southern privateering as further acknowledgment of Confederate belligerency. England had announced neutrality in good faith; but the proclamation raised more questions than it answered—including the reaction to the Confederacy's rightful claim under international law (as a belligerent) to send privateers with prizes into British ports. As a neutral, England would be obligated to welcome the privateers alongside Union vessels. Adams did not believe that the British government realized that the neutrality proclamation had made the "admission of equality."[7]

Adams tried to resolve the problem. In a meeting with Russell, he sought quick action against privateering. But the issue got lost in differences over interpretation. Adams thought he had won Russell's agreement to turn the matter over to Lyons, who would attempt to reach a settlement acceptable to the White House; Russell argued that his aim had been to secure American agreement on the other articles of the Declaration of Paris and not on privateering. Adams concluded that Russell was either remiss in his attention to detail or duplicitous. Whatever the truth, the problem came nowhere close to resolution, and the longer it lagged, the greater were the chances for conflict.[8]

But before the privateering issue could become explosive, it suddenly lost intensity. Part of the explanation lies in the Palmerston ministry's attempt to avert a confrontation with the Union by declaring that England would no longer allow privateers to bring prizes into its ports. But a more important reason for the decline of the privateering question was that the South in June had changed its maritime strategy from privateering to the actual destruction of enemy goods. The neutrality issue thus took precedence over privateering as the leading point of divisiveness. Adams remained unable to convince Russell to seek a revocation of the queen's proclamation. Such a move, the foreign secretary knew, would encourage greater license on the ocean—including that of his own people. With no rules governing maritime behavior during war, the chances of England's involvement in the American war would rise proportionately.[9]

Most Britons did not grasp the complexities in the American situation, nor should they have been expected to understand (or to attempt to understand) all the intricacies of those domestic issues. Once they regarded the struggle as a civil war, they correctly declared neutrality, awarded belligerent status to North and South, and expected to trade with both sides. The British refused to believe that a mere insurrection (as the Union called the South's action) could involve so many people and so much territory. Rather, the resistance mounted by the South constituted a full-fledged rebellion that sought to overthrow the government in Washington, and its own de facto government in Richmond entitled it to belligerent status. The Union did not agree. Given its stand on secession as an insurrectionary action that violated the Constitution, it could only regard the South's attempted withdrawal from the compact as treason. Northerners thus denounced England's extension of belligerent rights as a malevolent first step toward recognition of Southern independence. England insisted that its refusal to accept the South's claim to having established a de jure (legal) government was proof of an honest neutrality.[10] The British cited international law in defending their actions, and case after case upheld their views. But no code of law was applicable in a practical sense to the American question because, as in all wars, neither side would (or could) adhere to all the rules. The acceptance of any point by one antagonist automatically meant the rejection of that same point by the other. No matter what policy the British adopted, one antagonist or the other would criticize them for taking sides.

In practical terms, of course, the Lincoln administration had to admit that the South had belligerent rights, an admission that soon gave rise to what has become known as the dual status of the war. As both a rebellion and a public war—a definition upheld by the U.S. Supreme Court by a five-to-four majority in the *Prize Cases* of 1863—the dual nature of the American conflict permitted the Union government to claim sovereignty over the rebels as traitors while exercising over the Confederacy those belligerent rights emanating from international law.[11]

The governments in London and Washington thus headed toward a confrontation over neutrality that neither side wanted. The British insisted that the Americans had mistakenly attributed hidden meaning to the queen's proclamation. Neutrality was necessary to enable the London government to bar its people's participation in the American conflict. The war was a *justum bellum* in which England would not take sides while hoping to keep the contest within what Russell termed the "rules of modern civilized warfare." The proclamation, he insisted, "was designed . . . to explain to British subjects their liabilities in case they should engage in the war." The Lincoln administration complained that the British action had left it only sixty days to formulate a policy. Indeed, the British breathed life into the insurgency before it had proved itself on the battlefield. If the government's intention was to prolong the struggle, Adams gloomily declared, "I was bound to acknowledge in all frankness that . . . I had nothing further left to do in Great Britain."[12]

Continued disputes over recognition revealed the complexities involved in its interpretation. The Union and England agreed that no people deserved recognition as a nation until they had demonstrated a capacity to defend themselves and to maintain relations with other nations. But the two principals just as vehemently disagreed over whether the South had come close to that point. Adams insisted that the South had tried in vain to withdraw from the Union by an act of secession that was alien to the Constitution. Outside interference must not occur before the issue was settled and thus be instrumental in shaping that settlement. Russell stuck to his original policy of withholding a commitment either way until more time had passed and the outcome became clear. He could not give a pledge against recognition.[13]

While this debate rocked along, Adams discerned a division in British feeling caused by pressure from commercial groups interested in Southern cotton.[14] He was aware of the Confederacy's intention to use King Cotton as leverage in gaining recognition. By mid-May, in fact, the Confederate Congress had attempted to exert more pressure on Europe by prohibiting the exportation of cotton save through Southern ports. In truth, over 80 percent of Britain's cotton came from the South, and the threat of a sudden cutoff seemed to afford the Confederacy a distinct advantage.[15] But fortune had looked kindly on the Union: British manufacturers had a year's surplus. A protracted war, however, would cut into that surplus and necessitate either the use of inferior cotton from other countries or a combined effort by England and France to challenge the Union blockade and force open Southern ports. No matter what British sentiment might be toward the American question, the vital interests of their empire would come into play in about a year's time: Lancashire's cotton mills could not run without cotton.

The Lincoln administration continued to argue that British neutrality provided the South with hope for recognition. Adams remained uneasy because of the presence of the Southern commissioners and by their boastful claims to having had interviews with Russell. The foreign secretary assured Adams that the British had consulted with the French beforehand about whether to receive the Confederates and that both countries' custom was to receive them "unofficially." He did not expect to see them again. Russell understood the embittered American reaction to British neutrality, but he repeated that the only purpose of the queen's proclamation was to keep England neutral. Adams countered that the proclamation would prolong the war by raising the South's expectations of outside help.[16]

The Union's angry objections to British policy led the government in London to bolster defenses in Canada in the event of an Anglo-American war. Lyons had urged the ministry to take such protective action. In memos intended for cabinet perusal, Russell agreed that Seward's threatening behavior required a buildup in British North America, and Palmerston responded by recommending the dispatch of three battalions. Russell at first attempted to ease Adams's apprehensions about British troop movements in Canada. The area had been defenseless for some time, he explained, and the move was a precautionary measure caused by the chaos in the United States that might spill across the border. The Irish in New York City, he later added, would seize the opportunity to stir up trouble between England and the Union. But Russell also declared that he was unsure of the United States's motives. Seward was equally straightforward. The United States would entertain no hostile intentions toward England as long as it did not extend recognition, assistance, or sympathy to the insurgents.[17]

In response to Seward's assertions that British recognition of belligerency implied support for the dissolution of the Union, Russell drew on the past in an effort to show that the step involved no judgment of the quarrel in America but only an admission to the fact of war. Former foreign secretary George Canning had made similar statements in the Commons relating to Greek and Turkish moves toward independence during the 1820s. Belligerent rights, Canning maintained, were not a question of principle but of fact—"the size and strength of the party contending against a Government, and not the goodness of their cause, entitle them to the character and treatment of belligerents." To Lyons, Russell insisted that the British government could not treat millions of people like "a band of marauders." In support of British policy, Russell referred to a recent admiralty court decision in Washington, D.C. (the *Tropic Wind*, which was a British schooner), during which District Court judge James Dunlop declared that the president's proclamation of a blockade was a belligerent right that signified the existence of war. Further, Dunlop cited former Supreme Court justice Joseph Story as authority in concluding that there were no differences in belligerent rights between a foreign war (public war) and a civil war. The conflict between North and South, he concluded, was a civil war whose purpose was to determine whether the South would be independent. Such comment convinced Russell that British neutrality conformed with established practice.[18]

Although Russell's arguments were in harmony with international law, they nonetheless posed a serious threat to the Union's position. Dunlop had not upheld the South's argument for nationhood, but he had made clear that the struggle was a civil war and that the final status of the South was the great issue that remained undecided. By elevating the South's resistance from an insurrection to a civil war, Dunlop had, according to international law, stamped respectability on the Confederate cause and raised searching questions about the Lincoln administration's insistence upon restoring the Union by a war of subjugation.

THE ANGLO-AMERICAN ISSUES that kept coming to the surface—neutrality and the Union blockade, foreign intervention, the Anglo-French concert—were inseparable from the threat of recognition and were, for that reason, of vital concern and hence nonnegotiable. Thus the diplomats had the formidable tasks of smoothing over and postponing differences without hope of settling them and of desperately attempting to avoid confrontations that could end only in retreat or war. England adhered more closely to the rules of warfare than did the Union; but the Union could not be faulted for deviating from those rules if acceptance of them threatened its very survival.

Lincoln's blockade proclamation had raised numerous questions relating to international law. Had the president actually begun to implement a blockade? Or had his wording shrewdly indicated only the *intention* to blockade, thereby allowing him to change course if necessary? In either case, could the North close more than three thousand miles of coastline with fewer than a hundred vessels, only forty of which were steam-driven? Was not the result a paper blockade, made illegal by international law and more specifically by the Declaration of Paris? Seward argued that the proclamation was "mere notice of an intention to carry it into effect, and [that] the existence of the blockade will be made known in proper form by the blockading vessels." Lyons learned unofficially that merchant vessels in port would have at least fifteen days after the effective installation of a blockade to leave troubled waters. This was insufficient time, he believed. Blockading squadrons would be assigned to the mouths of rivers, where a small force could close the ports. In many instances the distance between ports and blockade stations was too great for a foreign vessel to leave in time. Moreover, the Union appeared to be making no effort to publicize closing notices. Seward maintained that the Union was acting in self-defense and expected England to respect a blockade. Adams assumed, as did the British, that the president had begun the process of implementing a blockade. In response to Russell's repeated misgivings, Adams assured him that Lincoln's proclamation had established an effective and hence legal blockade. Although the coastline was extensive, the Union could close the South because the region had few good harbors and even these were not easily accessible.[19]

Taking the president's proclamation at face value, the British during late May engaged in a series of debates in Parliament that made Adams hopeful of their compliance with a blockade. The British realized the danger of precedent in the long run: violations of an American blockade could ensure the same actions against a British blockade in some future war. But in the short run their refusal to respect a blockade would appear to be helping the South and thereby assure confrontations with the Union at sea. When Lincoln made his declaration pertaining to a blockade, some members of Parliament urged the government to comply. England, they declared, could become a defender of neutral rights and freedom of the seas. Adams, who was present at one evening debate in the Commons, noted rising sentiment for the United States among the upper classes. He caustically added, "It was never otherwise than favorable among the people at large." But he was unsettled by the shouts of approval that rang through the chamber after Sir John Ramsden (who had deserted his Liberal party for the Conservatives) sarcastically assured his fellow countrymen that they "were now witnessing the bursting of the great republican bubble which had been so often held up to us as the model on which to recast our own English Constitution." Russell countered that the Americans' problems had stemmed from slavery and blamed his own nation for throwing "the poisoned garment" around its former colonies. It did not appear appropriate, he emphasized, "that there should be among us anything like exultation at their discord, and still less that we should reproach them with an evil for the origin of which we are ourselves to blame." Adams remained concerned. Even though a large majority in the Commons condemned Ramsden's remarks, Russell won little support for the ministry's policies.[20]

The Lincoln administration soon announced an unorthodox procedure that ensured dangerous international repercussions. In accordance with Seward's statements to Lyons of the previous

March, it was preparing to close Southern ports under municipal law. The simplicity of the move had appeal. It might sidestep the legal complications caused by an ineffective blockade while affording time for the Union to implement a blockade that would deserve the respect of neutral nations. But trouble was certain. Whereas a blockade signified recognition of Southern belligerency, closing ports implied recognition of Southern independence. The Lincoln administration knew that the Constitution prohibited Congress from passing laws favoring one American port over another; therefore, ports could be closed only if the South were out of the Union. In seeking to apply municipal law to foreign nations, the United States would stir up additional heated controversies with England and other maritime nations. Seward defended the measure as a lenient blockade intended to prevent undue hardships on trade. Once the full blockade took effect, it would be enforced everywhere.[21]

The British saw danger that the Americans had not expected. Lyons had earlier grown uneasy about Seward's expressed interest in closing the ports and preferred a blockade because the international rules were clear and acknowledged. Russell likewise perceived the new threat and knew that France would see it too. Together the two European nations might ward off the Union's threat to commerce. He declared that the Union's attempts to close Southern ports would be a disguised paper blockade, guaranteed to heighten tension and raise the possibility of recognition. In this matter as in all others, he instructed Lyons, move in harmony with the French. Lyons agreed with this analysis. Further, he assured Russell, the Union's intention to close Southern ports did not adhere to international law. Not only did the Union expect to impose domestic legislation on foreign nations, but it would be establishing a system whereby no prize court could legally condemn a vessel for violations of that system. A blockade was a wartime power that the Union had implemented, Lyons declared, and yet the Lincoln administration persisted in its attempt to avoid calling the blockade a blockade and the South a belligerent. Seward had stubbornly declared that he would "close his eyes" to royal proclamations (which the British had issued and the French had not) and refuse to abide by extensions of belligerent rights that had not been formally announced to his government.[22]

In mid-June the blockade issue receded in intensity when the British showed no inclination to challenge it. Despite the Confederacy's efforts to convince England that the blockade was illegal and that it should intervene in the war to protect commerce, the loss of cotton would be less costly than war with the United States. Besides, the cotton question would not become serious until the end of the year: bountiful cotton exports in the three years before the war had left the British with a huge surplus. Further, enough other goods made their way through the blockade as to raise questions about the wisdom of confronting the Union on the issue. Finally, just two weeks before, the *Charleston Mercury* had irritated the British by urging Southerners to place an embargo on cotton exports. "The cards are in our hands," the paper declared, "and we intend to play them out to the bankruptcy of every cotton factory in Great Britain and France or the acknowledgment of our independence." William H. Russell heard numerous Southerners boast of certain British recognition and military assistance as if England were "a sort of appanage to their cotton kingdom." Charleston's fire-eating Edmund Rhett smartly claimed that England's "Lord Chancellor sits on a cotton bale."[23]

In the final analysis, the British preferred to wait out American events and found their strongest refuge in international law. Once they declared the Union's maritime restrictions an effective blockade, they were bound as a neutral to respect it. Besides, it was safer to adhere to a blockade than to become embroiled in dangerous hassles with the Union over port closings under municipal law. As long as England's cotton supply held out, the chances remained slim of its vessels running the blockade and provoking a confrontation with the Union.[24]

Before the American troubles had become serious, Palmerston cautioned Russell: "They who in quarrels interpose, will often get a bloody nose." Now, in mid-June, Russell adhered to that advice. He only casually referred to the blockade issue and made clear that naval commanders were under instructions to comply with the Union's procedures unless British subjects or properties were in danger. In a dispatch to Lyons, he referred again to the recent admiralty court decision in Washington that, he argued, substantiated England's acquiescence in a Union blockade. Judge

Dunlop had upheld the Union's seizure of the British schooner *Tropic Wind* in Richmond by declaring that a blockade became effective upon notice of its implementation, whether "actual or constructive."[25]

British tolerance of a blockade did not relieve the Union of its principal threat from abroad. Seward continued to fear intervention. And so did the chairman of the Senate Foreign Relations Committee, Charles Sumner, who considered Russell to be pro-South. To Union observers, a pattern of events pointed to recognition. First, Russell had refused to deny that possibility when former Union minister George Dallas raised the subject. Then the foreign secretary announced a concert between England and France—without consulting the United States—to follow identical policies toward the insurrection. The third sign was Russell's willingness to receive the insurgents' commissioners on an unofficial basis. The fourth was the proclamation of neutrality—issued on the day of Adams's arrival in England and in violation of a promised interview before the adoption of any decisive policy. The tone of the proclamation was especially objectionable, Seward declared, for it appeared "to recognize . . . the insurgents as a *belligerent* national *power*."[26]

On June 15 Lyons and Mercier alarmed Seward when they appeared unexpectedly in his office to notify him jointly and officially of their governments' position of neutrality and recognition of the South as a belligerent. The visit was in part a result of the secretary's recent statement that he would ignore British and French recognition of Southern belligerency without a formal announcement of such policy. The two ministers had determined to comply with his wishes by reading their instructions to him. Seward discerned deeper meaning to the episode. The joint appearance could be a subtle warning of a joint Anglo-French intervention in American affairs.[27]

Seward was working at his desk when he learned of their arrival, and he guardedly asked the messenger which minister had arrived first. "Lord Lyons, sir, but they say they both want to see you together." Seward refused to be intimidated by an apparent Anglo-French show of strength. "Show them both into the Assistant Secretary's room, and I will come in presently."

The secretary's assistant and son Frederick received them at his writing table and detected "an air of rather more than usual constraint and reserve in their manner." He directed them to the sofa, and a short time later the elder Seward entered the room, smiling and shaking his head. "No, no, no. This will never do. I cannot see you in that way."

When the two visitors stood, Lyons said, "True, it is unusual, but we are obeying our instructions." Mercier added, "And at least you will allow us to state the object of our visit?"

"No," Seward curtly replied. "We must start right about it, whatever it is. M. Mercier, will you do me the favour of coming to dine with me this evening? Then we can talk over your business at leisure. And if Lord Lyons will step into my room with me now, we will discuss what he has to say to me."

"If you refuse to see us together—" Mercier began with a shrug—

"Certainly I do refuse to see you together," Seward interrupted, "though I will see either of you separately with pleasure, here or elsewhere."

He asked for each minister's instructions and, after leaving the room to read them privately, returned to declare that he would not formally accept the papers. With nothing further to say, Lyons and Mercier departed. Seward, infuriated by the episode, alerted his emissaries in London and Paris about the Anglo-French concert and stressed the necessity of dealing with each country on an individual basis.

The Anglo-French understanding, Seward emphasized to Adams, must not influence Union policy. The two nations, Seward indignantly declared, had demonstrated a lack of respect for American sovereignty by reaching decisions without consulting the United States. The United States must reject outside involvement from anyone. The Constitution provided all necessary means for resolving the problem. A decade afterward in Paris, Seward was still bristling over the incident when he told Lyons, then England's ambassador to France, that "the three most impudent men in history . . . were Hernando Cortes, Lyons, and Mercier: Cortes for the way he treated Montezuma, Mercier and Lyons for the fifteenth of June, 1861."[28]

Seward warned that war could result from intervention. "The fountains of discontent in any society are many," and foreign meddling would cause more troubles. The government in Washington was using force to put down an insurrection. If foreign nations had the right to intervene in another's domestic affairs, world order would give way to continual war. In a July 4 conversation with William H. Russell, Seward warned: "If any European Power provokes a war, we shall not shrink from it. A contest between Great Britain and the United States would wrap the world in fire." If Seward was bluffing, he fooled Russell: "I could not but admire the confidence—may I say the coolness?—of the statesman who sat in his modest little room within the sound of the evening's guns, in a capital menaced by their forces who spoke so fearlessly of war with a power which could have blotted out the paper blockade of the Southern forts and coast in a few hours, and, in conjunction with the Southern armies, have repeated the occupation and destruction of the capital." Seward wrote Adams that America's domestic trial threatened to grow into a war involving the maritime powers because the United States and England had taken nonnegotiable positions. England could not deal with the Confederacy on any level without insulting the Union. The issue of America's integrity involved "nothing less than the life of the republic itself." [29]

From Washington's perspective, British actions took on the image of a concerted effort with France to move toward recognition of the Confederacy. Surely no other motive could have brought these longtime antagonists together except mutual self-aggrandizement at America's expense. The history of North America since the colonial era revealed consistent European interests in the New World. Russell assured his emissary in Paris that self-interest was not the ministry's primary goal and that the only chance for ending the American war without British involvement lay in a joint effort with France: "I am not disposed to walk alone in the hornets' nest at Washington." The stakes were too high for all concerned to allow the Union to separate England from France. But he could not convince the Union government that his chief motive was peace.[30]

England's relations with the Union continued to diverge. Both governments' vital interests had come into conflict with each other, which meant that the issues were not subject to negotiation. For security reasons, the Union could not allow commerce to flow in and out of the Confederacy; for economic reasons, the British had to maintain commercial relations with the South. If the war dragged on until England's cotton surplus was depleted, the mill workers in Lancashire might erupt in violence and put pressure on the government to force open Southern ports. A major confrontation with the Union navy would develop. Seward realized the danger. He assured the British that they would receive confiscated cotton from the South; and he continued to argue that the Palmerston ministry's failure to renounce any possibility of recognition kept the Confederacy's hopes alive and prolonged the very war that was in England's best interests to stop. Russell had grounded each decision in international law, but the neutrality he professed constituted a threat to the Union.

Ironically, Seward's fears were unjustified and Adams was probably correct: the British government leaned toward the Union—but for reasons having little or nothing to do with sentiment.[31] By late June Adams reported an upswing in British favor for the North, doubtless encouraged by the Union's warnings against involvement and by the growing realization that support for the South meant support for slavery. His son and private secretary in the London legation, Henry Adams, insisted that British sympathy lay with the Union. Since the Lincoln administration's angry reaction to the queen's proclamation of neutrality, the British government had seized every opportunity to prove its goodwill.[32] The younger Adams added, however, that the British ministry considered dissolution of the Union inescapable and that "even our warmest friends thought that this would be best for us as well as for themselves." Thus the British regarded the neutrality proclamation as the correct policy "to keep them straight with both sides." The American minister agreed with his son. The Union's complaints had caused all levels of British society to disclaim unfriendly intentions and to defend the proclamation as necessary to staying out of the war. Indeed, William Gregory in Parliament had withdrawn his resolution for recognizing the South because of insufficient support. The major explanation for improved British feelings, Adams maintained, was the Union's military buildup. William H. Russell upheld this view. Increasing numbers of Englishmen, he declared, were apprehensive that the North would win the war and turn on England.[33]

The steady decline of the port closings issue substantiated the elder Adams's observations. Even when, by mid-July, Congress had authorized the president to close ports in which the Union could not collect duties, Lyons called it a paper blockade but, in England's continued effort to avert a controversy over municipal law, allowed that the administration was buying time in an effort to establish an effective blockade. Lincoln admitted as much privately. After dinner in the Executive Mansion in late July, he told his friend and confidant Senator Orville Browning of Illinois that the avoidance of war with England rested on enlarging the navy and blockading only those ports that could be closed. From London Foreign Secretary Russell held a different view but also urged restraint. The Union had no legal power to close Southern ports and sought a way around a blockade. Even though Adams had admitted that the Constitution required all American ports to be open on an equal basis, Russell discreetly conceded that the Union might regard a rebellion as an exception.[34]

Adams had already concluded that self-interest would prevent the British from extending recognition to the South. Although many British observers seemed to prefer a divided United States, they would not help the Confederacy as long as the Union held the upper hand on land and sea. He also knew that neither the Liberals nor the Conservatives in England could support a slaveowning people. But he also realized that the British government remained poorly informed about American affairs and that few Englishmen understood the real issue of slavery and Union. One side believed that because the Union had not declared emancipation, slavery was not the issue. The other side argued that separation of North and South was consistent with abolition by isolating slavery in the South and forcing its eventual extinction. No one seemed to comprehend the Union's goal of protecting "liberty against reaction." Secession, Adams insisted, was not tantamount to simply dissolving a business partnership. He warned Seward that the best assurance against intervention was victory in battle.[35]

T H E N, in late July, attention suddenly turned to the battlefield. With Richmond as their goal, Union forces were poised at Manassas Junction in Virginia, preparing to launch the first major military campaign of the war against the main arm of the Confederate army, which was encamped about thirty miles from Washington and behind a stream known as Bull Run. Almost with relief, Lyons noted that the "long-expected battle is positively to be fought."[36]

3

Bull Run
and the Threat
of Foreign
Intervention

On July 21, 1861, Confederate forces routed the Union army at Bull Run, convincing many Englishmen that separation was a fait accompli and dramatically raising the South's hopes for recognition.[1] Lyons referred to the North's stunning defeat twice in one note to his superiors. "Bull's Run" should be known as "Yankee's Run," Palmerston crowed to colleagues. The "Bull's Run Races" demonstrated that the North's lack of resolution was attributable to its "fighting for an Idea chiefly entertained by professional politicians," whereas the Confederates were "fighting for what they consider rightly or wrongly vital interests."[2] Russell agreed. The Union defeat, he wrote Lyons, suggested the absence of a driving cause rather than a lack of courage. Charles Francis Adams feared that his prognostications had been correct: diplomatic recognition hinged upon the Union's "trial of fire" on the battlefield. Much of the British press, he bitterly recorded in his diary, seemed satisfied with the Union's humiliation and now spoke of recognition of Southern independence as a matter of course.[3]

IN THE emotional aftermath of Bull Run, impressions took precedence over realities and often distorted the truth. William H. Russell missed the battle but not the retreat. His stories in the *Times* of London described a Union army stumbling back into Washington in humiliating defeat, encouraging the feeling in England that the North could not win. Indeed, his letters printed in the *New York Herald* helped earn him lasting infamy among Northerners as "Bull-Run Russell." But American readers, seeking a scapegoat for the disaster, attributed the wrong meaning to Russell's words. Although many in England thought the war had approached its end, Russell did not. In his diary he prophetically wrote that "this prick in the great Northern balloon will let out a quantity of poisonous gas, and rouse the people to a sense of the nature of the conflict on which they have entered." But Russell was among only a small minority who felt that the Union could bounce back. In a dinner conversation with Mercier two days after the battle, Russell listened to the French minister confidently remark that Bull Run had proved him correct: the North could not subjugate the South and most certainly could not restore the Union.[4]

Many British observers were convinced that further fighting was pointless and that Bull Run had confirmed the South's secession from the Union. The Union's embarrassment had demonstrated its inability to govern a self-professed republic that sprawled from Canada to Mexico and from sea to sea. If the Lincoln administration swallowed its pride and made that admission, the fiasco at Manassas would go down in history as the first and last pitched battle of the war. The South was on the verge of independence.

Confederate leaders agreed, even though realizing that they needed to act with restraint. At such a crucial moment, they realized, they must not make a formal request for recognition without being sure of British acquiescence. But they might press for it. Taking advantage of the victory, the South's three commissioners then in London, Yancey, Rost, and Mann, wrote Russell a note asking for a treaty of friendship, commerce, and navigation. They assured the foreign secretary of their willingness to postpone a formal request for recognition of independence until the full meaning of Bull Run could become clear and justify their claim. England's antislavery sentiment should not be a consideration. Lincoln did not intend to free the slaves, they declared, but he was not above hypocrisy in enlisting British sympathies. He might even resort to instigating a servile war once he realized he could not restore the Union by any other means. The British government should recognize the government in Richmond. Restoration of the Union was impossible.[5]

But despite the popular conception of Bull Run, the British government would not alter its position: the South had not yet established its independence. In a written response to the Confederate commissioners, Russell again relied on international law in justifying neutrality. Agreement to any treaty, he knew, would be tantamount to granting recognition. If he gave in to this pressure, he would violate the dictates of caution as well as the precepts of international law. He also would place England in virtual alliance with the Confederacy and provoke a larger war. Russell continued to believe that either the battlefield or negotiations would have to determine the status of the American belligerents.[6]

Supporters of the Union were not surprised at the British public's reaction to Bull Run and expected a foreign policy crisis. Henry Adams did not know "whether to laugh or cry." His brother in the United States pleaded with him to "make the two countries understand each other." If the Confederacy won recognition, it would have to accede to the British desire for more cotton. A challenge to the blockade would result, causing war with the Union. Attorney General Edward Bates assured cabinet colleagues that England and France envied America's power and were exploiting every opportunity to deal it "a crippling blow." Frederick W. Seward tried to console the American minister in London by predicting a full range of European opinion before the war was over. His father remained at least outwardly confident. Despite the battle, the capital was safe and Union forces were growing in number. The blockade was working and disunion sentiment was not spreading as quickly. But the secretary of state prepared for the expected emergency.[7]

The Union defeat encouraged the Lincoln administration to avert a confrontation with the British over the port closings bill. In late July Lyons noted with relief that the president had not yet issued a proclamation closing the ports and that he might not do so. Bull Run, the minister thought, might have eased cabinet pressure for the move. Opposition to the proclamation came primarily from Seward, who had suddenly become less bellicose. He read Lyons parts of the dispatch to Adams in which the Union claimed the right to close the ports—a statement included in the event that Congress wanted to see the document. Seward then emphasized that the proposed act was "enabling" in that its passage did not mean that the president would close the ports but that he should have the power to do so. The interests of other nations, Seward assured Lyons, would have bearing on the president's final decision. Lyons was skeptical about Seward's calm demeanor and recommended a firm policy. England must "disabuse both Government and people of the delusion that they can carry their points with us by bluster and violence, and that we are more afraid of a war than they are."[8]

Russell realized that the port closings bill was dangerous enough by itself, but he also knew that combined with others it held even greater potential for trouble. He intended to avoid a confrontation at sea. War would endanger Canada and place his people on the side of the slaveowners. Yet he was pulled in more than one direction. The law of nations permitted the Union to collect duties at the port of delivery. But the port closings measure would violate international law by authorizing the president to order the seizure of foreign vessels and cargoes in areas not under blockade. A customshouse, Russell remarked, could not be on a vessel "at sea near the coast." The Union was attempting to establish a paper blockade. Yet Russell could not ignore economic realities. The loss of the coming fall's cotton crop would hurt England, even though the surplus on hand would smooth over the most serious difficulties for a while longer. Lacking viable alternatives, Russell concluded that the wisest strategy was to do nothing. He comforted himself with the notion that President Lincoln had the power to prevent acts offensive to maritime nations and recommended a continuation of England's watch-and-wait policy.[9]

During his ruminations, Russell came to suspect that Seward was using British opposition to port closures as a way to divide England and France. When the Anglo-American showdown came, Seward perhaps thought, France would not be at England's side. Surely even the impulsive secretary of state was exploiting this matter to show the Union's determination and thereby ward off outside intervention. But this risky strategy could encourage a maritime encounter involving honor. Russell noted another potential for trouble. If British merchant vessels were unable to enter Southern ports by agreement, they would find other entrances along the three thousand miles of coastline. Small vessels might even run out of creeks or bays for Jamaica or the Bahamas, "where the cargoes might be transshipped." The lord chancellor, Baron Westbury, had no patience with the Americans. He warned Russell against allowing "an arrogant & encroaching people" to violate international law. The resulting loss of British prestige in Europe would provide a precedent encouraging the North to demand more. He suggested ways out of the morass. If British leaders determined that the Union had an effective blockade, they could act honorably and within international law by barring their nation's merchant ships from blockaded waters. Should this measure prove unsatisfactory, the British government could approve the passage of vessels that paid Union duties. In no case, Russell concluded, would England condone American violations of international law. He was confident that France would adhere to England's policy.[10]

The port closings issue remained troublesome, rising and falling in relation to the Union's shifting faith in a blockade. Russell could not have known, but Seward had already reverted to his aggressive form. The secretary told Lyons that port closings were imminent. Lyons believed that Seward had learned of the recent buildup of England's Atlantic squadron and intended to show that the move had not cowed the White House. A week later, Lyons noted that even though the press and public supported the closings, Seward seemed to oppose the move. The secretary swung back and forth between closing the ports and upgrading the blockade. The successes of Confederate privateers running in and out of the ports had forced Seward to focus on the blockade. What he failed to see, Lyons believed, was that a strong naval squadron was essential to closing the ports, whether by blockade or by customs law. In either case, the Union blockade would never be effective. Consular reports substantiated its failure. With some trepidation Lyons warned that U.S. customs and port officers would as a matter of course interfere with British shipping.[11]

Meanwhile, another issue emerged that heightened the Union's fear of recognition. In mid-August Seward learned that a private citizen from Charleston, Robert Mure, was en route to New York and then to England, allegedly carrying dispatches from Richmond for the Foreign Office in London. Indeed, the South was responding to the Palmerston ministry's attempt to secure the Confederacy's adherence to all parts of the Declaration of Paris except the prohibition against privateering. But in the British government's attempt to keep commercial lanes open for neutrals, its diplomatic contact with Richmond further convinced the Union that recognition was imminent. Evidence was circumstantial though seemingly conclusive. It revealed that Mure, a colonel in the insurgents' military forces in South Carolina and a cousin of the British consul in New Orleans, also had dispatches for the Confederate commissioners in London and that he had acquired his passport from the British consul in Charleston, Robert Bunch. Seward ordered New York police to seize Mure and his papers— among them a sealed bag and a huge batch of private letters, all but four of them sealed. Mure also carried a letter of introduction written by Bunch and several unsealed copies of an inflammatory pamphlet lauding the South's victory at Bull Run.[12]

The Bunch affair infuriated the Lincoln administration. A British consul (whose responsibilities were commercial and not diplomatic) had apparently safeguarded Confederate dispatches and anti-Union materials in British diplomatic pouches. The papers, Seward contended, argued for disunion and were treasonable. If they were legal, Bunch should have sent them through Lyons, whose voucher would have assured their safe passage. Mure's letter of introduction emphasized the necessity of concealing the papers from Union officials. Seward read only those papers not under diplomatic seal and found them traitorous. He had not broken the seals of the others because of comity with the British government, propriety, and faith in England's "friendship towards the United States."[13]

To prevent a confrontation, Seward sought to leave Russell an honorable way out of the situation. The foreign secretary could disavow any knowledge of the papers or refuse to accept them if they were illegal. Seward sent the bag to Adams by special courier and with instructions to deliver it to Russell. Adams was convinced that both the British and French consuls were working with the Confederates and declared that if the papers were treasonable, Russell should recall Bunch. Seward had told Adams that Mure's letters implicated Bunch as a "conspirator" against the Union and suggested that the British had taken "the *first step* to recognition." Indeed, the French were involved. Bunch had collaborated with their consul in Charleston in sending an emissary to Richmond to discuss diplomatic matters. According to one letter addressed to a Confederate agent in Europe, "This is the first step of direct treating with our government."[14]

Russell denied Seward's allegations. Adams reported the foreign secretary's admission that Bunch had acted under "secret instructions, which are only now acknowledged because they have come to light." But Russell declared that nothing in the bag substantiated the charge of conspiracy. He reminded Seward that the Union's suspension of postal service from British subjects between North and South had caused a communications problem that Bunch had tried to ease by including private correspondence in consular bags. Further, in accordance with the Anglo-French agreement to maintain commercial avenues, Bunch had received instructions to inform the Confederacy that the British and French governments sought its acquiescence in all articles of the Declaration of Paris except that against privateering. Palmerston doubted that Lincoln would "draw the sword," but his administration had shown itself to be "so wild" that no action it took would be a surprise. Russell refused to recall his consul and denied that England had taken the first step toward recognition. The British, he emphasized to Adams, "have not recognized, and are not prepared to recognize the so-called Confederate States as a separate and independent State."[15]

Russell had no plans for recognition but had imprudently gotten involved in a risky enterprise that left the impression of an impending interference and thus lacked the full support of the ministry. The Union regarded any British communication with the Confederate government as a move toward recognition. Lyons was England's highest ranking diplomatic official in America and could not talk with Confederate officials without raising a storm; but no less suspicious was the Palmerston ministry's decision to authorize a nondiplomat, a consul, to conduct diplomatic business with a belligerent—the Confederacy. And the choice of consuls in itself did not seem wise. Bunch explained that Mure had assured him the packets contained only letters from mercantile friends and not dispatches from Richmond. Further, Bunch declared that Mure's so-called passport was only a paper certifying his authorization to carry British dispatches to London. But Russell was angry because Bunch had violated Lyons's instructions not to entrust dispatches to persons carrying private correspondence. Bunch was not prudent in forwarding all mail sent to his office in a consular bag. In peacetime such a plan would be inviting trouble; during the Civil War he was begging for it. The chancellor of the exchequer, William E. Gladstone, recognized the danger. He wrote Secretary for War George Cornewall Lewis that a consul must not serve as an "instrument in making any necessary arrangement with the Southern States." [16]

In Washington, Lyons defended the plan while admitting to its pitfalls. The ministry's attempt to assure neutrals' safety in the sea lanes was understandable, even though he knew that the Union would never acquiesce in London's making contact with Richmond to bring this about. An announcement of Confederate compliance with the Declaration of Paris would also have caused an uproar; but after the tumult had subsided, Lyons hoped, the North would realize that that compliance was not official—that under the pact of 1856 no signatory could negotiate a separate agreement on any of the declaration's terms with a nonsignatory. Lyons's reasoning was questionable. He hoped by "conciliatory words, by avoiding as far as possible abstract assertions of principle, and especially by never yielding an iota in practice, we shall by degrees accustom the government and the People here to see us treat the Confederate States as *de facto* independent." Bunch's effort to win Confederate compliance with most of the Declaration of Paris might have succeeded, Lyons mused, if the messenger had not been carrying "foolish private letters."[17]

When Russell refused to recall Bunch, the Lincoln administration revoked the consul's exequatur (written recognition of authority as consul given by the U.S. government), charging that his behavior had constituted another maneuver toward British recognition of the South. If Bunch was innocent of conspiracy, Seward contended, the consul had nonetheless violated the U.S. law prohibiting anyone below presidential authority from corresponding with a foreign government on political matters. Only diplomatic agents could make diplomatic communications. Bunch had no right to communicate with the insurgents and, in so doing, violated America's sovereignty. The "proceeding in which he was engaged," Seward declared, "was in the nature of a treaty with the insurgents, and the first step towards a recognition by Great Britain of their sovereignty."[18]

Russell accepted the White House decision but not without firing a parting shot that found an exposed target. After denying any wrongdoing, he shrewdly noted the irony in the Union's position. If the Confederacy was not a foreign state, as the Union had insisted, revocation of the exequatur did not apply because the action rested on a law prohibiting Americans from engaging in political correspondence with a foreign government. Bunch, Russell declared, was not an American and had no instructions to help foreign governments at odds with the United States. Although Adams insisted that the statute in question applied to anyone, not just Americans, he failed to convince Russell. In citing the statute, Russell continued, the United States appeared to admit that the Richmond government was a foreign government—"an admission which goes further than any acknowledgment with regard to those States which her Majesty's government have hitherto made."[19]

Union fears of recognition were exaggerated, but the claim that Russell's actions in the Bunch affair were not entirely neutral was correct. Though the foreign secretary acted in good conscience in trying to safeguard the commercial rights of neutrals, his effort to secure Confederate agreement (along with that of the Union) to all parts of the Declaration of Paris save that on privateering took on the appearance of bilateral negotiations with Richmond and hence constituted an admission of Southern sovereignty. Combined with British recognition of belligerent status, this new twist in diplomacy further convinced the government in Washington that its suspicions of England were well founded.

Indeed, the Confederate Congress in mid-August had agreed to England's requests regarding the Declaration of Paris. Technically, the Confederacy accepted the invitation of over forty nations to comply with all terms except the one on privateering. Union officials saw matters differently. According to their view, the British government had negotiated a treaty with the government in Richmond that constituted another step toward recognition.[20]

While the Bunch affair had been building in intensity, the Palmerston ministry made a curious change in its stand on the Declaration of Paris that suggested to the Union still another move toward recognition. In late August Adams reported failed negotiations with London over the privateering issue. Adams had taken the high-principled view of emphasizing that American acquiescence in the Paris terms would be for the purpose of establishing a permanent maritime code. Russell dismissed this claim as rhetoric intended to conceal the Union's efforts to outlaw privateering and, in that manner, to obligate all signatory nations to police the seas against Southern privateers while freeing the Union to tighten its blockade. Just as Adams was ready to sign, Russell wanted to add a written declaration that England "[did] not intend thereby to undertake any engagement which shall have any bearing, direct or indirect, on the internal differences now prevailing in the United States." Consent to this qualification, Adams complained, would imply that the U.S. government sought "some small temporary object" during its domestic trial. More so, he knew that Russell had devised a clever ruse for escaping the enforcement of anti-privateering responsibilities required by the Declaration of Paris.[21]

As in most controversies, the real bases for the opposing parties' differences were obscured by convoluted arguments that, even if valid, served purposes that only the inner circles of each government could know. The new article in the treaty, Seward declared, would permit the British (or any other nations) to alter their relations with the United States on the basis of its internal problems. In this instance England sought a "special rule" that would endanger America's welfare by relieving the Royal Navy of its responsibility to stop Southern privateering. Russell countered that England had declared neutrality during a civil war, and yet the U.S. government kept speaking of rebels and pirates. It logically followed that the Confederacy, recognized as a belligerent under international law, could authorize privateers. But by logic again, it followed that since the North insisted that Southern privateers were pirates, a European power signing a convention with the Union would be bound to treat those privateers as pirates. An exception proved necessary.[22]

Russell's argument was defensible, but it failed to stem Washington's suspicion that the British government was preparing to recognize a second North American republic. From London's perspective, its determination to stay out of the American war necessitated the qualifying statement. To the Union, Russell's qualification suggested that his government had decided against an agreement with the Union abolishing privateering and was sending a message to the Confederacy that England would take no action aiding the North in the war. The amendment would constitute a virtual announcement to the South that privateering was acceptable and that the natural next step would be to revoke the British prohibition against the entry of privateers with prizes. Though the Union apprehensions were unwarranted, Lincoln's administration could have interpreted the British action in no other way.

Like the trouble over the Bunch affair, the privateering problem was not subject to an amicable solution because of its integral relationship to the recognition issue. No matter which way the British turned, they would alienate at least one of the American antagonists. The British position exposed a danger about which specialists in international law had long warned neutrals: avoid any activity that could be construed as harmful to either belligerent in a war.[23] The British maintained support for the original pact in 1856, repeated their loyalty to international law, and then proposed a vaguely worded qualification that permitted them to make exceptions when needed. England's guiding principle remained to stay out of the war by adhering to neutrality. But it also kept a careful eye on events that would settle the question of whether the Confederacy had achieved separation and warranted recognition.

BY THE AUTUMN of 1861 the Union fears that the British had moved closer to recognition of the Confederacy seemed justified. Bull Run had encouraged the growing belief in England that Southern separation was irrevocable and that the Lincoln administration should end the war. The British military buildup in Canada continued, while below the Rio Grande River, in Mexico, another civil war endangered foreign citizens and property and invited armed intervention from abroad. In London, and over Union protests, Confederate agents purchased the fast-moving *Bermuda*, which ran the blockade into Savannah, Georgia. Confederate agents had resorted to subterfuge in contracting with shipbuilders in Liverpool for the construction of cruisers such as the *Alabama* and the *Florida*. Mobile journalist Henry Hotze, recently appointed a commercial agent by the government in Richmond, was preparing to publish a weekly journal in London called the *Index* in an attempt to mold pro-Southern sentiment throughout the country. And all the while the high Morrill Tariff wore on British merchants, threatening to drive even those sympathetic with the North into the hands of the South.[24]

During the summer of 1861 Russell had expressed dismay over the American war in a letter to his longtime acquaintance and former American minister to London, Edward Everett of Massachusetts. The foreign secretary's concern had often bordered on outright distress and by mid-July had nearly made him despondent. Port closings, the blockade, privateering, recognition—all were frustrating issues that had eaten away at his patience until he must have wondered about the feasibility of clinging to principle. He could not understand why the Union had not pronounced the American conflict for what it was—a war for abolition. He hated slavery and had seized every opportunity to destroy it. Had he not been a member of the cabinet that abolished the institution in the West Indies?[25] If the Union would admit that slavery was the primary issue driving the two sections apart, the basis for the war would become clear to outside observers and England could unite against the Southern proponents of slavery. But both American antagonists had instead focused on other matters and succeeded only in confusing everyone. In good faith the Palmerston ministry had announced neutrality and then quietly assured the Union that it had the sympathy of the British government and most of its citizens. But the Union wanted more. And when Russell refused to give anything more than honest neutrality (which Russell knew was, in practical terms, an advantage to the Union), he was accused of being pro-Southern.

Russell felt indignant. He had struggled to stay within the confines of international law, and he had maintained what he considered to be a strict and impartial neutrality. He had legally extended recognition of belligerent status to both sides in the conflict, and he had followed the law of nations in insisting that recognition of Southern independence would not come until the South had, in fact, won its independence. Why should he come under attack for the Union's failure to understand that the British intended to stay out of the conflict and allow the battlefield to determine the outcome? Yet his policies had earned nothing but criticism—even from his people at home.

Politically inspired attacks were part of the game, Russell knew; but many of the recent assaults arose from genuine concern over expected economic distress. The cotton surplus would be gone by autumn 1862—or were the mill owners lying about their stocks, holding back production and taking advantage of import cutbacks in an attempt to drive up prices? And the Confederacy had imposed an embargo on cotton that aided its enemy's blockade effort while hurting the country it needed to befriend. Southerners offered the explanation that they had barred cotton from Atlantic ports out of fear of Northern confiscation. But whatever the truth, workers in Lancashire were growing increasingly uneasy about shortened workweeks and a certain rough winter. Poor law assistance and public works programs could not hold back violence forever. And with that violence could come a demand to challenge the blockade that would bring the war with the Union that Russell sought to avert.

Russell was not in an enviable position. Intervention in the American conflict could bring it to a close, or it could incite a war with the Union. A third possibility existed: failure to intervene might prolong the struggle and force an intervention for both economic and humanitarian reasons. International law, Russell knew, permitted nonbelligerent nations to encourage those at war to settle their differences. Indeed, American blood would be on England's hands if it ignored its moral and legal duty as a civilized nation to take every action possible toward securing peace. The North had seemingly satisfied principle by fighting to preserve the Union; the South had nonetheless established its claim to secession. Continued fighting would destroy both sides—and for no purpose.

But if Russell sought consolation and understanding from Everett, he found neither. In early September, at the same time as the Bunch affair, Everett's reply reached the Foreign Office. As if the letter had first gone through Adams's hands for approval, it contained all the familiar arguments the American minister had presented after his stormy arrival in London the previous May. Everett had found it difficult to express these hard feelings. He had fond memories of the long hours of whist and other social amenities he enjoyed while in London; but, like a friend betrayed, he was now deeply hurt and upset with the British. Russell, Everett declared, had underestimated the extent of Americans' dissatisfaction with British policy. They were angry with the quick granting of belligerent rights and the lack of sympathy with the United States during its crucial hour. Russell had not been convincing when he compared British recognition of Southern belligerency with the United States's and England's recognition of South American republics. Whereas both countries had waited years before taking that action, in the present case, the British held off a mere four to five weeks after the fighting had begun before extending recognition of belligerency and receiving the Southern commissioners. The Union had not expected the British to declare war on the Confederacy. But it did want them to renounce any possibility of recognition. Instead, England adopted an air of "cold neutrality" although part of the British press was decidedly favorable to the Confederacy.[26]

Everett insisted that the British misunderstood the American situation. Russell, like many of his countrymen, failed to see the relationship of slavery to the war for the Union. The Lincoln administration had thought that England's views on slavery would prevent any action encouraging to the South. The British, however, had set aside their antislavery sentiment, failed to grasp the importance of the Unionist issue, and then, incredibly, welcomed the Confederacy's drive for independence. Despite disclaimers from both North and South, Everett wrote, this war grew out of slavery. Russell was wrong in asserting that the war served no moral purpose and that Lincoln should have let the South go in peace. Only a national convention (which would have taken a long time to assemble) could have made separation constitutional. To prevent such a meeting and other peace attempts, the South had attacked Fort Sumter. Everett had heard from a reliable authority that the Confederate commissioners had urged Russell not to receive Adams—that by the time he arrived in London the Union capital would be in the Confederates' hands and "they would be the United States." Russell, Everett concluded, had approached the brink of recognition by announcing neutrality and extending belligerent rights before Adams had had a chance to present the Union case.[27]

Despite appearances, Russell was not secretly pulling for the South. Again he felt that his views, particularly about slavery as a cause of the war, had been misrepresented. And his forbearance was already in short supply because of implications arising from Seward's concurrent complaints about Bunch's behavior. Russell had not spoken of Southern separation out of pro-Southern sympathy; nor had he done so out of ill feeling toward the North. He simply wanted the North to recognize the South's independence as an accomplished fact and call an end to the war. To Russell's credit, he knew that slavery was a vital part of the war—perhaps *the* vital part. But abolition was not the answer. He still had not grasped the crucial connection between the maintenance of the Union and the ultimate end of slavery.

Russell's adherence to neutrality was buttressed by an undercurrent of English support for the Union that opposed any thought of recognition. In the cabinet, the Duke of Argyll, who was lord privy seal and outspokenly pro-Union, expressed alarm that the ministry might consider recognizing the South. At present, he insisted, "no one can say that the result of the contest is in sight." Parliamentary member William E. Forster from the Liberal party also opposed recognition. The son of a Quaker missionary and nephew of the renowned antislavery spokesman Thomas

Fowell Buxton, Forster publicly approved the international impact of Harriet Beecher Stowe's best-selling abolitionist novel in America, *Uncle Tom's Cabin*, and denounced the South's treatment of black people. British neutrality was beneficial to the Union, he declared, while urging Russell's under secretary of state for foreign affairs to oppose involvement in the American war. If England were to violate international law by recognizing the South prematurely, a war could ensue in which Northern privateers would harass British commerce and block the flow of cotton. Worse, England would be in the position of "fighting for slavery." The North would then instigate a slave rebellion and cause a race war that would spread throughout the South. Forster refused to believe that Russell "would commit any such insanity."[28]

Despite the Union's assessment, the greatest pressure for intervention came not from England but from the European side of the English Channel. Since the earliest days of the Civil War, France had expressed interest in intervention. Whether to secure a toehold in North America or simply to garner a heavy share of Southern cotton, Napoleon III consistently demonstrated a strong interest in American affairs. In doing so he followed the example of his illustrious uncle, Napoleon I, who had dreamed of building a French empire in the New World that would relegate its English competitor to a secondary position in the world power structure. The first Napoleon had not been secretive in his schemes, and Napoleon III was equally open and adventurist in his own machinations. From across the Atlantic in 1861, an opportunity appeared from below the Confederate border: Mexico was in civil war and vulnerable to foreign intervention because of its indebtedness to European nations. As events transpired, the Union soon feared that a joint intervention in Mexico that included England and France would provide an entrée into the Western Hemisphere as well as a precedent for further action above the Rio Grande.

Russell realized that France would have preferred to act alone in any New World enterprise; but he also knew that Napoleon was no fool. The French emperor was mounting a serious challenge to British naval power, and Russell had noted increased criticisms of England by the French, leading him to wonder if they were tiring of the British entente. The Crimean alliance with France had deteriorated after their war with Russia of the mid-1850s, and the Palmerston ministry had tried to restore the ties before being left out of the political and economic changes then sweeping across Europe.[29] Both the British and the French realized that their concert regarding American affairs rested only on mutual self-interest. They also knew that a multilateral intervention was wiser than a unilateral move. A joint intervention made it less dishonorable to pull out in the event of failure, and it did not leave the intervening nation's chief rival free to exploit other ongoing hot spots of the world, particularly those in Denmark and Italy.

The French effort got under way in early October 1861, when Mercier met with Lyons to make a case for intervention in the American war. Mercier had returned to Washington in late September, after a much publicized tour of both North and South with Prince Napoleon Jerome Bonaparte. The visit had caused an angry stir in the Union, where longtime apprehensions regarding French intentions in North America seemed to be substantiated. Surely, Northerners complained, the Emperor Napoleon had sent his cousin (second in line of succession) to the Confederacy in an attempt to demonstrate friendship and to assess the feasibility of recognition. In early August, just two weeks after Bull Run, the prince had applied for a pass to see the battlefield. Seward had had misgivings, even though he approved arrangements to escort the young man to Southern lines. William H. Russell put his finger on the problem when he recorded in his diary that Union supporters regarded the prince's arrival in the South as "a recognition of the Confederates as a belligerent power." Now, back in Washington, Mercier gave Lyons a summary of a private letter from Foreign Secretary Thouvenel that the prince had brought with him to America. France's need for cotton had become so serious that Thouvenel sought an understanding with England on taking some action. Mercier had a disquieting recommendation: England and France should recognize the South and then warn the Union against any interference with their trade.[30]

Lyons listened as Mercier reported his communiqué to Thouvenel that intervention might end the war. Several Americans, Mercier declared, had assured him during his tour with the prince that recognition of the Confederacy was the only way to stop the fighting. They insisted that the move would attract the support of a large number of Northerners who were searching for a way to stop the war. Recognition by the European powers would prove the futility of the struggle. But Mercier did not think the time opportune. Like Lyons, the French minister still had not comprehended the Union's resolution after Bull Run. Mercier believed that the North had only momentarily recovered from that military disaster and was again building a false sense of security. The number of recruits was increasing, military preparations had resumed, successful naval expeditions along the coast had raised hopes, and news had arrived of Union advances in Kentucky and Missouri. The North would agree to a separation, he insisted, after it had erased the humiliation suffered at Bull Run.[31]

Mercier thought that the optimism in the North would soon collapse again and provide the moment for intervention. At that point England and France might intervene with a strong policy that would win Northern support and bring an end to the fighting. Mercier counted on British cooperation because, unaware of the surplus on hand, he thought their need for cotton more serious than that of the French. Actually, both nations were heavily dependent on Southern cotton. Like England, France had a surplus of cotton because of the bountiful Southern harvests during the three years preceding the war. But whereas England received 80 percent of its cotton from the South, France's draw was 93 percent. When Lyons expressed doubt that his government was ready to recognize the South or break the blockade, Mercier reminded him that Confederate foreign policy rested on denying cotton to Europe until it extended recognition or freed the South from the blockade.[32]

Mercier had taken a long step toward intervention but just as boldly retreated: if England was not ready to act, "France would not act alone." As if he intended the joint interventionist proposal as a stratagem for winning British trust, Mercier denied French self-interest in the New World and expressed concern for England's welfare. The French would do nothing without British approval, he promised.[33]

Lyons forwarded the matter to London but warned that for recognition to end the war, the intervening powers must be prepared to use military force in the event the North refused to lay down arms. He agreed that the time was not auspicious for such an extreme measure. If the Union came to realize the impossibility of restoring the South, Americans on both sides might feel compelled to welcome Anglo-French intervention. But Lyons was convinced that as long as the Union saw a chance for victory it would resist European involvement. Upon granting recognition, England (and France) might avoid conflict with the United States only by amassing a great naval force and acting without hesitation. Recognition would not end the war unless the intervening powers took the extreme measure of negotiating "a defensive (if not also an offensive) Alliance with the South."[34]

Almost within the hour of the receipt of Lyons's dispatch, Russell took it to Palmerston, who agreed with his emissary in Washington that the best British policy for the present was to stay out of the contest. The only pretext for interfering would be to protect the interested nations from war's harm. The European powers, Palmerston declared, could not now argue that the war in America threatened their welfare. The steadily dipping cotton supply would not justify interference unless the situation became more serious. Some American cotton would reach England, and more than usual amounts would arrive from other areas of the world. Russell could not have forgotten what Palmerston had told him less than two weeks earlier: "This cotton question will most certainly assume a serious character by the beginning of next year; and if the American civil war has not by that time come to an end, I suspect that we shall be obliged either singly or conjointly with France to tell the northerners that we cannot allow some millions of our people to perish to please the Northern States and that the blockade of the South must be so far relaxed as to [allow] cotton loaded ships to come out."[35]

Although Palmerston sounded emphatic, he remained tentative: "A Rupture with the United States would at all times be an Evil," especially in winter because ice and snow in Canada would hamper communications and troop mobilization. In addition, he found it wise to keep the French at arm's length. They had less to lose in a war with the Union. They had no direct line of contact with the United States, their naval power was stronger than the

Union's, and they had less commerce to risk. We should "lie on our oars," Palmerston insisted. As he argued to Russell's under secretary, it was too early for a decision. The war's operations "have as yet been too indecisive to warrant an acknowledgment of the Southern Union." [36]

Palmerston's caution resulted from other considerations as well, particularly the ongoing negotiations with France and Spain pertaining to intervention in the Mexican civil war. Rumors were correct: the three European nations were working out the details of a joint venture that would arouse further Union suspicions of the Old World nations' intentions. Would France and England (and even Spain) use a Mexican intervention as precedent for intervening in the United States? Adams thought so. European control of the Mexican coast all the way north to Matamoros would permit an evasion of the Union blockade and lead to Old World intervention in American affairs. Since September the three European governments had been trying to decide how to undercut the Union's recent offer of a loan to Mexico in exchange for securities in the form of public lands and mineral rights. They opposed the American proposal. As Palmerston wryly remarked, "a mortgage of Mexico to the United States . . . would certainly lead to foreclosing." [37]

The idea of a Mexican expedition did not appeal to everyone in the Palmerston ministry. Russell had told the queen that England should send a naval force to the Mexican coast to help take Vera Cruz—but not to include ground forces for an occupation. In either case, Russell considered it essential that the United States agree to the venture and that, out of concern that France might pervert the agreement, England renounce any intention to interfere with the Mexican government. To do otherwise would violate the British doctrine of nonintervention, embroil England in a vicious internal struggle, and alienate Americans. Secretary for War Lewis objected to joining France and Spain in what the newspapers were calling an all-out war in Mexico. He considered it unjust to use force in collecting debts from "a notoriously bankrupt, dishonest, & unsettled government." Fighting a people in a state of anarchy would be "like fighting with the Arabs of the desert." He added sarcastically, "It seems from the tone of the newspapers that this is to be a Foreign Office war, in which the Cabinet is to have no voice." Lewis appeared to be correct. His brother-in-law the Earl of Clarendon had recently complained that to declare war on Mexico without going before the cabinet would be "Palmerstonian." When he had urged Palmerston to take the matter of the Vera Cruz blockade before the cabinet, the prime minister had quipped: "Oh, ah! the Cabinet . . . very well; call one then, if you think it necessary."[38]

Over public and private opposition, England joined France and Spain in signing the Treaty of London on October 31, establishing a military expedition to Mexico and inviting the United States to join. Although the three European governments offered assurances that they sought only "the redress of grievances," Seward was not sure and quickly turned down the invitation. If, in retrospect, he should have lodged a strong protest of the Mexican intervention, he did not think it wise at the time. Mexico, he believed, had made advances toward self-government and would eventually prevail over its Old World monarchical invaders. Seward had other considerations as well. Saddled by one war and remembering the opposition to his April memo, he decided against challenging the Europeans' action. Resistance to the Mexican expedition might draw its participants northward and, in so doing, help the South destroy the Union. Once the Union was restored, Seward thought, the United States would deal with the European intruders.[39]

The events following Bull Run made clear that the United States would have to survive its domestic and foreign challenges on its own. The Anglo-American rapprochement had endured numerous difficulties, but the present troubles were potentially more serious. When the Union's moment of trial came in 1861 the British appeared undecided about which American antagonist should receive their support. Charles Francis Adams wrote his son in the United States that the *Times* of London had admitted to what he already knew—that if the United States were permanently divided, it would no longer be a threat to Europe. Henry Adams complained that the Union's friends in England had been "lukewarm," whereas the South's supporters openly praised its call for independence. A little later, the young Adams was more distressed. No European government would help the Union, he wrote his brother. "They all hate us and fear us. . . . We must depend wholly on ourselves."[40]

The Adamses, like many other Americans from the North, were too hard on the British government and people. Despite the widespread belief in the North (and South) that British calls for conceding the breakup of the Union were signs of sympathy for the South, the ministry and its people held on to neutrality while regarding separation as the only way to stop the bloodshed, re-open the cotton trade, and, at least in Russell's thinking, bring an eventual end to slavery. In a view that never gained support from his colleagues but was popular with Lord Robert Cecil and a good number of other Conservatives, Russell argued that separation of the South would be advisable because, as the sole slave nation in North America, it would come under enormous internal and external pressure to grant emancipation rather than see the slaves escape into surrounding free countries. Restoration of the Union was not desirable. If the South returned to the Union, Russell declared, it would demand guarantees for slavery. "For this reason I wish for separation."[41]

Russell's thoughts on slavery and Southern separation underlined his failure to grasp the intensity of the American conflict. North and South had gone to war over the very issues that he thought were soluble by merely accepting separation and allowing slavery to end peacefully. The North would never make peace at the cost of permitting Southern separation or safeguarding slavery, and the South would never lay down its arms without a guarantee of independence and protection against emancipation. Southern independence with slavery would constitute a total defeat for the Union and a total victory for the Confederacy. No hope existed for a compromise.

From the Union's vantage point, the British government had opened the door to intervention by the autumn of 1861. Bull Run had combined with other Anglo-American difficulties to enhance the fears of recognition. Even though Russell insisted that the ministry's neutrality remained intact, the possibility of recognition of the Confederacy seemed alive, especially because of a potential alliance of pro-Southern enthusiasts and equally strong proponents of neutrality who believed Southern separation a fait accompli.

SUPPORTERS OF recognition received a sudden boost in early November, when a Union cruiser stopped a British vessel in the Caribbean and removed the Confederacy's newly appointed ministers to London and Paris. British neutrality was about to undergo its most severe test yet.

There never was within

memory such a burst of feeling.

—*An American in London,*

November 29, 1861

4

The *Trent* Affair
and Recognition

During the winter of 1861–62 the Confederacy's hopes for recognition soared as the Union and British governments appeared poised for war over the *Trent* affair. The government in Richmond had recalled its three commissioners and replaced them with two higher ranking ministers plenipotentiary: James Mason of Virginia to London and John Slidell of Louisiana to Paris. They were to press England and France for disavowal of the blockade and recognition of the South. The two emissaries ran the blockade out of Charleston in mid-October, en route for Havana, where they booked passage on the British steamship *Trent*. Under the presumed safety of the neutral flag overhead, they intended to travel to St. Thomas, where they planned to board a steamer to Europe. But Captain Charles Wilkes of the USS *San Jacinto* was in Cuban waters and had learned that Mason and Slidell were on the *Trent*. Spotting the vessel in the Bahama Channel on the

James Mason, Confederate minister to England
(National Archives)

afternoon of November 8, he fired two shots across its bow and brought it to a stop. Then, in a move unprecedented in admiralty history, he ordered an officer to remove Mason and Slidell as the "embodiment of dispatches" (hence contraband) and bring them aboard the *San Jacinto*. The *Trent* was allowed to resume its voyage, while its former passengers and their two secretaries were taken to Boston and incarcerated in Fort Warren.[1]

John Slidell, Confederate minister to France
(National Archives)

Northerners rejoiced over the seizure of Mason and Slidell. Starved for good news after Bull Run, they praised Wilkes for avenging that humiliation and all British maritime encroachments with one blow. The seizure of these two Southerners in particular drew a triumphant response. Mason had been a principal advocate of the hated Fugitive Slave Law and the Kansas-Nebraska Act, and Slidell had earned a reputation as one of the most dedicated secessionists in Congress. Americans reacted with a "cackle of joy," according to Charles Francis Adams, Jr., as he prepared for duty in the Union army. "I remembered the last exhibition I saw Mason make of himself in the Senate-chamber; and I smacked my lips with joy." William H. Russell noted that Slidell was "one of the most determined disunionists" in the South—"subtle, full of device, and fond of intrigue." At Fort Warren, Russell predicted, Slidell "would conspire with the mice against the cat sooner than not conspire at all." The capture of these two rabble-rousers, Northerners believed, had vindicated Bull Run and restored the nation's honor.[2]

But after the instant celebrations began to wane, Americans became concerned about England's reaction. Many observers admitted that the act was a violation of their own country's opposition to search and impressment. Moreover, Wilkes had violated international law: a human being had never been considered contraband, and the vessel had not been heading for an enemy port. Wilkes had not searched the *Trent* for contraband goods; had he done so, he might have discovered that the British commander had cooperated with Mason in hiding a Confederate mail pouch from the boarding party, a violation of the vessel's neutral standing that made it subject to capture and prize adjudication. Despite the books on international law in Wilkes's cabin (including those by Vattel and Wheaton), he had been unable to find a precedent for his action. He had acted illegally in seizing diplomatic envoys from a neutral ship bound for a neutral port.[3]

The certain storm from across the sea was slow in coming because the Atlantic cable was not working and the British did not learn about the *Trent* for nearly two weeks; but when the steamer bearing the news arrived in England it set off a furious outcry over what was regarded as a gross infringement of British honor. An American in London wrote Seward: "There never was within memory such a burst of feeling. . . . The people are frantic with rage, and were the country polled, I fear 999 men out of a thousand would declare for immediate war." Another American in Edinburgh wrote: "I have never seen so intense a feeling of indignation exhibited in my life." Adams sped back to London from the country, only to be embarrassed by having to admit to Russell as he rushed into a hastily called cabinet meeting that he had received no information from Washington on the affair. England, Adams lamented as he walked the streets of London in despair, "would have been less offended if the United States had insulted her a great deal more." He told equally distraught members of the legation that they would be home in a month. His assistant secretary, Benjamin Moran, had earned his reputation for acerbity after serving for several years in London and was like many Americans in initially praising Wilkes's action; but upon reflection he realized that it could undermine Adams's efforts to keep England out of the war and from recognizing the Confederacy. The *Trent* affair would "do more for the Southerners than ten victories, for it touches John Bull's honor, and the honor of his flag." From the United States, Charles Francis Adams, Jr., was so unsettled that he asked his father whether Seward intended to start a war, while in London Henry Adams moaned that "all the fat's in the fire." England "means to make war."[4]

The Palmerston ministry had at first found news of the *Trent* difficult to believe. Seward had often threatened war with England, but Russell had joined Lyons in suspecting that the secretary's actions were primarily for domestic political effect. Surely Seward had not ordered Wilkes to remove Mason and Slidell from the vessel. Wilkes had committed an egregious error that the Lincoln administration would have to disavow. Palmerston was irate. The Americans, he told the queen, had violated the British flag and would have to make reparations. He fumed to Russell that they had intended this "deliberate and premeditated insult" to "provoke" a quarrel. Russell called for a strong stand and warned that the Americans were "very dangerous people to run away from." Westbury angrily complained about violations of British neutrality, and even Argyll, who was decidedly pro-Union, called the act a "wretched piece of American folly."[5]

If Seward wanted a fight, Palmerston seemed prepared to accept the challenge. According to some accounts, the prime minister opened an emergency cabinet meeting on November 28 with the declaration: "I don't know whether you are going to stand this, but I'll be damned if I do!" After a series of strained meetings, Russell completed the draft of a strongly worded dispatch to Seward but first showed it to the queen, who, in turn, asked her consort, Prince Albert, to read it. Rising from his sickbed, he toned down the missive and convinced the foreign secretary to allow the United States a graceful way out of the crisis by expressing the ministry's willingness to accept a statement from Washington that Wilkes's act had been unauthorized. Russell agreed to this concession, but he instructed Lyons to seek reparations, the immediate release of the two captives, and a formal apology. Further, in a show of force, the ministry sent more troops to Canada and enlarged the British fleet in the Atlantic. War would probably result, Palmerston thought. He could not wait long for compliance. If the United States failed to do so, Lyons was to return home. "What we want," Russell instructed his minister, "is a plain Yes or a plain No to our very simple demands, and we want that plain Yes or No within seven days of the communication of the despatch." Conflict seemed certain, causing the American stock market to plunge and the British government to impose an embargo on the sale of saltpeter (the primary component of gunpowder) to the United States.[6]

Meanwhile, the South eagerly waited for a certain conflict that would bring an equally certain alliance with England and, as a matter of course, diplomatic recognition.[7]

T H E *Trent* affair threatened to have explosive repercussions, for it could cause an Anglo-American war that might lead not only to a defeat for the Union but to the additional calamity of Southern independence. News of the *Trent* had given added impetus to Palmerston's earlier move to upgrade the defense of Canada, for its provinces seemed incapable of resisting the huge and impressively equipped army gathered on the Potomac. And he could not see how England could derive the same commercial profits from a divided North and South as from a unified nation. The *Bee-Hive* of London, whose editor strongly favored Southern separation because of the North's restrictive trade and tariff policies, had no doubts about the need to exploit the situation by breaking the blockade: it called for a British alliance with France and war against the Union. Not only could the British settle all debts accrued from Union affronts to their national honor, but they could promote the end of slavery. In a view similar to Russell's, the journal argued that Southern separation would mean repeal of the Fugitive Slave Law, eventually forcing Southerners to accept emancipation. William Lindsay, a leading London shipowner and staunch Confederate sympathizer in Parliament who had once talked with Napoleon III about establishing a direct trade route between France and the South, favored war if the North did not return Mason and Slidell to England. If war were declared, Russell should first secure an offensive and defensive treaty with the Southern commissioners. Had the British recognized the South after Bull Run, Lindsay remarked, they would have avoided this trouble.[8]

The French seized upon the *Trent* affair as an opportunity to renew their call for joint intervention in the Civil War. Mercier believed that intervention would work if Russia, which was openly pro-Union, participated in the project. Even if Russia's view of the American conflict had derived from its ongoing imperial rivalries with its former British and French antagonists in the Crimean War, surely, Mercier reasoned, the tsar saw the advantages for everyone in ending the American war. But Lyons doubted that the Union would be receptive to intervention, even if the proposal were made while the South held the upper hand on the battlefield. He was less sanguine than Mercier about American public support for mediation, and he also was not comfortable when Mercier called for "intimidation" of the North. As Lyons realized, a threat once made became useless if not carried through. Intimidation would not work unless the British government convinced the Union that rejection of intervention carried "serious consequences." Besides, the blockade was the critical issue. The North believed it could not win the war without the blockade, whereas the South would not agree to an armistice without an end to the blockade. Lyons added another sobering consideration: Lincoln would soon instigate a race war by calling for emancipation. War with the North would place England on the side of slavery.[9]

Even though the Palmerston ministry distrusted Napoleon, its relationship with France tightened during the *Trent* crisis. Wilkes, the Paris government declared, had violated international law and England deserved reparations. Mercier supported Lyons's demands made to the United States, and Lyons, in turn, kept Mercier informed of all discussions with Seward. Palmerston and Russell remained worried that Napoleon would exploit Anglo-American difficulties to seek advantages in both the Old World and the New. They were aware of Union resentment over the European expedition in Mexico and feared that a combination of these troublesome events with the present crisis could lead to war. If a break in diplomatic relations occurred between his government and that in Washington, Russell did not want the French minister to leave the United States along with Lyons. "The insult is to us," Russell wrote his ambassador in Paris, "& I think we must be left to resent it—in the first place at least." England's honor was at stake. The Union's behavior had been foolish, for it would have less chance of winning the conflict with the Confederacy if war developed between the Atlantic nations and the North had to forgo the blockade to deal with the British fleet.[10]

Despite the Palmerston ministry's fears, the French did not take advantage of the *Trent* affair to reap benefits in Europe and North America. Napoleon's venture in Mexico, his desire to avoid a naval encounter with England, and domestic considerations that included widespread popular support for the British position all combined to strengthen Anglo-French ties during the *Trent* crisis. Russell was satisfied. Except for Russia and perhaps Prussia, "all the world is disgusted by the insolence of the American Republic." [11]

Throughout the tumult over the *Trent*, Russell grew increasingly exasperated with the Americans while remaining fairly confident that the Atlantic nations could avert war. He thought it probable that the Americans would "like to draw in their horns and be disagreeable to us at the same time." Lincoln wisely refrained from mentioning the *Trent* in his annual message to Congress, but Russell feared congressional opposition to a sensible solution that would necessitate England's having to take strong measures to safeguard honor. By early December Russell had become more optimistic. Even the "most foolish" editors of the American press realized that the Union's only chance of defeating the South was to keep England and France neutral. Further, Russell had learned from a British diplomat that the Lincoln administration had not authorized Wilkes to stop the *Trent*. According to Percy Doyle, Union general Winfield Scott (whom Doyle had met in Washington and in Mexico) admitted that orders had gone to other warships in the area to seize Mason and Slidell, "dead or alive," but only, Scott insisted, if the men were on board a Confederate vessel. Wilkes had acted on his own. Russell hoped that Scott would urge Lincoln "to send our passengers back." Ironically, the Union's army seemed more amenable to reason than did its civilians. Russell had received word that General George B. McClellan told Lincoln that there was no justification in the seizure. "I wish McClellan could be made Dictator." [12]

Yet the Union, for both domestic and foreign reasons, could not back down easily. On December 15 Senator Orville Browning was with the president when Seward arrived with the dispatches from England confirming the administration's worst fears: the Palmerston ministry accused the United States of violating international law and demanded an apology and restoration of the men. War or national dishonor seemed to be America's only alternative. Browning could not believe that England would do "so foolish a thing." But if England was determined upon a war, he just as foolishly exclaimed to Lincoln and Seward, "We will fight her to the death." The next day Congress debated whether the United States should retain Mason and Slidell and thereby redeem the nation's honor or retreat before British demands under the guise of reason and international law. That evening Seward seemed to opt for honor. He appeared haggard and worn at a party hosted by the Portuguese legation and, surrounded by his own cigar smoke and perhaps braced with brandy, warned a small group that if England made war, "We will wrap the whole world in flames!" Among the listeners was William H. Russell, who was visibly shaken by Seward's remarks. Another guest pulled Russell aside to offer an assurance that was probably correct: "That's all bugaboo talk. When Seward talks that way, he means to break down. He is most dangerous and obstinate when he pretends to agree a good deal with you." [13]

Close observers found the American position both ludicrous and dangerous. Charles Francis Adams, Jr., worriedly wrote his brother in London that the United States had "capstoned" its "blunders by blundering into a war with England" that would result in Confederate independence. Henry Adams was aghast at his people's behavior in the United States. "What a bloody set of fools they are! How in the name of all that's conceivable could you suppose that England would sit quiet under such an insult. *We* should have jumped out of our boots at such a one." To his brother, he complained that the United States had adopted England's despicable search policies. "Good God, what's got into you all? What in Hell do you mean by deserting now the great principles of our fathers; by returning to the vomit of that dog Great Britain? What do you mean by asserting now principles against which every Adams yet has protested and resisted? You're mad, all of you." Poor communication between Washington and London posed an additional problem. As of December 11 the senior Adams had still heard nothing from Washington. On that day he complained that the White House's failure to apprise him of the situation had placed him in an awkward position. Henry muttered that if his father saw Russell walking down the street, he would "run as fast as he could down the nearest alley."[14]

Less than a week before Christmas, Charles Francis Adams considered war imminent and worried that it might spread throughout Europe. He had earlier noted war preparations in British depots and magazines and warned Seward that if the United States did not comply with British demands the ministry in London would recognize the South and refuse to adhere to the blockade. Adams had finally heard from Seward, who at that late date informed his minister only that Wilkes had not acted under instructions and that the Lincoln administration would send more information once Lyons revealed his government's position on the affair. But Seward added an ominous note: he authorized Adams to warn the Palmerston ministry that recognition of the Confederacy would undoubtedly lead immediately to war with the United States.[15]

Adams felt distraught. If in a crisis his home administration failed to keep its highest-ranking representative in England informed, how could he counter the accusations of American warlike intentions? If Washington exerted no leadership, how could he encourage negotiations when he did not know the direction to take?

And he had similar problems regarding the British government. "Where is the master to direct this storm?" Adams moaned. "Is it Lord Palmerston or Earl Russell?" The British considered Seward the bête noire who sought to insult them into war. This nonsense he could not dispel because Seward was too gifted an actor. His emotional outbursts had caused Lyons to send one alarmist dispatch after another, and now the secretary's continual threats of war had taken on substance with the *Trent* affair. The only way out of this confrontation over honor was to admit error. Adams expressed relief that the administration had neither authorized Wilkes's action nor condoned it. But now, he insisted, the White House must disavow the act and return the captives. "I would part with them at a cent apiece!" [16]

Meanwhile, the ongoing tension over the blockade compounded the excitement over the *Trent* and, according to American and British observers, raised the potential of forcing recognition. In a diary published in the *Boston Courier* in mid-December, Henry Adams told of his visit to Manchester, during which merchants and a newspaper editor warned that pressure would grow for challenging the blockade and extending recognition if the American war continued into the spring of 1862 and inflicted economic harm on people outside the United States. The South's commissioners in Europe assured President Davis in Richmond that the British and French would demand that the North lift the blockade as a condition for settlement of the *Trent* crisis. The commissioners, in fact, had hurried to London and Paris to be there when the expected news arrived of the Lincoln administration's capitulation and the European powers responded by announcing recognition of the South. In Parliament, John Bright and Richard Cobden, both Liberals and supporters of the North, were disconsolate as they pronounced the blockade a failure: it would not bring down the South and might cause a quarrel with England. Fortunately, for the moment, Bright noted, Lancashire had sufficient cotton and there was no sentiment in England for breaking the blockade. But the economic situation was already precarious. In November 1861 a published survey of 836 textile mills showed that of 172,000 workers, only 64,000 were fully employed and 8,000 had been released. The remainder was on short time that ranged from one to three days' less work a week. If matters worsened—and they would in time—the ensuing demand for cotton would promote a new crisis. Challenging the blockade, Bright warned, "would be an act of war."[17]

Further pressure for defying the blockade came from British businessmen, who complained about the North's recent decision to sink old ships filled with huge stones (the "stone fleet") in Southern channels to close the ports. Though Russell realized that international law condoned such action as long as no permanent damage resulted, he again demonstrated his inability to grasp the severity of the American conflict when he denounced the Union's cruelty. Further, he did not realize that in Charleston, one of the targeted port cities in the program, the Union had left two channels open. Cobden likewise failed to grasp the serious nature of the war and called the forced port closings "barbarous." Seward assured Lyons that the damage was temporary and that the stone fleet was designed only to facilitate the blockade. But this small controversy, combined with the ongoing problems over the *Trent*, worked to heighten Anglo-American emotions.[18]

The United States soon found itself alone on the *Trent* affair and had to retreat from its hard-line stand. Mercier warned Seward not to expect help from France. Contrary to popular belief, Mercier insisted, Napoleon did not want to see England locked in a struggle with the United States while he made gains in Europe and Mexico. On December 21 Browning had a long discussion with Lincoln during which both men alluded to a call for arbitration suggested by Charles Sumner. But England demanded immediate satisfaction, and the president rejected that approach as too time-consuming. In truth, the chances for England's accepting arbitration would have been minimal at best. Bright and Cobden had joined numerous British church groups in urging the ministry to submit the matter to arbitration, but Palmerston and Russell staunchly refused to permit another nation to pass judgment on their government's behavior.[19]

On Christmas Day the president invited Sumner to meet with him and the cabinet to seek an honorable way out of the confrontation. Despite Seward's warning of war and no hope of French support, Lincoln had refused to release Mason and Slidell. Perhaps he realized the political cost; or he might have been concerned about the impact on Union morale. The probability is that he wanted to go on record as standing in opposition while knowing that eventually he would have to turn them over and acknowledge a violation of international law. He had already referred to Mason and Slidell as "white elephants." In any case, their incarceration would have satisfied his people's need for a victory over the South while he skirted a war with the British. The task seemed somewhat easier, for Sumner bore letters from Bright and Cobden, both of whom insisted that England opposed war. The next day, the cabinet met for four hours and, persuaded by the British letters and surprisingly hearing no objection from the president, recommended that he free the men. Seward was perplexed by Lincoln's change of heart and pursued the matter after the others had left the conference room. The president smiled as he conceded that Seward had been correct: "I found I could not make an argument that would satisfy my own mind, and that proved to me your ground was the right one." [20]

Seward now had the onerous task of preparing a note to Lyons that would save American honor by disguising the capitulation to England. On December 27 he hosted a dinner for the two congressional committees on foreign affairs, after which he invited them into the drawing room to announce the administration's decision to release Mason and Slidell. Few were pleased, but all agreed with the move. That same day Seward informed Lyons that even though Wilkes had acted without authorization from Washington, he had rightfully seized Mason and Slidell as contraband of war. But since Wilkes had not taken the *Trent* to prize court and had instead allowed the vessel to resume its voyage, he had committed an illegal act that cost him legitimate claim to the captives. The United States would extend no apology, but it would grant reparation for the misdeed. In taking this action, Seward declared, the United States was reiterating its long-standing support for neutral rights that the British now so clearly had observed. "We are asked to do to the British nation just what we have always insisted all nations ought to do to us." As for Mason and Slidell, Seward remarked, they were of "comparative unimportance" and would be "cheerfully liberated." [21]

Seward's argument salvaged his nation's honor by concealing America's surrender in a fog of legal arguments that, perhaps unnoticed at the time, carried important ramifications. To those in England who complained that Wilkes had violated their neutral rights, the secretary of state emphasized that the decision to free the captives reiterated America's long-standing opposition to any maritime actions (including impressment) that infringed upon freedom of the seas. Thankfully, he indicated, the British had at last come to accept these same principles. But Seward's note did not rest on solid legal ground. International law was by no means clear on the legality of removing diplomatic envoys sent by a belligerent that had not won recognition as a sovereign nation. More important, however, Seward had implicitly conceded both the neutral status of the British and hence the belligerent status of the Confederacy by referring to Wilkes's act of search as legal in halting a neutral vessel carrying contraband. The very usage of terms such as *neutrality* and *contraband*, according to international law, signified the existence of war between belligerents. Settlement of the immediate crisis, however, outweighed the long-range implications of the arguments used. By the time each side sorted out the complexities and ambiguities, the Civil War and all accompanying matters would have swept the nations beyond the *Trent* and into other controversies.

MEANWHILE, in London, the Lincoln administration's decision to release the men remained unknown and the war scare drummed on at a rapid beat. Moran acidly noted that most British journals criticized the Union and reveled in its troubles, whereas Adams reported that numerous papers wanted a conflict. When Parliament assembled in the new year, spokesmen for the "war party" would put pressure on the ministry to satisfy honor. If not successful, they would demand more stringent guidelines for blockade law and less rigid restrictions on extending recognition. Adams was uneasy about how long Russell could withstand the pressure. The Duke of Newcastle in the Colonial Office had joined Palmerston, Russell, Lewis, the admiralty's Duke of Somerset, and others as a special cabinet War Committee for only the fourth time in England's history. Adams's fears were not unfounded. Already, Newcastle had received memorials from Canada, Nova Scotia, and New Brunswick, all three British provinces pleading for assistance in building an intercolonial railway to facilitate protection against a feared American invasion. Newcastle, along with Lyons and Sumner in Washington, had convinced many British at home that Seward wanted war. If that were true, Adams declared, all Seward would have to do was to *"insult the British government* in his answer."[22]

Adams believed that the Union had many British friends, but he was certain that few of them were willing to come forth until its leaders performed more creditably on both the military and diplomatic fronts. The British had made clear that only progress in these areas would ease the hostilities caused by the *Trent*. Under calmer circumstances, he believed, the British would realize that the succession of events actually undermined the South's arguments by showing that the American conflict was "the ever-recurring one in human affairs between right and wrong, between labor and capital, between liberty and absolutism." Henry Adams placed much of the problem at Seward's feet: he "shaves closer to the teeth of the lion than he ought."[23]

By the beginning of the new year, however, more British spokesmen had become guardedly optimistic about escaping war. Argyll thought the Union did not want war and wanted Wilkes to admit that he had acted without orders. In a war, Argyll reminded his colleagues, they would be an ally of the South and of slavery. Lewis was concerned about the tangled events that would transpire in Europe should the United States and England go to war. If a civil war broke out in troubled Germany while England was fighting the Americans, he warned, Napoleon would take advantage of British preoccupation in Canada to exploit the unrest in Europe. Lewis was not worried about Canada coming under Union attack—Lincoln's hands were full with the South. Yet Americans were "singularly reckless & unscrupulous." Russell remained anxious, but surely the Americans knew that England was "not likely to eat dirt." To Palmerston, Russell wrote: "I am still inclined to think Lincoln will submit, but not till the clock is 59 minutes past 11."[24]

Cobden and Bright likewise realized that the *Trent* crisis and its ramifications extended beyond the present danger. Though often at odds with the Palmerston ministry, they also were Liberals with considerable influence in Parliament because the ruling Liberal party lacked a strong majority, thereby allowing the two men to determine the balance of power between it and the Conservatives.

Cobden feared that Canada's defenses were poor and that his government could not amass an army large enough to ward off an American invasion. But he was more worried that the *Trent* affair would lead to British involvement in the North-South struggle. Even if England and the United States resolved their troubles, he declared to Bright, all Europe would soon demand the opening of the Mississippi River. Either British or French recognition would come in six months if the North did not win decisively on the field. To keep the American conflict from dragging in other nations, the North must open the Mississippi River and other ports for all but contraband goods. But Cobden, like many others in England, doubted that the North was capable of subjugating its adversary. A glance at a map showed this to be impossible. "Is not the war hopeless?—How can they ever lie again in the same bed?"[25]

Bright and Cobden expressed concern that the Union blockade would force British intervention in the American war. Bright feared that the British government would "conspire" with France to allow it to take the initiative so that England would not appear responsible. Surely, he exclaimed, France would not make itself the "Cat's paw of England." But regardless of which nation led the way, interference in the contest would not assure a remedy to Europe's economic troubles. Bright agreed that the quickest way to resolve a certain cotton crisis was for the Union to open Southern ports. Cobden did not believe that France and England would jointly interfere in the war. Instead, they would plead economic distress, which made the blockade the "hinge of the whole affair." No intense pressure existed for cotton, although that situation would soon change. Indeed, a January 1862 survey revealed that the number of unemployed had jumped more than three times what it was in November and that those on short time had increased over 50 percent. Workers in England were suffering, but the spinners and merchants still had sufficient cotton stocks to last until June 1862. Bright and Cobden hoped that by then Northern occupation of New Orleans and Mobile would open the South's main cotton ports and undermine any call for challenging the blockade. Recognition of the South and breaking the blockade, Cobden warned, would lead to a "war without the excuse of the 'outrage'—& indeed with no excuse, as long as the North grows in power."[26]

The views expressed by Cobden and Bright paralleled those of others in England and suggested a growing interest in recognition. Even though these two men favored the North, they were in uncomfortable agreement with those in England who considered disunion a fait accompli. Cobden believed that nearly everyone in Parliament would favor recognition. Yet he and Bright feared that economic interests in England and other European states would ultimately compel violations of the blockade that would lead to war in the Atlantic. British humanitarian and economic concerns were not entirely unrelated—particularly when they were in harmony with the national interest—and they therefore seemed more important than a prolonged battle in America over differing interpretations of constitutional principles.[27] Once both American antagonists had denied slavery's role in bringing on the war, the issue became clear to the British: the South wanted independence, whereas the North wanted empire. The Union's resistance to recognition remained on shaky ground. All sorts of people in England were tiring of a conflict that they believed had been settled at Bull Run when the South—or so it seemed—demonstrated its right to independence.

Meanwhile, the news of America's compliance with England's demands arrived in London and, just as quickly as the crisis had arisen, instantly eased the pressure for war. Adams praised Seward for the settlement and maintained that his decision to publish the foreign correspondence had helped to dispel the belief that he was hostile to England. Moran expressed relief over the surrender of Mason and Slidell but characteristically warned that the *Times* of London would attempt to "goad the nation on to a war with us now on the blockade question." Even though Henry Adams felt confident that most members of the British cabinet favored neutrality, he warned that the war party had shifted tactics and not its goal. "You must not misunderstand Palmerston. He means disunion, but not war unless under special influences." Lewis likewise was apprehensive. "I do not believe that the Americans will cherish the *Trent* affair in their hearts, & will watch the moment of our weakness in order to be avenged." Lyons hoped the Americans would not now seek additional "abuse of England" and called for a strong military force to remain in Canada to discourage an American attack. Palmerston was pleased with the *Trent* settlement, whereas Russell, who also was satisfied, referred to Vattel and Wheaton in insisting that the Union must discard its argument that Mason and Slidell were rebels and, in doing so, assist England in its neutrality by calling them "enemies of the United States at war with its Government." Russell managed to find a redeeming feature in the crisis. "The unanimity shewn here, the vigorous despatch of troops & ships—the loyal determination of Canada may save us a contest for a long while to come." Seward did not have "any animosities" toward England. It was, as Lyons put it, "all buncome." [28]

Despite the turn toward peace, other issues kept surfacing in the period afterward that repeatedly raised the possibility of recognition. Charles Francis Adams thought the peaceful resolution of the *Trent* affair had stiffened the war party's determination to work out a deal with the South that could lead to recognition. Henry Adams detected quiet maneuvering that could lead to trouble over the blockade and eventual British recognition. Almost everyone thought that France was trying to persuade England to challenge the blockade, whereas France insisted that England was exerting pressure on Napoleon to do so. The Palmerston ministry, Adams suspected, was deeply divided. In truth, it seems that England remained torn over the blockade and whether slavery was the central cause of the American war. An assembly of London workers in late January condemned Mason and Slidell as slaveholders and thus the "sworn enemies" of workers everywhere. But Henry Adams remained skeptical that Englishmen would see the truth. "We talk emancipation in vain now." The key to preventing recognition, he wrote the editor of the *New York Times*, Henry J. Raymond, was victory on the battlefield. "Without that our fate here seems to me to be a mere question of time." [29]

Henry Adams warned that the British war party's next battle for recognition would take place in Parliament in early February. The "reprobates," he declared to his brother in the United States, expected the Palmerston ministry either to extend recognition or to resign. The South's friends would point to the great number of vessels that had run the blockade; the North must show an equal number captured or chased. Adams saw a glimmer of hope. Russell had recently told the son of France's King Louis Philippe that the North would win the war. "If he thinks so,"

Adams declared, "he surely won't countenance interference. And if the Ministry are firm, we are safe." But as Parliament went, Adams feared, so would go British society and ministry.[30]

The elder Adams agreed with his son and thought the Palmerston ministry "notoriously feeble" in Parliament. The South's supporters in that body would probably claim that the Union had not yet put down the rebellion and that recognition was due. He had the impression (erroneous) that the Conservatives favored recognition, even though only one or two newspapers expressed that view and he did not consider them trustworthy. It was impossible to determine the feeling in the House of Commons because the matter had not become a party issue and each individual voiced his own opinion. The Conservatives, Adams wryly remarked, were strong only when they stood in opposition to something. Most members of that party seemed to be waiting for Palmerston's demise and his expected replacement by Lord Derby of the Conservative opposition.[31]

Settlement of the *Trent* crisis eased the threat of war, but it did little to dissuade those British spokesmen, who, for varied reasons, seemed to want intervention in the Civil War. Mason came to believe this shortly after his arrival (with Slidell) at Southampton on January 29. The great number of Englishmen who wanted to end the American conflict for either humanitarian or economic reasons remained interested in intervention and would now, Mason predicted, shift their focus to challenging the blockade. Equally important, the British government suspected that slavery would soon emerge as the principal issue and set off a race war in the South that would intensify the pressure for intervention. Impressions threatened to become reality, for in mid-January President Lincoln told Senators Browning of Illinois and Garrett Davis of Kentucky that to save the Union he would, if necessary, stamp out slavery. Whether or not Lyons was aware of Lincoln's feelings, he wrote Russell just two days later, "The question is rapidly tending towards the issue either of peace and a recognition of the separation, or a Proclamation of Emancipation and the raising of a servile insurrection." Russell expressed alarm that the president should want "a war of emancipation."[32]

In the Union's view, British recognition of the South remained a possibility, a fear that seemed warranted on the basis of continued suspicions of British intentions. The probability of more bloodshed (and England's humanitarian aversion to it), the growing need for cotton, the concern over slave rebellions leading to a racial war, the heightening call for accepting separation—these considerations threatened to combine and bring about the formation of a strange coalition with pro-Confederate groups that might put pressure on the ministry to recognize Southern independence.

But despite the appearance of widespread British sympathy with the South, the Palmerston ministry remained neutral and, perhaps, more careful about dealing with the South. At a time when the government in London might have exploited the emotional situation to challenge the Union blockade, it had chosen instead to reiterate its compliance with the commercial strictures. In a letter to Mason, Henry Hotze, the Confederate agent in England, discerned the real importance of the *Trent* affair: it had hurt the South by allowing the British government to curry considerable political favor at home and thereby make itself less vulnerable to criticism in handling foreign affairs. Charles Francis Adams made the same observation, though adding a cautionary note. The Palmerston ministry, he wrote Seward and Everett, had been strengthened and would be able to act more independently and firmly. The Union must therefore avoid any issue that might provide a pretext for either the Liberals or the Conservatives to exploit America's internal troubles. England would continue to "sit as a cold spectator," Adams assured another acquaintance, "ready to make the best of our calamity the moment there is a sufficient excuse to interfere."[33]

BRITISH NEUTRALITY remained the chief guarantee against intervention, and yet this reality continued to escape observers in the North who feared that the *Trent* settlement had won only a reprieve from British recognition of the Confederacy.

It is when the Americans

feel sure of us that they

take liberties.

—Lord Lyons,

February 11, 1862

5

Trials of
British
Neutrality

The *Trent* crisis had passed, but the Union government remained concerned about British recognition of the Confederacy. The war threat during the winter of 1861–62 had encouraged British observers to consider some action intended to bring the American conflict to a close before another confrontation—perhaps more dangerous—developed between the Atlantic nations. The Confederacy, many Englishmen continued to believe, had proved its mettle by routing the Union army at Bull Run. The Union owed it to humanity to let the Confederacy go in peace. Yet, as the British saw things, the Lincoln administration was unreasonable in expecting to force the South back into the fold. Even though the Palmerston ministry maintained its aloofness from the American conflict, British figures outside the center of power resumed their appeals to the government to bring peace. Much of Europe suffered severe economic hardships caused by the demise of American trade, and the conscience of civilization demanded some form of intervention before the war drew in other nations.

IN THE aftermath of the *Trent* excitement, the British government reiterated its adherence to neutrality. Seward remained cautious. Now that calm had returned, he hoped that England would realize that the conflict had matched the duly established Union government against rebellious slaveholders who refused to conform to the modern age. In early February 1862, Lewis in London noted that the cabinet was under no real pressure to interfere because the Lancashire workers had "behaved with wonderful forbearance and moderation."[1] Russell attempted to soothe the Union's hard feelings. As of February 6, he informed Lyons, no ships of war or privateers from either side would be allowed in British home or territorial harbors. In Parliament Russell aroused no disapproval from either party when he declared the government's intention to adhere to noninvolvement. Even Moran, who remained critical of England, discerned a less hostile attitude in Parliament toward the United States. Yancey's dispatch to Russell asking for recognition had been made public and was, Moran declared, "remarkable" for its "flat impudence." It was ridiculous for Yancey to insist that the issue in America was taxation and not black freedom; the British would soon realize that the Northern stand against slavery was serious. But Moran's brief flirtation with optimism gave way to his unbending belief that the recognition question would remain as long as the Union failed to achieve a decisive victory on the battlefield.[2]

Northerners again became alarmed about British intervention when they learned that Russell had met with Mason, albeit on an unofficial basis. In December 1861, during the height of the *Trent* crisis, the foreign secretary wrote the three Confederate commissioners then in London that he refused to engage in "any official communication with them." But peace had prevailed, and in early February 1862 he invited Mason, recently arrived in London, to meet with him "unofficially" at his house. Given Russell's oft-expressed sympathies for the Union and his abhorrence of war, he probably was trying to demonstrate his neutrality. "At all events," he insisted to Lyons, "I am heart & soul a neutral." But, as in the Bunch affair, Russell had again failed to grasp the importance of impressions. Any meeting with Mason would have a negative effect on the North.[3]

On February 10 Russell received his guest with what Mason called a "civil and kind manner" that, he admitted, betrayed no tendency to help the South. The meeting proved awkward. When Mason offered his credentials, Russell refused to accept them because of the meeting's unofficial nature. Once seated, Mason read that part of his instructions seeking recognition and disregard for the blockade, but he chose not to say anything about cotton until England's expected shortage had become acute. He also did not emphasize recognition, although he insisted that the South would never realign with the North. The Confederacy, he assured the foreign secretary, had enough men and resources to pursue the war for as long as the North resisted Southern independence. Then, in an effort to show that the South had already won nationhood and could stand on its own, Mason took an ill-advised stand: he proclaimed no interest in material assistance or a military alliance, thereby virtually helping to close the door on the only real possibility the South had of winning independence.[4]

For the most part, Russell listened, although he inquired about the status of Kentucky, Missouri, and Tennessee and about the South's alienation from northwestern Virginia. Mason's reply must have aroused Russell's skepticism. The three states, Mason insisted, were part of the Confederacy, and the upper corner of Virginia remained loyal to the South despite the Lincoln administration's attempt to delude everyone into believing the opposite. Mason came away from his meeting with an unsettled feeling. He was convinced that Russell's personal sentiments did not lie with the South and that his policy would remain "in-action." Russell repeatedly confirmed this assessment. As Mason's predecessors had learned, Russell would allow events alone to determine his course of action.[5]

Americans in the North, not yet knowing of Mason's meeting with Russell and thinking that the British threat of intervention had eased after the *Trent* crisis, turned their concern toward the French. Lyons noted the Union government's apprehensions about French aims regarding the blockade. In late January Napoleon had hinted at his country's willingness to use its good offices to promote an end to the war; but, Lewis declared with dissatisfaction, the American government strongly opposed any such proposal. Even though many of his countrymen believed that the North wanted an honorable pretext for recognizing Southern independence, Lewis remained unconvinced. He saw no sign of Northern interest in ending the war. The Union had made clear its intention to rely on military force. The French consul general in New York thought differently. He had assured his superiors in Paris that as soon as the Union had won a major battle and reestablished respectability, Lincoln would acknowledge Southern separation. Russell suspected, however, that such a victory would stiffen the North's drive for reunion. His consolation was that England had lost interest in the American question and relations with the Union had improved. European affairs now commanded England's attention.[6]

Lyons knew that the American war was not nearing its end. His government must keep the Americans guessing: "It is when the Americans feel sure of us," he warned Russell, "that they take liberties." Seward's request that England withdraw recognition of the South's belligerent rights was premature. To win over the British, Seward even implied that the Union would sink no more stone-laden vessels in Southern harbors and would relax the blockade. Yet he also had hinted to Mercier that if the Union allowed trade with Confederate ports, such trade must be solely in ships of the United States. Mercier showed no interest in such a proposal because, Lyons explained, European nations would find it more advantageous to remain neutrals between belligerents than friends with a government attempting to put down a rebellion. In the latter instance they would have to submit to trade restrictions imposed by the Union government on ports considered part of its territory. They would have to accept Southern port closings by congressional acts and not by a blockade. But as neutrals, those same European nations would not have to submit to municipal restrictions because they fell outside the purview of international law. Neutrality reduced the chances of conflict with the Union because the rules were clear. Lyons agreed with Mercier. The Union had not achieved a major victory, and no one could maintain that the war was nearly over. Seward was not justified in seeking the withdrawal of belligerent rights from the South.[7]

Then, in mid-February, the tide of war seemed to change. In the Tennessee heartland, Union forces led by Ulysses S. Grant captured Fort Henry on the Tennessee River and then took Fort Donelson, twelve miles to the east on the Cumberland River. Within a few days Nashville fell. The Union controlled Kentucky and major parts of Tennessee and stood poised for an assault on the Mississippi River that, if successful, would divide the South, expose New Orleans to attack, and eventually open that city's port and ease foreign pressure for ending the blockade. The *New York Tribune*, which reflected the Union's ebullient mood, predicted the imminent end of the war. News of Fort Henry hit the British like a "flash of lightning," according to Moran. England would "desert her slave-driving allies now." Adams agreed. The Union's victory at Fort Donelson was the greatest military event of the war and would ease the threat of intervention. Mason admitted that the news had "an unfortunate effect" on the South's English friends. John O'Neil, a weaver in Lancashire, perhaps expressed the views of fellow workers when he praised the Union's capture of Fort Donelson as a major step toward ending the war.[8]

The Union's victories in the West aroused great interest in England, for by early March the American war had begun to have a mixed effect on the British textile industry. In slowing cotton importation into England, the war helped the mill owners, who profited from the higher prices resulting from the sale of surplus finished goods that had stockpiled after the overproduction of the past three years. A mill owner in Clitheroe, James Garnett, expressed concern that because of the huge supply of cloth on hand, a sudden end to the American war would cause the loss of "a serious sum of money." To cut losses, he and five other manufacturers in Clitheroe had decided to run the mills on short time. Now, with the fall of Fort Donelson, Garnett was worried that the value of his stocks would plummet because of an end to the war followed by a sudden infusion of cotton. Another mill owner noted a near panic in Manchester. O'Neil was an employee of Garnett's and offered a different perspective. As early as November 1861, O'Neil had lamented the widespread distress in the manufacturing areas caused by reduced work hours. During the *Trent* crisis, he had observed that the economic impact of short time had combined with the threat of war with the United States to assure fewer deliveries of cotton. The end of the American war would hurt mill owners while benefiting workers. Not surprisingly, the Union triumph at Fort Donelson aroused Garnett's concern and drew O'Neil's praise.[9]

The news from America had arrived while Parliament was meeting in early March and added to the South's problems in winning support against the blockade. During Mason's February interview he had given Russell 126 pages of documents covering the period May 3, 1861, through February 17, 1862, all intended to prove the ineffectiveness of the blockade. Russell had sent the documents to Parliament. On March 7 William Gregory, an outspoken proponent of the South, presented a motion in the Commons calling for renunciation of the blockade. That Gregory was a strong advocate of recognition further underlined that question's inseparability from the blockade issue. He presented the statistics gathered by Mason and buttressed them with reports by the British consul in Charleston of successful blockade running. But close perusal of the documents revealed that Mason's figures referred only to the time before October 31, 1861, which raised suspicions that the blockade had later become effective and therefore contributed to the Confederacy's difficulties in keeping up-to-date contact with its representatives in Europe. Forster demonstrated that Gregory's references to blockade runners distorted the truth. Those vessels making it through the blockade, Forster maintained, were small coastal steamers that hovered close to land en route to the West Indies. Moreover, he argued, the soaring cotton and salt prices in England proved the effectiveness of the blockade. The British could either continue neutrality and peace or break the blockade and ally with the South in a war for slavery. Sitting in the galleries was Henry Adams, who observed with great satisfaction that Gregory's suddenly dispirited speech sounded like a "funeral eulogy." Almost everyone considered the blockade acceptable. Gregory withdrew his motion.[10]

Succeeding events confirmed the difficulties in using the blockade as a lever for bringing about British recognition of the South. Instead of expending so much effort in denouncing the Union's naval efforts as a paper blockade, the South might have been wiser to have exploited the situation by mortgaging its cotton for foreign loans that would have tied Europe's welfare more closely to a Confederate victory. Further, Mason's efforts were sometimes counterproductive. Moran noted that in the previous evening's parliamentary session, William Lindsay criticized Seward and drew a loud cheer from Mason that offended parliamentary decorum. Mason's boorish behavior, Moran remarked with glee, had hurt his cause, for it was "out of place" and "indecent" and provided justification for expelling him from the Commons. Lindsay introduced a motion to break the blockade, but it was withdrawn without a vote. Two days later, on March 10, the Lords likewise debated the blockade. Russell, now an earl and therefore a member of that body, seized the opportunity to declare that the Union was succeeding in closing down the South. A week earlier his legal advisers affirmed what he knew already: an "actual and effective blockade by a competent force" meant the "actual presence of an adequate naval force, either stationary or sufficiently near to each blockaded port to cause an evident danger of capture." Whether or not the blockade had become effective, the Palmerston ministry had declared it so, thereby confirming its desire to avoid a confrontation at sea with the Union navy.[11]

Russell then introduced another potential development of the war for the Lords' consideration: British assistance to the Confederacy might cause the Union to instigate a slave rebellion in a desperate attempt to emerge triumphant. Be patient, he urged his peers; within three months the American war would end on the basis of a separation. Russia's ambassador to London, Baron Philip Brunow, thought that Russell counted on the Union's recent conquests in the West to solidify the border states' loyalty and cause them to promote a peace based on permanent division of the Union. Russell's warning regarding a race war suggested his growing fear that if the American conflict did not end soon, it would reach another level of ferocity that might increase the pressure for British involvement.[12]

Other observers drew their own conclusions about recent events. Mason gloomily conceded that the South had lost the battle over the blockade and saw the possibility of British intervention fast dimming. By no coincidence did he include in this same dispatch his remarks about the negative effect of the taking of Forts Henry and Donelson on the South's friends in England. John Slidell reported a similar lack of progress in Paris. Despite his earlier feeling that Napoleon III had great influence on British policy, the Southern minister now was convinced that England had to take the initiative. The emperor considered England's goodwill so important that he would do anything to keep it. The situation was exasperating, Mason thought. The British believed reunion impossible and yet refused to extend recognition. He tried to find solace in a hollow claim that the North had only captured outposts in taking Forts Henry and Donelson. Their fall, he insisted, did not foreshadow Southern defeat.[13]

Another of the South's representatives in England, Henry Hotze, exhibited an amazing capacity for self-delusion regarding the Southern position. In his efforts to drum up support for the South, Hotze argued that the fall of Fort Donelson had *benefited* the Confederacy by showing the British public that, despite the certainty of separation, Southern victory would not come easily and that intervention was now more necessary than ever to shorten the war. Even if the North overran Virginia, North Carolina, Missouri, Kentucky, and Tennessee, Hotze told British editors, the Confederacy would stand as Lincoln had found it on Inauguration Day. Much blood and treasure would have been expended in gaining only temporary possession of Southern ramparts, for "the citadel would still remain untouched." The British, he assured the Richmond government, believed that conquest of the South was impossible. The *Trent* affair, admittedly, had hurt the South by making the British government less vulnerable to public criticism of its foreign policy. But Hotze reported that several members of Parliament were preparing to make a major effort to secure recognition. "I am for the first time, almost sanguine in my hopes of speedy recognition."[14]

The outcome in Parliament allayed the apprehensions of the American minister, but he warned that the Union's battle with England over recognition was not over. The discussions had revealed the animosity felt by many members toward the United States. They were not interested in the welfare of either North or South but in seeing America's overall political strength undermined by a permanent division. Even Russell seemed to lean this way. His speech in the Lords suggested a belief in the ultimate breakup of the United States that would be followed by recognition of the South. Fear and jealousy, Adams insisted, dominated the thinking of England's ruling classes. They had grown increasingly concerned that the United States would challenge their nation's control of the sea and therefore welcomed a division of the United States that would allow them to play off one group of Americans against the other. At least one member of Parliament claimed that the Commons agreed with Gregory's remarks about the economic problems caused by the blockade and yet at the same time, Adams noted, that member approved the ministry's policy of neutrality. Only the Union's recent military successes had eased the pressure for interference.[15]

The root of the troubles between the Union and England lay in their different understandings of the American conflict rather than in any alleged pro-Confederate design by the Palmerston ministry. No question can exist that in outbursts of anger and perhaps even in moments of quiet contemplation, Palmerston agreed that disunion would be a blessing for Britain. But his innate anti-Americanism never altered his pragmatic response to the war. He and others knew that an American peace was more in accordance with the British interest. Slavery was less important to the London ministry than were matters affecting British security. European affairs, in particular, seemed more vital to the welfare of the empire. Still, Palmerston realized that a prolonged war in America might necessitate an intervention that would have a major impact on the balance of power in the New World. Indeed, the reverberations would probably be felt in the Old World as well. The issues in the American contest were not clear-cut. Domestic considerations had restrained the Lincoln administration from focusing on slavery as a cause of the war, and the South, in an effort to promote its bid for British recognition, had emphasized matters other than slavery in justifying secession. Consequently, when the London government failed to see the rationale in preserving the Union, many in the North attributed shadowy purpose to British motives. From the Union's perspective, neutrality seemed tantamount to favoring the South.

The British stand on separation grew not only out of strategic interests but also from economic and humanitarian concerns. No wise country would act against its own interests, of course, and Russell was not willing to endanger his government for the sake of some ideal. But there is no reason to doubt that he was sincere in wanting to end the war for humanitarian reasons. Determination of motives is difficult if not impossible. But again and again Russell offered assurances of Union sympathy; repeatedly he stressed the inhumanity of continuing a war that had demonstrated the futility of reunion. He had legitimate concerns about the imminent cotton shortage at home. Yet even if he was moved more by economic than humanitarian concerns, the two interests were not incompatible. The Union was dissolved, he insisted. For the benefit of all concerned, the most realistic course was to accept that fact. To do so did not signify favor for the South. In his thinking, to put the Confederacy on its own might force an end to slavery.

Seward disagreed with Russell's reasoning on slavery but realized that the subject was becoming a major concern to all parties involved. Freedom could not live in harmony coterminous to slavery, the secretary of state declared; nor could freedom and slavery live in peace together. Adams had recently warned that Mason and Slidell had intimated the possibility of an offer to England and France that, in exchange for recognition, the South would agree to gradual emancipation. Though clearly a deception, Adams believed the story dangerous enough "to demand the most active and immediate efforts at counteraction." The White House should publicize the fabrication throughout the South and announce the Union's opposition to slavery. Thus Russell would have to give up his claim that the war was one of empire against liberty. Seward, however, remained fearful that abolition would intensify Southern resistance; besides, if the South really did adopt emancipation, as its emissaries had claimed, the insurrection would die because of the South's opposition to abolition. Yet he realized that the Union could no longer ignore the slavery issue. "The time has probably come for the practical determination of the great issue which has thus been joined." Seward's allusion to emancipation suggests a growing realization within the administration, though yet unvoiced, that the time was fast approaching to make clear the inseparability of slavery and Union in the war.[16]

In late March still another problem developed when Russell had to deal with naval affairs involving the Union and Confederacy. Ships that had been privately contracted by the South in the summer of 1861 were now nearing construction in British yards, and one, the *Florida*, had left Liverpool despite Northern protests. Russell maintained that without evidence that the ship had been equipped for war in England it was not subject to seizure under the Foreign Enlistment Act. Russell's free trade views and legalistic approach were difficult to overcome even in the face of certain trouble. Like Lyons, Russell rejected Union demands that he believed were efforts to win advantages over the South. If England gave in, the Union would want more. Russell intended to persuade other governments to give a similar reply.[17]

A dramatic maritime encounter between Northern and Southern ironclad vessels undercut Russell's hopes for an early end to the war. According to Moran, the British had exulted over the feats of a new ironclad owned by the South, the *Virginia* (formerly the *Merrimack*). A decisive Confederate victory "would enable John Bull to swallow rebels, slavery and all." Russell welcomed the news of the South's naval success, for it confirmed his assurance to Lyons that the Southern "spirit may be invincible." In late March, however, London learned of a naval clash at Hampton Roads between the *Virginia* and the Union's own ironclad, the *Monitor*. A standoff had resulted that, according to Moran's jubilant observation, "dumfounded and dismayed all England." From Lancashire's working population, O'Neil hailed the news as the coming end of the war. Nothing could have caused so much excitement in Europe, Moran proclaimed. "John Bull is sorely frightened at the manifest weakness of his own navy and is very civil at once."[18]

Northerners believed that the *Monitor*'s activities revealed British concern about the Union's strength at the end of the war. "John Bull is now the worst armed nation in the world," Moran joyfully (if only wishfully) declared. Adams noted that the Union navy's new prowess exhibited at Hampton Roads had caused a sensation in England and would probably force a buildup in its own navy and fortifications. He also believed that the Union's military power had neutralized British interest in intervention. That same evening, puffed up by the day's good news, Adams attended a reception held by Lady Palmerston and engaged in a brief conversation with Lewis, who uncharacteristically lost self-control and lashed out at the North for seeking to subjugate the South. Reconstruction of the Union was impossible, Lewis exclaimed. Adams cut short the heated exchange by remarking that British desire to see the United States divided was the most compelling argument against allowing that event to take place. Whether or not the Union's perceptions of British concern were accurate, British interest picked up in early April regarding the construction of a railroad in Canada that would connect Halifax and Quebec and thus join the three principal provinces of British North America. But Gladstone warned that the railway would not guarantee safety against the United States.[19]

Americans' assessment of British fears was doubtless exaggerated, but there can be no question that the Palmerston ministry wanted to avert a war with the Union. From the British vantage point, war with the United States was an uninviting prospect—which was all the more reason for overlooking the economic impact of the blockade and bringing the American conflict to a halt.

The hesitant British stance regarding recognition had upset the South as well as the North. The new Confederate secretary of state, Judah P. Benjamin, complained that by not extending recognition, England prolonged a devastating war by encouraging the North to believe that it could subjugate the South. Recognition would bring the opposition Democratic party to power in the North and force an end to the fighting. As long as England appeared to doubt the South's capacity to maintain its government, the North would continue the war. British policies, Benjamin insisted, were undermining the chances for peace and thereby hurting their own interests based on trade with the South. Recognition would put an end to the struggle without endangering England.[20]

Ironically, the Union government presented much the same argument but with the logic turned around. Seward was so optimistic about recent military events that he sent Adams a map with a lengthy dispatch (meant for Russell's perusal) explaining how the North would continue to win territory and open Southern ports. The end of the war would come sooner, Seward noted, if England and France would announce they had no plans for recognizing the South. Adams worked to keep Russell in an untenable position by complaining about the *Florida*'s escape and the British merchants who had run the blockade. Moran expressed elation over Adams's

*Judah P. Benjamin, Confederate secretary of state
(Library of Congress)*

performance. "This kind of *honest* British neutrality and flat lying in the face of their own written reports," Moran recorded in his diary, "received such an exposure that his Lordship [Russell] had nothing to say in defence of his officers, the facts being too plain to be quibbled out of." But Russell did not change his position, and the war showed no signs of coming to a close. Even the opening of ports meant little because the Confederacy placed more limits on cotton exports and U.S. customs laws blocked payments in specie for products.[21] Although the expected cotton flow remained a mere trickle and the British supply continued to fall, it had not yet reached a critical level. England would continue to abide by neutrality.

AFTER ENGLAND and the Union had refused to go to war over the *Trent*, the Southern government decided to increase the economic pressure on Europe by unofficially withholding cotton. Even though Southerners attributed the threatening shortage of cotton to Europe's refusal to overturn the blockade and added that they lacked the ships to do it themselves, Russell was not convinced. He believed that the South had further complicated matters by using King Cotton diplomacy with a vengeance. His people in the mill areas, he knew, would soon begin to hurt— and badly.[22]

The South's use of cotton as a lever for winning recognition had always had the potential of backfiring. In conversation with Adams, Russell angrily declared that the cutback on cotton owed less to the blockade than to the South's attempt to deny the product to England and France and force them into recognition. The foreign secretary was upset with the South's attempt to pressure a decision regarding a question based on "great principles, & not merely immediate interests." Indeed, not until 1863 did the Confederacy negotiate a deal (with a French banking firm) to float cotton bonds in Europe. Earlier uses of cotton had aimed at winning independence by diplomatic and political means, rather than by securing weapons and supplies. Russell knew that unless the Union closed all Southern ports, England could acquire cotton in Cuba and Nassau. But such a supply would not meet the larger needs of late summer or early fall of 1862.[23]

The approaching cotton shortage also revealed the tenuous

nature of the Anglo-French relationship. Adams noted increased economic hardship in both nations that might force an intervention by the fall. In early April Napoleon told the Union minister in Paris, William Dayton, of France's growing need for cotton and expressed no opposition to withdrawing belligerent rights from the South; but he added that France and England had agreed to act in harmony regarding the United States and any change must come first from England. Perhaps, he groused, he had been wrong in granting belligerent rights before Southern separation had been assured. Adams saw an advantage in pursuing this transparent goad to action, for if England rejected the move, the blame would fall on the Palmerston ministry. But an hour-long talk with Russell achieved nothing. Adams confided to his diary that Russell's arguments were shallow, though honest and well-meaning. Napoleon, in an effort to widen the breach between the Union and British governments, later told Dayton that he regretted the premature recognition of the South as a belligerent but that England had brought it about. Napoleon now proclaimed his willingness to withdraw recognition of belligerent rights if England would do so. The British were not naive about their understanding with the French. Palmerston wrote Gladstone that the French "hate us as a nation from the Bottom of their Hearts, and would make any sacrifice to inflict a dark Humiliation upon England." Napoleon intended to build an army more than six times larger than England's and a navy equal to England's or better. For the time being, however, England found it expedient to move in concert with France in American matters.[24]

The tripartite expedition in Mexico had also presented a severe test to Anglo-French harmony and Union-British relations. Problems within the European alliance over the occupation of Vera Cruz had become evident in January 1862. The French had marched on to Mexico City with the objective of overthrowing the republican government and establishing a monarchy with a European prince on the throne. Both the British and the Spanish decided that this move had nothing to do with the collection of debts and was therefore in violation of the Treaty of London of 1861. Napoleon's perfidy had not surprised Palmerston; he took great pleasure in the thought of the French emperor becoming entangled in his own web as he tried to subjugate Mexico. Not only could the British prime minister relax his vigilance against French schemes in Europe, but he also was pleased that the French involvement in Mexico would limit American expansion.[25]

Bitter Union feelings toward the Mexican intervention put additional pressure on England to withdraw from the country and the pact. Charles Francis Adams warned Washington that the military expedition to Mexico City "may not stop until it shows itself in the heart of the Louisiana purchase." In early March Lyons had had a frank discussion with Seward about Mexico, after which he reported to Russell that Americans considered the intervention objectionable and the installation of a monarchy offensive. Russell had already grown concerned about the venture. The advantage Palmerston saw of curbing American adventurism in Mexico did not concern Russell nearly as much as did the likelihood of a war in that country fostered by Napoleon's dangerous policies. Russell believed that France had made demands of Mexico with the expectation that they would not be met. Intervention appeared to be a pretext for occupation. England and Spain therefore negotiated separate arrangements for reparations from Mexico and withdrew from the country on April 9, 1862. The French remained.[26]

The Union's military successes in Tennessee had encouraged Mercier to attempt a peacemaking mission to Richmond. After the news of Forts Henry and Donelson, Thouvenel instructed his emissary to ask Seward whether his nation's prestige had been restored to the point that it might now accept intervention. But at a meeting in early April, Seward was so exuberant about the recent positive turn in the war (including the Union's victory at Shiloh or Pittsburg Landing) that Mercier decided not to bring up the matter. Instead, he remarked that he ought to visit Richmond for a firsthand inspection of conditions and morale. Seward surprised Mercier by accepting his suggestion and offering a pass through Union lines. Mercier then invited Stoeckl to accompany him on the mission, but the Russian minister declined, explaining later to his superiors in St. Petersburg that he saw no chance for success. Secretly, however, Stoeckl supported the French effort for peace because of his own government's opposition to involvement and the inability of the British to win the trust of the Union. Lyons frowned upon the venture. His well-known opposition to communicating with the South would make it appear that Mercier's visit signified a break in the Anglo-French accord. But Lyons relented when Mercier agreed to assure Seward that the two European nations were in agreement.[27]

Mercier informed Seward that he would emphasize to the South that it could expect no alliance with Europe and should consider an armistice in view of recent military setbacks. Seward approved, and Mercier (without having notified Paris of his decision to visit the Confederate capital) arrived in Richmond on April 16. The discussions proved disconcerting. Mercier talked with Benjamin, an acquaintance from prewar days, who made clear that the South's resistance remained firm and that only continued fighting could determine the verdict of the war. Mercier, according to Benjamin, was exasperated: "How can anybody talk to either side?" he blurted out to Benjamin. "I dare not utter to you a single sentence that does not begin by the word 'independence,' nor can I say a syllable to the other side on any other basis than union." Benjamin tried to reply in good humor while keeping the discussion on a private and unofficial level. "Why should you say anything to either side? I know your good feeling for us, and we require no proof of it. But you know we are hot-blooded people, and we would not like to talk with anybody who entertained the idea of the possibility of our dishonoring ourselves by reuniting with a people for whom we feel unmitigated contempt as well as abhorrence." After a three-day stay, Mercier returned to Washington on April 24 and reported his findings to Lincoln and Seward, who were sorely disappointed with the South's continued defiance.[28]

News of Mercier's visit to Richmond had met with some favor in England and so had the Southern version of the battle of Shiloh. The British had expressed relief after the South's claim to victory, even though the truth was that Grant had rallied his badly demoralized forces in a two-day battle near and along the banks of the swollen Tennessee River and barely salvaged a narrow victory for the Union. Especially shocking was the casualty figure—a combined total of twenty thousand, which far surpassed the number of men lost in previous battles and was a portent of the ghastly direction the fighting had taken.[29]

The initial British reading of the battle of Shiloh infuriated Adams. English merchants, he bitterly complained, were like the Dutch during the American revolutionary war, who "would, if money were to be made by it, send supplies even to hell, at the risk of burning their sails." It was "a trial of patience" to watch European nations cast judgments on American affairs. Moran remained concerned. In Russell's last note, he claimed that his nation had hurt its own economic interests by adhering to its responsibilities to the Union. Moran was appalled by what he considered to be a bald-faced lie. "If it be one of Great Britain's duties to a friendly nation to declare rebels belligerents before they have a flag afloat, and another to aid those rebels covertly in every possible way in an unholy war for slavery, then she has certainly performed her neutral duty." He warned that an "impartial posterity" would view events differently. Adams told Russell that he feared for the future more than the present, for great bitterness would result from the assistance given to the South by Englishmen who professed neutrality. Russell did not reply.[30]

Lyons's premonitions about slavery were meanwhile taking form, for the government in Washington had begun to make slavery a stated issue in the American conflict. Congress had passed the Confiscation Act in early August 1861, which authorized the seizure of property—including slaves—used directly in the South's war effort. In February 1862 Congress considered a second confiscation bill that caused Lincoln much concern. According to the bill, those slaves in rebellious areas who escaped to Union army camps would be free after sixty days, providing slaveholders with the option of ending resistance and winning back their slaves. The president feared that the new measure would alienate the border states by inviting slaves everywhere to walk off the plantations. He would support the measure only in areas where it did not impede the Union's restoration. Then, in early March, Lincoln addressed the border state problem. He asked Congress for a joint resolution supporting gradual and voluntary emancipation with compensation stemming from federal money awarded to states that voluntarily freed their slaves. Adams hailed Lincoln's action as the most important step yet taken in the war. Its impact on Europe, he believed, would probably be greater than on America. Russell, however, remained concerned about a servile insurrection and expressed skepticism about Lincoln's purpose in moving against slavery.[31]

Another sign pointed to an emerging Union consensus against slavery: in Washington on April 7, Seward and Lyons signed a treaty opposing the slave trade, which resulted from the Union's foreign affairs needs during the Civil War but suggested a new direction in the conflict. The pact called for what the British had long wanted and could not now oppose—the mutual right of search off Africa and Cuba. Had there been such a treaty in 1808, Seward wrote Adams, "there would have been no sedition here, and no disagreement between the United States and foreign nations." Lyons believed that the real objective of the treaty was political—to maintain the president's credibility with his party should he have to make concessions to the Confederacy in an attempt to reconstruct the Union. In truth, the domestic and foreign ramifications of the treaty were inseparable. The Union demonstrated its long-standing opposition to the slave trade while suggesting, if only inadvertently, that to intervene in the war on the South's behalf would help maintain slavery.[32]

The Lincoln administration's antislavery momentum continued to build as it focused on emancipation. Three days after the treaty with England, on April 10, the president signed a bill providing for gradual emancipation with compensation. Congress had encouraged the confiscation approach by forbidding officers from assisting the return of fugitive slaves to the South. Lincoln preferred the moderate alternative and called on the border states to participate in emancipation and to persuade the South to do the same. The ensuing debate revealed resistance by the border states, although the measure passed by good margins in both houses of Congress. Soon thereafter, on April 16, Lincoln signed another bill, authorizing compensation and colonization for slaves now declared free in the District of Columbia.[33]

Some basis exists for believing that Lincoln had relations with England and France in mind when he considered emancipation. In September 1861 the U.S. minister in Spain, Carl Schurz, assured Seward that an antislavery pronouncement by the Union would unite Europe against the South because no country would help slaveholders. The following January, Schurz returned to the

United States and talked with the president about using the anti-slavery issue to thwart outside intervention. Lincoln thought for a moment and replied: "You may be right. Probably you are. I have been thinking so myself. I cannot imagine that any European power would dare to recognize and aid the Southern Confederacy if it became clear that the Confederacy stands for slavery and the Union for freedom." If Schurz was correct in his recollection of Lincoln's reaction, the president's policy did have a foreign policy purpose and, whatever its other motives, was having a favorable effect on antislavery groups in England. On the morning of April 16, 1862, a large delegation of the Anti-Slavery Society, including a member of Parliament, met with Adams to praise the Lincoln administration's antislavery views.[34]

Then, in early May, news arrived in England that the Union had seized New Orleans and had seemingly taken a climactic step toward ending the war. Dixie diarist Mary Boykin Chesnut was disheartened: "New Orleans is gone, and with it the Confederacy! Are we not cut in two? The Mississippi ruins us if it is lost." With measured relief, Adams expressed optimism over the fall of New Orleans and the concomitant knowledge that McClellan was en route to Richmond. The British were incredulous over the fall of New Orleans, Adams noted. The port city's collapse, Moran triumphantly declared, constituted one of the greatest blows sustained by the South. The English "refuse to believe it, simply no doubt, because they don't want it should be so." Miles away, in Clitheroe, Garnett recorded his apprehension (and perhaps that of other mill owners) resulting from the Union's capture of New Orleans and accompanying reports that the South was burning cotton in an effort to force British intervention. The war appeared to be reaching its end—and with a scarcely believed Union victory.[35]

The fall of New Orleans perhaps discouraged even the slightest chance of a French intervention engineered by William Lindsay. Earlier that same April he made three unauthorized visits to Napoleon III that further strained the Anglo-French understanding. Napoleon agreed with Lindsay's allegations that the Union blockade was ineffectual and repeated his recent claim that he would have lifted it had England agreed. Twice the British government showed no interest in his quiet inquiries. In two to three months, Napoleon noted with concern, the suffering of French labor groups would become unbearable. Recognition of the South, Lindsay interjected, would help the situation. Napoleon proclaimed that he would send a fleet to the Mississippi River if England would do the same. Two days later he met again with Lindsay and asked him to relay the French position to Palmerston and Russell, as well as to Conservative opposition leaders Lord Derby and Benjamin Disraeli. Lindsay thought Napoleon wanted immediate action. The emperor's agitated manner revealed extreme dissatisfaction with his role as subordinate to England and suggested that he might act alone.[36]

Lindsay's optimism disappeared when he attempted to fulfill his mission in England. Russell refused an interview and declared that he could not receive any foreign communication except through formal diplomatic channels. Lindsay returned to Paris, this time accompanied by Mason, where he told Napoleon on April 18 of Russell's rebuff but noted that even though Derby had been too ill to discuss the matter, Disraeli had agreed with the French stand. Indeed, Disraeli expressed suspicion (never substantiated) that Russell and Seward had struck a private deal whereby England would respect the blockade and hold off recognition. Napoleon was so upset by England's refusal to reciprocate his friendly involvement in the *Trent* affair that he seemed prepared, according to Lindsay, to open the ports, by force, either alone or with England.

The South's friends had again demonstrated their wont for self-delusion. Thouvenel was angry with Lindsay's unorthodox actions and with the emperor's dangerous diplomacy, and in a discreet yet pointed way expressed his displeasure (and that of the French ambassador in London, Count Charles de Flahault) to Napoleon. The emperor had spoken without support from his advisers and felt compelled to retract his alleged offer of help. More important, Russell had not altered his stand on neutrality. In a face-saving effort, Napoleon declared that recent events in New Orleans had forced a reassessment. According to Slidell, the collapse of the port city was the crucial consideration in restraining French intervention.

In the meantime, even as Lincoln proclaimed the opening of New Orleans and other ports after June 1, an ironic and unexpected development was under way: rather than convincing the

British (and French) that intervention was not necessary, the victory at New Orleans had provided a further impetus to foreign involvement. Many British observers believed that the Union had satisfied honor and would surely accept mediation. In France, Thouvenel discussed the wartime situation with Slidell, who admitted to the negative consequences of the fall of New Orleans but nonetheless insisted that his people's iron will would prevail. Outside intervention, he insisted, would hurry the inevitable outcome. In exchange for European recognition, the South would agree to a six-month armistice that included a relaxation of the blockade. Although both Napoleon and Thouvenel were upset over Mercier's unauthorized mission to Richmond, they realized that his reports of Southern resilience were accurate. Thouvenel concluded that his government should maintain neutrality and continue waiting for the proper moment to offer mediation.[37]

BOTH EUROPEAN NATIONS were disappointed that the Union victory at New Orleans did not yield the expected results. The Mississippi River was not yet entirely open, and the capture of its Southern gateway did not automatically release a flow of cotton, nor did it satisfy the Union's craving for a restoration of honor. Instead, the victory assured the Union that subjugation of the South was probable and signaled the certainty of long and bitter fighting in both the western and eastern theaters. Adams and others had not been correct in declaring that Union victories on the battlefield would guarantee against outside interference. The Union's military successes had left open the possibility of foreign intervention.

Seedtime
of British
Intervention

In the summer of 1862 the Union underwent another period of severe trial. Despite victory at New Orleans, the talk of European intervention persisted and for the first time became the central issue in an emotion-packed meeting of Parliament. The Union's control of the mouth of the Mississippi River cheered the American legation in London for only a short time. The euphoria came to an abrupt end when Charles Francis Adams was rebuffed once more in his appeal to Russell to withdraw belligerent rights from the South. During their conversation, Russell again argued that England's policy benefited the Union by permitting it to buy arms and military stores from British firms. Adams had learned of these arms deals some months earlier and had argued to Seward that they undermined the Union's protests against

British policy and had succeeded in stopping further purchases in England and shifting them to Austria, which did not aid the insurgents. The foreign secretary, however, maintained his pledge of neutrality and, to Adams's chagrin, repeated that the policy was "exceedingly advantageous" to the North.[1]

Thus at the instant of the Union's greatest victory, the outcome had combined with England's growing economic problems to encourage legislators to consider intervention. As Union officials perceived matters, military successes had the reverse effect of heightening the chances for an intervention that would promote disunion. Whether the Union won or lost in battle, the British seemed bent on accepting secession. In truth, these fears were not entirely unfounded. Concern had grown in England that a long war would pull in interested foreign parties and lead to an international crisis. The cotton surplus would diminish to a critical stage by autumn, and in France the shortage was already becoming alarming. To challenge the Union blockade would mean confrontation with the Union. The only alternative, according to some British observers, was a joint mediation followed by a negotiated end to the war. Richard Cobden, who was no friend of the South's, recommended to Charles Francis Adams over breakfast that a joint intervention by European powers might be the solution. Adams warned, in return, that those intervening powers must have a workable peace plan to suggest. Slavery, he emphasized to Cobden, was the central issue in the war, and the North would never accept peace as long as that system remained in place. The North would not allow *dis*union; the South would not accept *re*union. No basis for compromise existed. "It was the failure to comprehend this truth," Adams recorded in his diary that evening, "that clouded every European judgment of our affairs."[2]

THE LINCOLN ADMINISTRATION joined Adams in fearing that British interest in intervention had grown after the fall of New Orleans. Rumors of Anglo-French intervention, Lyons noted, forced the U.S. government to moderate its attitude toward England. The Americans, in an effort to ease their fears, called on England and France to renounce any intentions to intervene. But Seward, Lyons added, also held to the belief that the Mexican affair would ward off the interventionist danger in America by undermining the Anglo-French entente. The French, however, were growing anxious for an end to the war in America. Mercier continued to favor intervention, Lyons noted, but remained perplexed about how to do so in a way that would assure the acquisition of cotton. The French minister feared that the South would not quit fighting until it was desolated and that the North would soon declare immediate emancipation and stir up such upheaval in the South that cotton production would grind to a halt. Lyons agreed with Mercier that failure to intervene would assure more troubles, though he did not see how the measure would do any good. As Union forces advanced, Southerners would probably follow the pattern set in New Orleans of destroying cotton in hope of pressuring England and France to intervene. The only chance for peace, Lyons insisted, lay in a major Southern military victory that might turn more Northerners against the war. Russell agreed and expressed regret that the Union's success at New Orleans had mistakenly "portend[ed] the conquest of the South." The North still would not allow separation, which was the only "fair solution."[3]

Lyons's forebodings of a long war, in a paradoxical sense, encouraged the chances of a British intervention that he actually opposed. Only the broken will of the Union—which was not in evidence—would make intervention palatable. Lyons continued to believe that a defensive alliance with the South offered the sole possibility of convincing the North to call off the war. Such an agreement might even include the use of force to keep the Union's army and navy away from the plantations to allow cultivation of cotton and permit British ships to carry the product from the ports. But a pact with the South, Lyons also knew, carried the distinct possibility of causing war with the United States. A bloodless intervention could succeed only when either the North or South was willing to have peace "*at any price.*" And yet, he keenly observed, intervention would not then be necessary because one antagonist would have conquered the other. Mercier concurred. Like the British, he realized that intervention—and Lyons thought that Mercier meant with recognition—would have its desired effect only when the North was exhausted militarily. Lyons was in ill health and hoped to be in England soon, where he could discuss the matter with the ministry. "The war," he assured Russell, "has become one of Separation—or Subjugation."[4]

Unaware of the intricacies confounding Anglo-French considerations of intervention, the Lincoln administration feared that England and France had moved toward involvement and took steps to block such a measure. In mid-May an unsigned article entitled "Rumoured Foreign Intervention" appeared in the *Washington National Intelligencer*, warning that the only acceptable approach was a "moral intervention" aimed at restoring the Union. In forwarding the article to Russell, Lyons wrote that just three days before, Seward had expressed the same ideas to Lyons and that the article probably spoke for the government. The writer of the article opposed any plan resting on satisfaction of European industrial interests and approval of Southern separation. Such a proposal would constitute an Anglo-French military alliance with the Confederacy. If Europe's desire for cotton led to recognition of Southern independence, such intervention would constitute an "act of hostility to The United States, and as such would not only be resented, but resisted to the last extremity." When Lincoln opened the ports, the South burned cotton. This would be an unusual time for an intervention aimed at independence—when the South was desperate. "Can a rebellion claim recognition by virtue of its weakness, or sympathy because of the recklessness of its leaders?" Intervening nations would be accused of self-interest and have no right to extend recognition. The Confederates had not "vindicated their independence among the commonwealth of States."[5]

The international situation appeared so precarious during the spring of 1862 that Seward attempted to counter the threat of intervention by warning England that its involvement in American affairs could set off a slave revolt that would spawn a race war in the United States. Before the fall of New Orleans, he wrote Adams in a dispatch meant for Russell's later perusal, Europe speculated about an intervention that could only have benefited the South. Runaway slaves regarded the Union army as the chief means toward freedom. If the Confederacy tried to stop their escape, who could prevent the present conflict from "degenerating into a servile war?" A European intervention premised on

Southern separation would guarantee such a war and thereby disrupt the economy and destroy all European interests in America. Should England prepare to intervene, Adams was to use this note in an attempt to stop the move.[6]

As an indication of the touchy situation, in early June a minor dispute erupted that fused with other Anglo-American difficulties to increase Adams's concerns about intervention. The previous month in New Orleans, female resistance to Union occupation had become so embittered that General Benjamin Butler announced that any female who insulted his soldiers would "be treated as a woman of the town plying her avocation." Palmerston sent Adams an angry private note denouncing Butler's ill-advised "woman order" that, in the context of the times, suggested to the American legation that the prime minister was instigating a problem with the Union as a pretext for intervention in the war. But Russell managed to calm the ruckus by assuring Adams that the note was unofficial and suggested no change in government policy. Though Adams felt comforted by Russell's intercession, the episode proved costly to the Adams family. For some time Palmerston did not speak to the American minister, and Lady Palmerston no longer invited him and his wife to receptions at which Adams had previously learned much from unofficial conversations with British dignitaries.[7]

Thus the fear of imminent British intervention had not receded, even though the government maintained its opposition to such a move. Lindsay, in fact, had announced his intention to introduce a motion in Parliament calling for diplomatic recognition of the South. Mason was jubilant. "All this I hope," he wrote Richmond, "indicates that some movement is to be made at last." Russell assured Adams that Lindsay's motion would "come to nothing," but the American minister remained apprehensive. Indeed, he chose this time, June 20, to show Russell the note from Seward warning of slave revolts. The Union alarm was misplaced. Russell assured Adams that the ministry did not contemplate mediation despite pressure from the press and other sources. Although some have charged (then and later) that the *Times* was pro-South, the truth seems to be that the London paper agreed with the Palmerston ministry and numerous others in England who wanted a settlement based on Southern separation. Only the North stood in the way. And yet the British never seemed to understand that from the Union's perspective, the call for separation was equivalent to supporting the South. Palmerston made his stand clear when he declared to Russell that "no intention at present exists to offer mediation." Such a move would be tantamount to asking two boxers to end their fight after only "the third round." The war itself must convince the North that reunion was impossible.[8]

At this critical juncture the lack of military progress in the eastern theater of the war hurt the Union's cause in England and on the Continent. McClellan's failure to take Richmond had combined with England's unanticipated reaction to the Union victory in New Orleans to intensify the public interest in intervention. To European observers, McClellan's futile efforts in the Peninsular Campaign had reinforced the belief that the Union could not defeat the Confederacy. Even Moran admitted that McClellan's reversals outside Richmond damaged the Union's credibility in Europe. Henry Adams interpreted the reaction in England as heightened pro-Confederate feeling. Lyons, now in London, wrote the British chargé in Washington regarding McClellan's setback on the Peninsula: "I'm afraid no one but me is sorry for it." The war would continue and with it the growing appeal for intervention. A parliamentary debate would not be appropriate, he thought. "I do not think we know here sufficiently the extent of the disaster to be able to come to any conclusion as to what the European Powers should do."[9]

The Lincoln administration's fears of European intentions, whether or not exaggerated, continued to mold policy. The Union renounced the pessimistic reports from the Virginia battlefield, but it could not dissuade the Palmerston ministry from believing that neither victory nor defeat could induce the Union to accept the South's separation. Both the British and the French were disturbed by the Union's unbending resolve in the face of adversity. Following McClellan's retreat from Richmond, Mercier broached Seward with the possibility of mediation. The minister offered assurances that Europe's response to Union conquests rested solely on its interest in ending the war. Mercier drew Seward's solemn reply: "Do not believe for a moment that either the Federal Congress, myself or any person connected with this government will in any case entertain any proposition or suggestion of arrangement or accommodation or adjustment from within or without upon the basis of a surrender of the Federal Union." Lest there be doubt, Seward proclaimed: "We will not admit the division of the Union." [10]

To the Union, the path to British intervention seemed clear as Lindsay prepared in July to introduce his motion for recognition. In accordance with Russell's request, Lindsay informed Mason, he had sent the foreign secretary a copy of the motion, accompanied by a note alleging that 90 percent of the Commons supported immediate recognition and that the majority would vote for the motion with or without government support. Lindsay told Russell that the government had a "*right*" to extend recognition and assured him that the move would not lead to war. In an argument that demonstrated both Lindsay's wishful thinking and his failure to comprehend the Union's resolve, he told Russell that most Northerners would welcome British recognition, as would Seward, who wanted out of the war.[11]

Despite the Union fears, the Palmerston government remained uninterested in extending recognition—especially at this time. The prime minister considered it a strange moment to push for recognition when all the American coast and major internal rivers belonged to the North and one of the South's large armies was "split into Fragments." The South would probably continue the contest "but we ought to know that their separate independence is a Truth and a Fact before we can declare it to be so." To intervene now would put England on the side of the Confederacy in the war. He did not believe that Lindsay had sufficient parliamentary support. That same day, at a late afternoon conference with Adams, Russell again dismissed Lindsay's motion as inconsequential.[12]

Even though Adams held to his belief that Union victories on the battlefield would prevent recognition, he again failed to understand the position of the London ministry.[13] It had distinguished between accepting Southern separation and extending recognition to an independent nation. Although Palmerston and Russell believed that the Confederacy had established its claim to separate status, they remained dubious of its capacity to stand as a sovereign nation. To the British leaders, the only purpose of mediation (if it occurred) would be to resolve differences between belligerents and not between nations. The Union saw no distinction and regarded mediation as meddling in domestic affairs. Given this mutual lack of understanding, any British action hinting at intervention would necessarily raise Union protests.

The British ministry continued to feel pressure, for cotton was becoming a serious consideration. Adams had another private conversation with Cobden regarding intervention that stemmed from England's growing concern over the diminishing cotton supply. The workers, Cobden declared, had discussed the use of political tactics to persuade the British and French governments to make a "joint representation" to the U.S. government. Cobden warned of considerable sympathy for the South and emphasized that a half million bales of cotton might ease the pressure. In reading Adams's account of this conversation, Seward understood how European leaders believed that intervention could take place without hurting anyone. But they failed to realize how sensitive Americans were about sovereignty and honor. Intervention, he insisted, would inspire a greater devotion to the Union and prolong the war, leading to the abolition of slavery through violence and, by totally disrupting the South's economy, putting an end to cotton exports.[14]

The Union government's continued fear of intervention tested its forbearance, particularly in view of conflicting signals from European figures. Exasperated by recent developments, Adams met with Lyons in London and emphasized that Russell misunderstood the situation in America. Lyons, much to Adams's relief, acknowledged that foreign involvement would worsen matters. From Paris, Dayton reported that Napoleon remained skeptical about the North's ability to restore the Union. The British, Seward complained, were also difficult to convince. Despite recent Union military successes in Louisiana and in the West, they pointed instead to setbacks at Richmond and Corinth and to the dearth of Union sentiment in Norfolk and New Orleans. "Ah, well! Skepticism must be expected in this world in regard to new political systems, insomuch as even Divine revelation needs the aid of miracles to make converts to a new religious faith." Corinth, Seward wryly observed, fell to the Union on the same day that the British people declared that the South's hold on the city meant that the Union was broken. In England, Adams noted that accounts assuring impending Union control of the Mississippi River had quieted the call for intervention. Moran countered that in England the news of the Union navy's imminent conquest of Memphis would be downgraded in importance. The British aristocracy, Adams declared with disgust, continued its "ill-disguised antipathy" for the Union. When in July Mercier again raised the subject of mediation to Seward, the secretary of state could contain himself no longer. He warned that "the Emperor can commit no graver error than to mix himself in our affairs. At the rumor alone of intervention all the factions will reunite themselves against you and even in the border states you will meet resistance unanimous and desperate." Mercier advised his home government that intervention could lead to war.[15]

T H U S in the summer of 1862 the Union government thought its cause in England was in serious trouble. No amount of valor on the battlefield guaranteed against intervention, and the economic situation in England had become markedly worse. Almost half of the country's industrial work force was unemployed, cotton stocks were only a sixth of what they were in 1861 and prices were rising rapidly, almost a third of the mills were closed or preparing to do so, and crops in general were poor. Henry Adams insisted that the only remedy was for the Union armies to crush the South.[16]

At the same time, Confederate hopes that England would defy the Union blockade were fast dissipating. Mason informed Russell of Davis's surprise at finding in the recently published correspondence before Parliament that the British government had added to the Declaration of Paris these words in declaring a blockade effective: "*or to create an evident danger of entering or leaving it.*" England, Mason indignantly declared, should have officially notified the Confederacy of this change and given it a chance to respond. Such a stipulation hurt the South because the British now maintained what Russell had already told Mason on an unofficial basis—that the escape of ships through the blockade did not necessarily make the blockade ineffective. Mason enclosed long lists of ships entering and clearing Southern ports and argued that neutral nations must not acquiesce in a paper blockade. "Not one in 10, in the large number of voyages so made, it is believed, has been captured." Mason attributed much of the hardened British attitude to what he dismissed as unfounded rumors fostered by the Union government that the South had ordered the destruction of cotton. The truth was, however, that the Confederate Congress in March 1862 had sanctioned crop destruction in an effort to exert further pressure on England and France. Perhaps not yet informed of this decision—which would suggest the difficulties experienced by the Confederacy in running both goods and information through the blockade—Mason made a statement that belied the facts. The South, he declared to Russell, had not burned or held back cotton in an effort to extract foreign concessions. If the supply was low in England and Europe, "it is because Europe has not thought it proper to send her ships to America for cotton." Southerners, Mason insisted, had kept cotton from the seaboard because of the small demand and to save it from Union confiscation. If the North adhered to international law in designating the blockaded ports and maintaining a sufficient force to keep them closed, cotton would flow through those other ports necessarily left open for trade.[17]

Then, in an action long anticipated by the British, the Lincoln administration shifted the focus of the war toward the end of slavery. Perhaps to signal this change in policy, the president some months earlier had called on Congress to do something never done before by the United States: to extend recognition to black governments—those in Haiti and Liberia—and on June 5 he signed a bill authorizing the appointment of commissioners to those countries. On July 12 Lincoln met in the White House with congressmen of the border states and advocated compensated emancipation. In a move demonstrating his longtime support for the solution set forth by the American Colonization Society, he argued that South America could accommodate free blacks. But Lincoln's arguments failed to persuade his listeners. Then, on July 13, he won the support of Seward and Secretary of the Navy Gideon Welles when he told them that he intended to proclaim emancipation in an effort to "strike at the heart of the rebellion." The move, Lincoln explained, was "a military necessity, absolutely essential to the preservation of the Union."[18]

Lincoln's turn toward emancipation seemed timely: by mid-July the situation on both sides of the Atlantic pointed to a coming showdown over recognition. Cobden continued to believe that only a massive infusion of cotton from the Mississippi

River could prevent foreign intervention. Palmerston sought to calm disgruntled cotton workers with food and other forms of relief. Mason discerned a change in British attitude that suggested the imminence of recognition. Slidell was also optimistic about France. In Washington the British chargé, William Stuart, sensed that the United States had approached a turning point in the war. People in Louisiana thought Lincoln was preparing to make a stand against slavery. From New Orleans, Reverdy Johnson, who had been sent there by the State Department, informed Lincoln that the move toward emancipation had undermined Union sentiment.[19]

Charles Francis Adams supported Lincoln's action against slavery by declaring that English observers regarded McClellan's reversal as a sign of impending Union defeat and felt that the time had come for intervention. Indeed, Adams confided in his diary, the expectant atmosphere in London was similar to that following Bull Run. Lindsay had meanwhile disclosed his stratagem to incorporate both intervention and recognition into his motion before Parliament. Mediation, he emphasized, should come in conjunction with other powers. Adams did not think that the ministry or leading opposition members favored mediation. "But it is a good deal nursed by the rank and file of the latter, and by a portion of the ministerialists." He was not sure how long the Palmerston government could resist the pressure.[20]

Adams urged the officials in Washington to clarify the higher purposes in the war. He was certain that the big powers had discussed the American situation but had not yet agreed upon any specific action. He warned, however, that all signs pointed to mediation. Even if the step took "'the most benevolent aspect possible, the effect would be to concentrate in a degree the moral sense of the civilized nations of Europe in its behalf." The Union must stress its interest in freedom and thereby undermine the accusation that it sought empire. Adams's concerns were justified. Mason had informed Russell that the Confederacy welcomed a British offer to help end the North's effort to subjugate the South.[21]

England appeared to be moving toward intervention. Even though the Palmerston ministry did not support Lindsay's motion, its objection rested not on substance but on timing. The prime minister emphasized in the House of Commons the need to maintain his government's independence of action in accordance with the constantly changing situation in America. He had come under pressure from Gladstone to offer mediation in an effort to bring the war to a close. And, of course, no guarantee existed that the ministry would defeat Lindsay's motion. He had prepared well by publicizing his views and by working with his colleague and fellow Southern sympathizer John Roebuck and with the Conservative opposition leader in the Commons, Benjamin Disraeli.[22] Even though the Palmerston ministry continued to distinguish between separation of the South and its status as a nation, the Union considered the gap between them so small that either classification portended danger.

As the day arrived for Parliament's debate on Lindsay's motion, the importance of McClellan's failures in Virginia loomed larger. Some enthusiasts mistakenly termed them a capitulation. Mason wrote Slidell that very day of July 18: "I am happy to say that the rout before Richmond has had the happiest effect here in all quarters, and things look well for Lindsay's motion tonight." From Richmond, Confederate secretary of state Judah P. Benjamin urged Mason to seize the moment and push for recognition. Such a triumph, he declared, would stimulate domestic investment in the war effort and yield many related benefits. The British permanent under secretary for foreign affairs, Edmund Hammond, felt satisfied that the North had sustained a thorough defeat. He added, however, that it still had not been "sufficiently humbled to seek for peace." The South deserved recognition, he declared, and yet only the need for cotton would lead to intervention before a Northern surrender. Charles Francis Adams thought that someone had fabricated the stories of a McClellan debacle in an effort to sway the House of Commons. If so, the attempt seemed successful. His son Henry observed that anti-Union sentiment was "rising every hour and running harder against us than at any time since the *Trent* affair."[23]

The air was pulsating with excitement when Palmerston joined Parliament on the evening of July 18 to discuss Lindsay's motion. Mason had entered the chamber with what Moran derisively called "two or three vulgar looking Confederates." After a brief dispute over seating, Mason and a companion were permitted on the floor below the gallery (where Moran sat) while the others trucked upstairs. Suddenly a member of the Commons rushed in with an evening paper carrying the headlines: "Capitulation of McClellan's Army. Flight of McClellan on a steamer." As a crowd gathered to hear the details, Henry Adams (who was in the chamber) dismissed the story as the product of "Southern liars." The American legation, he knew, had received reports denying McClellan's surrender that were dated two days after the present account. When the legislators returned to their seats, Lindsay took the floor to proclaim an irreparable break between North and South and to argue for the justice of the latter's cause. Cleverly sliding around the nettlesome problem of recognition, he focused on mediation. Lancashire needed cotton, he declared; its workers told him that the South deserved independence. Lindsay, however, was a poor speaker who so blatantly twisted the truth that many members soon left the chamber. After an hour-long attack on the Union, he revealed his motives by declaring that he "desired the disruption of the American Union, as every honest Englishman did, because it was too great a Power and England sh'd not let such a power exist on the American continent." According to Moran, "Old Mason spat tobacco more furiously at this than ever, and covered the carpet." Moran thought that the Confederate emissary had failed to realize that Lindsay had declared the South to mean nothing to him and that his only objective was to destroy the entire United States for the benefit of England.[24]

As the debate roared on, Moran sensed doubt in Parliament about the wisdom of intervention. To encourage this feeling, he circulated a private telegram to prove that the stories of McClellan's capitulation were erroneous. "It seemed to me," Moran noted, "that fear of us, and fear alone, was the check to action." P. A. Taylor, a new member from Leicester who belonged to the London Emancipation Society, stood to defend the ministry but met howls of derision from the Conservative opposition. Those who had walked out on Lindsay now returned, and Palmerston, who had pulled his hat over his eyes during Lindsay's speech and seemed asleep, doffed his shield and listened intently. Taylor drew jeers when he insisted that the American war centered on the struggle between slavery and freedom. When Taylor praised Lincoln, Moran noted a "burst of horse-laughter and ridicule" that was a "disgrace to the age." Taylor shouted above the tumult that any support given to the South put England on the side of slavery. Lord Adolphus Vane-Tempest, son-in-law of the Duke of Newcastle, came to Lindsay's defense but appeared drunk and more than once nearly fell over the back of the bench in front of him. William E. Forster, the strong Union advocate, then delivered a short but effective speech in behalf of the ministry, perhaps suggesting his close relationship with Charles Francis Adams by warning that intervention would encourage a servile war.[25]

The debate did not reach a decision point until well into the morning hours, when Palmerston rose to proclaim his opposition to intervention. As if to remind members of Parliament that his ministry had been effective during the *Trent* crisis and that they again should stay out of foreign policy, he put the interventionist matter to rest in three minutes. England's only objective regarding the American war, Palmerston insisted, was "that it should end." Though supporters of both North and South had expressed feelings that would receive warm acceptance by their favorites in America, he warned that these same members of Parliament had uttered disparaging remarks that would antagonize both belligerents and that it was "human nature to think more of things that are offensive, than of things which are gratifying and friendly." Any decision either for or against mediation and recognition belonged to the government and not to the House of Commons. Only the ministry could deal responsibly and knowledgeably with such a delicate matter "according to the varying circumstances of the moment." But it could take no interventionist course until Southern independence was "firmly and permanently established." Precipitous recognition would not establish a nation unless the step "were followed by some direct active interference." And this approach would lead to "greater evils, greater sufferings, and greater privations." Never in history had there been "a contest of such magnitude between two different sections of the same people." Mediation at this point would fail because neither North nor South was prepared to lay down its arms. The House must withdraw Lindsay's motion. The government must maintain the discretionary power to decide "what can be done, when it can be done, and how it can be done."[26]

Silence gave way to applause. Lindsay withdrew his motion, declaring bitterly that he would "wait for king cotton to turn the screws still further." Moments after adjournment Moran filed past Mason, who was sitting by himself, "looking sullen and dejected." Confederate sympathizer William Gregory soon joined Mason in leaving the chamber. The morning's press confirmed that McClellan had not surrendered and proclaimed its approval of Lindsay's decision.[27]

Americans in London praised Palmerston's speech but warned that the prime minister had scarcely hidden his belief that Confederate military successes could lead to intervention. Charles Francis Adams had the impression that the recognition question was dormant, not dead, and remained convinced that the upper classes still wanted to inflict permanent damage on the United States. Mixed signals from the battlefield were responsible for the confusion, he thought. Despite the victory at New Orleans, the Union had been unable to capture Richmond and the British felt certain that it never would. Henry Adams had earlier warned that if the Union was still fighting in Virginia in July, foreign interference would become certain. The only obstacle has been the inability of the European powers to unite in a mediation offer. A Union stand against slavery, he emphasized, would deter intervention.[28]

British reaction to the American war rested on more than news from the battlefield. Cotton had become an even greater concern, for by autumn the supply on hand would sink to an emergency level. But even though economic considerations had risen in prominence, the British government harbored ill feeling toward the Confederacy for withholding cotton. More important was another aspect of the military situation. British leaders remained opposed to challenging the Union blockade and risking war with a nation that had an army larger than England's and that now had ironclad vessels. Mediation seemed to provide the only feasible avenue toward ending the war—but only if the North realized the impossibility of subjugating the South. Thus, according to British reasoning, the call for a Southern military victory did not necessarily prove pro-South sympathy. Such a triumph might convince the Union that its objectives were not attainable and that the only alternative to mutual destruction was an armistice followed by negotiations aimed at peace.

MEDIATION OFFERED the most attractive solution to concerned groups and individuals, both inside and outside the British government. Mediation would satisfy the humanitarians who believed the war a purposeless bloodletting that civilized nations had a moral duty to end. It would meet the needs of businessmen who required not only Southern cotton but Northern grain.[29] It might mollify the antislavery spokesmen who believed that the way to kill the institution was to prevent its spread. But in reality, the key to mediation remained a convincing Union defeat that would undermine its will by demonstrating the war's futility. The Union, however, turned to something higher for help. Perhaps the key to preventing intervention lay in its proclaiming a moral purpose in the war.

7

Emancipation by the Sword and the British Decision to Intervene

In early August 1862 a variety of forces converged to force leaders in England to move with France toward a joint mediation in the American war. Recent news from the United States, particularly the unfounded rumors of the Confederate capture of Baltimore, had caused great anticipation in England. Perhaps such a conquest, Russell noted, would finally break the Union's spirit. Most Englishmen continued to believe that separation would help both North and South. Although interest in mediation had grown, the ministry felt no public pressure to extend recognition. The mill workers, it was generally conceded, could withstand the hardships until March or April 1863. Russell nonetheless felt troubled.

Union conquest of the South remained doubtful and still Seward had done nothing "to prevent the cry that may arise here, from the obstinacy & passion of the North." Mason received word from Slidell that his July interview with Napoleon left the impression that he might act without England. A similar assessment came from Washington, where Stuart reported that France seemed prepared to advocate recognition. Mercier thought that by October American public opinion might be receptive to a joint mediation.[1]

For a host of reasons, the British government, or more properly Russell and Gladstone, showed interest in a joint mediation designed to curtail a war that appeared unending. Cotton had not yet become a prime consideration, though a critical shortage loomed on the horizon. By the spring of 1863, unless the Union marketed the more than 3 million bales its army had confiscated in the South, King Cotton diplomacy might become a reality. While this concern continued to grow, Stuart reported from Washington that the Union had shifted its wartime objective to the abolition of slavery. He feared that the North might instigate a servile uprising to undercut the South. The Union's call for stronger war measures now included confiscation, emancipation, and arming the slaves. Many Americans, Stuart declared, believed that a full-scale slave rebellion would break up the Confederate army by forcing the soldiers to return home to protect their families. Seward's warning regarding slave insurrections deeply troubled Russell. Indeed, in Russell's anxiety he misinterpreted Seward's note to believe that the Lincoln administration was prepared to stir up a slave rebellion in a desperate effort to ward off foreign intervention. So serious were Russell's fears that Stuart read Russell's dispatch to Seward and later gave him a copy. The possibility of a race war, Russell insisted, would "only make other nations more desirous to see an end of this desolating and destructive conflict."[2]

The Union's move against slavery not only alienated the British but tended to encourage the very intervention the Lincoln administration sought to prevent. Most British observers did not believe that the Union advanced emancipation as a moral measure. When the war began, they had been surprised when Lincoln emphasized that the conflict did not concern slavery. Even if Lincoln was worried about the domestic political consequences of fighting a war against slavery, he also took the side of many of his countrymen—including those outside the Republican party as well as those within—who had condoned slavery by refusing to make a stand against it. The British now regarded emancipation as sheer hypocrisy—a desperate effort to save the Union by encouraging the South's slaves to rebel and bring down the cotton kingdom from within. The only remedy to this demonic action, from England's perspective, was an intervention aimed at Southern separation.

The Lincoln administration expressed anger with the British. The "slaveholding insurgents," Seward told Adams, had asked other nations to help overthrow the American government, and then, in an effort to safeguard slavery, they stabbed these same nations in the back by blocking the cotton flow. The South's actions were not only treason against the Union but a war against humanity. How could England fail to grasp these truths? Nothing the Union did, Seward lamented, had a favorable impact on Europe. Victory "does not satisfy our enemies abroad. Defeats in their eyes prove our national incapacity." And now the Union's stand against slavery had failed to arouse support, even in England. "At first the [Union] government was considered as unfaithful to humanity in not proclaiming emancipation, and when it appeared that slavery, by being thus forced into the contest, must suffer, and perhaps perish in the conflict, then the war had become an intolerable propagandism of emancipation by the sword." Seward insisted that humanity was at stake. The Union sought only respect for its sovereignty. If other nations intervened, the American conflict would become "a war of the world." [3]

The Union and British governments had taken different roads that nonetheless led to the same destination. Each was convinced that the other's policies assured a war of atrocity that could become racial in the United States before it became international. As the Union officials warned that intervention would prolong the war, raise the tempo of the fighting, and ultimately spread the conflict beyond America's boundaries, so did the British come to believe that failure to intervene—and soon—would guarantee the same results.

LINCOLN WAS NOT aware of this potential collision over slavery and had moved toward emancipation. At the urging of

Secretary of War Edwin M. Stanton, the president met on July 22 with prominent New York attorney and Democrat Francis B. Cutting, who had supported slavery but now favored its eradication as part of the war effort. During a two-hour discussion, Cutting insisted that emancipation would ward off recognition of the South and mollify the growing number of antislavery adherents. That same day Lincoln told the cabinet he intended to proclaim emancipation. As a "necessary military measure" for ending the war, the president declared in the draft he read to his advisers, all slaves in states still in rebellion by January 1, 1863, would become free.[4]

The cabinet response was mixed but cautiously favorable. Postmaster General Montgomery Blair was the only one who objected. Emancipation, he feared, would turn over Congress to the Democrats in the fall elections. Yet in a letter the following day he allowed that the measure might be valuable in halting foreign intervention. The secretary of the treasury, Salmon P. Chase, had long favored abolition by any means. The president, Chase thought, could achieve emancipation more quickly by authorizing generals to arm the slaves. Stanton likewise had argued for arming the slaves and now supported an immediate proclamation of emancipation. Seward counseled delay. He had once claimed that he did not like "to proselyte with the sword" and now feared that emancipation might provoke intervention by appearing to be an attempt to stir up a slave insurrection. Seward urged the president to hold the announcement until the Union achieved a victory on the battlefield. Otherwise, the secretary warned in a statement that later rang true in England, emancipation would appear to be "the last measure of an exhausted government, a cry for help . . . our last *shriek*, on the retreat." Lincoln agreed to postpone the proclamation until the Union won a battle.[5]

The president had come to believe that the war's demands made it necessary to seek the "forcible abolition of slavery." He believed himself patient and forgiving. "Still I must save this government if possible. What I *cannot* do, of course I *will* not do; but it may as well be understood, once for all, that I shall not surrender this game leaving any available card unplayed." To New York financier and Democrat August Belmont, Lincoln wrote: "This government cannot much longer play a game in which it stakes all, and its enemies stake nothing. Those enemies must understand that they cannot experiment for ten years trying to destroy the government, and if they fail still come back into the Union unhurt." Belmont agreed with Lincoln's proposition but warned him to muffle the blow with as much dexterity as possible. Confederate spokesmen had already accused the Union of seeking "conquest and subjugation" and, in so doing, had undercut the chances for awakening a dormant Unionist sentiment in the South. A heavy-handed attack on slavery would take on a vengeful appearance and thereby aid the Southern cause. But Lincoln was not inclined to be careful—even when dealing with the loyal slave states. He impatiently told a Union supporter in the South that the insistence by slaveholders in the border states "that the government shall not strike its open enemies, lest they be struck by accident," had caused the "paralysis—the dead palsy—of the government in this whole struggle." Lincoln could wait no longer: "The truth is, that what is done, and omitted, about slaves, is done and omitted on . . . military necessity."[6]

Thus on the simplest level (as the British suspected, but for the wrong reason), emancipation provided a means to an end—another instrument for winning the war. Whether through confiscation or emancipation, growing numbers of Union spokesmen believed that the exigencies of the war licensed the president to pull out the cornerstone of the South. If the slaves walked off the plantations, would not their departure bring down the South from within? Lincoln did not wish to cause a slave rebellion, but he realized that any wartime move against slavery could grow into widespread resistance to the institution that would not abate until all blacks were freed. And he understood that the chances for a servile uprising would increase as a result of emancipation. But the lack of significant progress in the war dictated a change in strategy.[7]

In retrospect, it seems indisputable that even if emancipation was first and foremost a military measure, almost everyone involved in the process recognized that the president's war measure would facilitate an end to slavery. During a cabinet meeting on Sunday, August 3, Chase insisted that the time had passed for trying to put down the rebellion without interfering with slavery. And, Chase noted with satisfaction, Seward had thrown aside his hesitancy to favor any step that won freedom for the blacks. Lincoln himself declared that he was "pretty well cured of objections to any measure except want of adaptedness to put down the rebellion." In the western theater General Ulysses S. Grant, fresh off a series of victories at Forts Henry and Donelson, Shiloh, and Corinth, argued that confiscation was vital to victory. One of his officers declared that "the policy is to be terrible on the enemy. I am using Negroes all the time for my work as teamsters, and have 1,000 employed." Grant told his family that he sought only "to put down the rebellion. . . . I don't know what is to become of these poor people in the end, but it weakens the enemy to take them from them."[8]

The threat of foreign intervention confirmed Lincoln's decision to move toward emancipation. Seward had given him a letter from the French writer Count Agénor-Etienne de Gasparin, who expressed surprise over the Union's inability to win the war and asserted that he had tried to counteract the threat of a European involvement that had prolonged the fighting. America's chief danger came from Europe, for without hope of intervention the South's revolt would have ended long ago. The Union must emphasize its drive for liberty. If Europeans could argue that the Union had no interest in abolition, the supporters of intervention would succeed. Lincoln concurred. The Union had to raise a cry for black freedom that would discourage European intervention.[9]

Such a move against slavery would have to come quickly, for Lincoln was undergoing pressure from all sides of the emancipation issue. Many white Northerners had no interest in or even humanitarian concern for the blacks and would refuse to spill blood on their behalf. Others either silently approved of slavery or felt no responsibility for nonwhites. Working groups resented free black competition. Abolitionists would denounce his government for refusing to end slavery without compensation, whereas moderates would urge him to make haste slowly. If slavery became the central issue in the war, the latter group warned, the Democrats would push for peace at any price and take the border states with them. Both the War and Peace Democrats opposed emancipation. Northern Democrats accused Republicans of fanaticism and pointed to antiblack riots in Northern cities during the summer of 1862 as a result of this interference in racial relations. Numerous stories from Union troops registered their opposition to a war against slavery. Lincoln had long been disturbed by slavery though he felt bound by law to protect the institution. But he now had to confront the question within the context of all-out war. Ideal and reality had merged, forging an alliance between those who opposed slavery on moral or economic grounds and those who would resort to any expedient to win the war. At this point in the conflict, Lincoln discerned, the border states seemed secure and he could move toward an emancipation policy that would encourage a Union victory while satisfying humanity's demands to bring slavery to a close.[10]

While Lincoln contemplated the slavery issue, Mason continued his efforts for British recognition. Russell's response to Mason's written entreaties underlined the British government's dilemma: "Any proposal to recognize the Southern Confederacy would irritate the United States, and any proposal to the Confederate States to return to the Union would irritate the Confederates." British neutrality would continue until the war rendered its own verdict. Mason persisted. The Confederacy, he declared, had demonstrated "the capacity and the determination to maintain its independence." In a statement that must have puzzled Russell, Mason insisted (as he had done in their February meeting) that the South sought "no aid from, nor intervention by, foreign Powers." If a self-professed nation proved "both its capacity and its ability" to maintain its government, Mason argued, other nations were obligated to extend recognition. He sought an interview with Russell to discuss the matter. After consulting the cabinet, Russell saw no reason for a meeting.[11]

Mason did not stop his pleas for recognition. If England believed its own public pronouncements that Southern separation was final, he warned Russell, then the ministry's failure to extend recognition prolonged the war. The North must know that other nations had accepted the South into their community and that the Lincoln administration's attempt to restore the Union was destructive to all concerned. The world must realize that "for whatever purpose the war was begun, it was continued now only in a vindictive and unreasoning spirit." To withhold recognition would hurt Europe as well as all America.[12]

If Russell was considering mediation, he remained opposed to recognition. A crucial difference existed between the interventionist measures. Mediation, in his view, sought only to end the war, whereas recognition would bestow nationhood on the South. He insisted that constitutional questions regarding secession belonged to Americans alone and that the British had never made a judgment on whether the South had withdrawn from the Union. The outcome of the war remained uncertain. The ministry had tried to steer British policy between Mason, who claimed eighteen months of success, and Seward, who argued that in the same period the Union had restored much of the South to the Union. England must maintain neutrality. "In the face of the fluctuating events of the war, the alternations of victory and defeat . . . ; placed, too, between allegations so contradictory on the part of the contending Powers, Her Majesty's Government are still determined to wait." Recognition, Russell emphasized to Mason in a note, would come of "an independence achieved by victory, and maintained by a successful resistance to all attempts to overthrow it. That time, however, has not, in the judgment of Her Majesty's Government, yet arrived." [13]

Mason received Russell's reply two days later and bitterly assailed the British government for ignoring all evidence showing the impossibility of the North's subduing the South. Like Russell, Mason finally realized that the path to recognition ran through the battlefield.[14]

Despite the ministry's opposition to recognition, the South had reason to hope for mediation, for both England and France showed interest in that approach during the summer of 1862. A combined offer by the two nations (and perhaps in concert with Russia, Austria, and Prussia) would exert pressure that the Union could not ignore. Mediation, Mason knew, might lead to recognition. He wrote his wife that he expected intervention soon. And in Paris less than a week later, Slidell declared: "I am more hopeful than I have been at any moment since my arrival in Europe." Gladstone had moved closer to intervention. After expressing again the growing public opposition to the war, he declared to a friend that "this bloody and purposeless conflict should cease." The prime minister, Gladstone wrote his wife, "has come exactly to my mind about some early representation of a friendly kind to America, if we can get France *and* Russia to join." [15]

Even though Russell still attributed the ministry's inaction to the war's uncertainty, his reaffirmations of neutrality left open the possibility of mediation. Such an approach seemed the only way to encourage the two American antagonists to lay down their arms and negotiate their differences. Hammond supported mediation but preferred that the fighting continue until the South convinced the Union of the impossibility of subjugation. If Europe left the North alone, he declared, it would lose the war and accept England as peacemaker. Lyons also appeared interested in England's assuming responsibility for ending the war. The opening of New Orleans and other ports, he feared, would fail to relieve the need for cotton, thereby stirring up pressure from the manufacturing areas for intervention that would prove too much for the government to withstand.[16] Whether or not Russell leaned toward mediation, his perceived indecisiveness (by both North and South) left the impression that some form of intervention was possible.

IN TRUTH, a further delay in intervention seemed no longer feasible, particularly in light of the deterioration in Union-British relations over still another issue—that of Confederate shipbuilding efforts in England. Charles Francis Adams had urged Russell to put a stop to this illicit business, which had begun in the summer of 1861, but the foreign secretary replied that his country's laws restrained such action. According to the Foreign Enlistment Act of 1819, Russell explained, the ships must be equipped and manned for warlike purposes in England or its dominions. To win a favorable verdict in British admiralty proceedings, he must have proof that the vessels were being equipped specifically as warships for the Confederacy. But Russell's appeals to municipal law did not assuage Union anger over perceived violations of British neutrality. In June 1862 Confederate agents signed contracts with Laird Brothers of Liverpool for the construction of two rams, which were armored vessels fitted with a seven-foot-long "piercer" three feet below water for disabling wooden ships blockading Southern ports. That same month Adams lodged complaints that Laird was building a huge vessel called No. 290 (later named the *Alabama*) that had fittings cut for cannon. As a result of Adams's long and bitter protests, the crown's law officers on July 29 finally recommended detaining the *Alabama* for investigation and two days later sent orders to that effect. But word of the government's impending action had somehow gotten to Liverpool and the *Alabama* left the dock on the same day of the crown's decision.[17]

The Lincoln administration was irate with the British for risking the Union's welfare over what appeared to be technicalities in a law. Stuart attempted to placate Seward by insisting that England had done all it could legally do. The ministry could not act without proof. Union consul Thomas Dudley in Liverpool was upset over the escape. Now, he declared, "we are more in danger of intervention than we have been at any previous period. . . . They are all against us and would rejoice at our downfall." Not all Englishmen agreed with their government's behavior. The under secretary of state for foreign affairs, Sir Austen Henry Layard, saw the danger of war and thought Liverpool's businessmen should halt this commerce. It caused ill feelings among Americans and subjected England to charges of "bad faith" for violating the spirit of the queen's proclamation of neutrality. Eventually the Palmerston ministry clamped down on such shipbuilding activities but not before both physical and diplomatic damage had occurred. Years afterward, Russell regretted his decision not to act sooner. "In a single instance, that of the escape of the 'Alabama,' we fell into error." He had thought it his duty to wait for the law officers' report, but he now realized that he should first have detained the vessel.[18]

Seward feared that the Palmerston ministry had moved closer to intervention and sought to halt such an action that could ultimately lead to a break in diplomatic relations. In a portion of a dispatch sent to London that the secretary chose not to include in documents later given to Congress, he highlighted the hazards stemming from British involvement in any form. If Russell offered to "dictate, or to mediate or to advise or even to solicit or persuade," Seward instructed Adams, "you will answer that you are forbidden to debate, to hear or in any way receive, entertain, or transmit any communication of the kind." If England acted alone or in collaboration with other powers in recognizing the South, Adams was to "immediately suspend" his functions as a diplomat. If England followed recognition with "any act or declaration of War against the United States," Adams was to break diplomatic relations and return home. "You will perceive," Seward solemnly

William E. Gladstone, British chancellor of the exchequer
(H. C. G. Matthew, ed., The Gladstone Diaries, *9 vols.*
[Oxford: Clarendon Press, 1978], 6:frontis.)

noted, "that we have approached the contemplation of that crisis with the caution which great reluctance has inspired."[19]

Seward's fears were not misplaced, for Gladstone was among several British observers of the American scene who now expressed heightened interest in intervention and searched for terms of a settlement. Not only were economic and humanitarian considerations involved, Gladstone argued, but the war increased the chances for other nations' involvement that would, in turn, lead to a clash over their own competing interests. His diary reveals several attempts to gather information that might suggest provisions for peace. The day following the *Alabama*'s sudden departure, he engaged in what he intriguingly called a "most interesting conversation" with Henry Hotze, the Confederate propaganda agent who published the *Index* in London in an effort to win British favor for the South. That night Gladstone talked with a "Southern Gentleman" (not named in the diary) about the difficulties in resolving the border issue between "Northern and Southern Republics." He also read a popular 1861 publication favoring British intervention. Entitled *The American Union* and by 1862 already in its fourth edition, it was written by James Spence, a Liverpool merchant who served as a financial agent of the South and who denied that slavery had a role in bringing on the war. Secession was justified, Spence insisted, as was recognition of the Confederacy.[20]

Gladstone's primary concern was to end the war, even though he showed little or no understanding of or real interest in its origins. He left a cabinet meeting of August 2, 1862 with "a bad conscience" because his colleagues refused to support recognition until *both* North and South wanted it. Such a stand, he wrote the Duke of Argyll, had no precedent and was morally wrong. If England waited until the war's verdict was clear, both antagonists would have been irreparably damaged and the European nations would bear considerable responsibility. The North was the central obstacle. England should suggest a joint and friendly intervention that involved France and Russia. "Something, I trust, will be done before the hot weather is over to stop these frightful horrors." More than thirty years later Gladstone insisted that he had supported intervention as "an act of friendliness to all America."[21]

The call for intervention from the British press added to the Union's concerns. The *London Morning Post* joined Gladstone and others in demanding a swift end to the fighting in America. The war, it said, provided "a history of mistakes on the Federal side. Blinded by self-conceit, influenced by passion, reckless of the lessons of history, and deaf of warnings which every one else could hear and tremble at, the people of the North plunged into hostilities with their fellow-citizens without so much as a definite idea what they were fighting for, or on what condition they would cease fighting." In statements revealing its inability to understand what was at stake in the American conflict, the *Morning Post* declared that the Union "went to war without a cause" and "without a plan" and was "still prosecuting it without a principle." The fighting had settled into a "suicidal frenzy" that had a "ferocity unknown since the times when Indian scalped Indian on the same continent."[22]

The autumn of 1862 seemed to be the time of crisis for the Union. Palmerston saw the day of intervention fast approaching and won the queen's approval when he advised her that October seemed opportune. An appeal for an armistice, the prime minister now declared, seemed the proper approach. Not only did recent events dictate remedial action, but a halt in the fighting over the winter would provide the antagonists time for reflection. Russell agreed. Just before departing for a brief stay on the Continent, he wrote Palmerston: "Mercier's notion that we should make some move in October agrees very well with yours. I shall be back in England before October, and we could then have a Cabinet upon it." The threat that the North might incite a servile war, Russell hoped, would stiffen other nations' resolve to end the conflict. Further, the border states were unhappy with Lincoln's policy and might join the South or call for a settlement. Finally, Russell thought the North's confidence was seriously shaken after McClellan's failure to take Richmond. The terms of settlement would be a problem, Russell warned Palmerston. "I quite agree with you that a proposal for an armistice should be the first step; but we must be prepared to answer the question on what basis are we to negotiate?" If in October the Northerners remained determined to fight, "it will be of little use to ask them to leave off." Russell hinted that at that point, more resolute action (of an unspecified nature) might become necessary.[23]

For the first time in the American war, the three most powerful men in the British ministry—Palmerston, Russell, and Gladstone—leaned toward mediation. Another cabinet member, Earl Granville, opposed mediation but thought that momentous step was certain because of its support from his three colleagues. On a separate matter he wrote Stratford Canning some months earlier: "He [Gladstone], Johnny [Russell], and Pam [Palmerston] are a formidable phalanx when they are united in opposition to the whole Cabinet in foreign matters." Granville eventually became convinced that a majority of the cabinet favored mediation even though he considered it "decidedly premature" and "a great mistake."[24]

The ministry received a mixed reaction to its initial public explorations of a joint mediation with Europe. On August 5 Russell informed Parliament that the ministry was considering such a move and that it might include Russia because of its known sympathy for the Union. The pro-North Argyll did not think that England, even in collaboration with Europe, should interfere until the Union betrayed "some symptoms of doubt & irresolution." He shared Russell's apprehensions that if intervention was premature, the next step would involve "*armed* interference." Argyll doubted the Union's capacity to defeat the South, but he did not believe that the American struggle had reached the point that both sides would accept intervention. Bright was perplexed about the ministry's intentions. He wrote Cobden, "I don't quite understand Lord Russell's American Declarations [in Parliament] last night." Bright could not recall for certain, but he had received assurances from either Charles P. Villiers or Thomas Milner-Gibson from the cabinet that Russell was "quite Northern in feeling & wishes." If so, Bright remarked, Russell seemed "very unwilling to let anybody discover this from his official sayings." In any case, Bright noted, Russia would not participate in any action opposed by the Union. Indeed, it might behoove humanity if the war continued until slavery came to an end. Cobden repeated his argument presented earlier to Adams: a joint appeal by all Europe would be the "safest form of intervention."[25]

Despite Seward's bellicosity, the chances had increased for intervention. Even though Parliament was prorogued on August 7 and the queen's speech was noninterventionist in thrust, the British government had moved toward serious discussions regarding mediation. The danger was clear. Though Russell and others distinguished between mediation and recognition, they failed to heed Union warnings that any form of intervention constituted an interference in American domestic affairs and that once a mediation process began it had the potential of moving beyond an attempt to halt the war and into recognition of Southern independence. In either case, mediation implied the existence of two entities, and even this much the Union refused to concede. Intervention by any other name was still intervention.

Adams remained apprehensive—and for good reason. Even though Russia's participation in any interventionist effort was unlikely because of its ties with the Union stemming largely from the United States's making its good offices available in the Crimean War, the government in St. Petersburg had not closed the door. Tsar Alexander II had freed the serfs in March 1861 and looked with favor on emancipation in America, and he opposed any form of rebellion against the established order. More important, he realized that Russia's economy was agricultural and not hurt by the Civil War, and he regarded the Union as both a friend and an important balance against British and French interests. The Russian minister in Washington, Baron Edouard de Stoeckl, was a veteran observer of American politics, for he had lived in the nation's capital for twenty years and had married an American woman. Demagogues, he believed, had brought on this horrendous war, and the Union most assuredly would reject any hint of recognition. Stuart had learned from Stoeckl that, in Stuart's words, "a simple offer of good offices from one or more Powers, without allusion to ulterior action, would be simply declined" by the Lincoln administration. Yet the Russian minister thought the North was nearly exhausted. For that reason, he did not think that war would automatically result from recognition or even from an offer made with the alternative of forcing open the cotton ports. The risk would be great because the Union would refuse to bend to such a threat, but a mediation proposal from two or more European powers did not guarantee a war. At the same time, Stoeckl confessed to being unable to gauge a people as unpredictable as the Americans. Stuart was not yet aware of the ministry's growing focus on mediation and allowed his anti-Union propensities to cloud his judgment. Recognition of the South, he argued, might enhance its "respectability" in the North. "Peace might thus be accelerated."[26]

The Union government realized that its military failures in Virginia encouraged intervention and made every effort to show that it would not quit the war. The *Times* of London declared that the Union's reversals at Richmond had revealed its assumed military prowess to be only a facade. In the Foreign Office Hammond praised the South for doing everything right—especially its building of rams and ironclads. Stuart believed that the North's false hopes necessitated a series of major defeats before it would consider mediation. From his cabinet post Lewis expressed fear that the Union's determination to crush the South would lead Washington to exploit any mediation offer as a means of securing more recruits against an external as well as internal threat. Seward angrily claimed that outside nations had only one weak argument for intervention—that a civil war was "inconvenient" to them. But intervention in any form, they did not realize, "might be fatal to the United States." Adams knew that he was to suspend diplomatic functions should England extend recognition or decide to mediate. Moran noted that the situation was so dangerous that he had "placed the despatch [containing these instructions] under lock and key for security's sake."[27]

As intervention seemed certain, the Lincoln administration continued its move toward emancipation as a wartime and diplomatic measure but with the realization that its implications extended beyond the war. In late August Lincoln responded publicly to Horace Greeley's editorial on behalf of emancipation addressed to the president and printed in the *New York Tribune* under the title "The Prayer of Twenty Millions." In his letter in the same paper on August 25, Lincoln clarified his position on slavery. "My paramount object in this struggle," he declared, "*is* to save the Union, and is *not* either to save or to destroy slavery." He continued: "If I could save the Union without freeing *any* slave I would do it, and if I could save it by freeing *all* the slaves I would do it; and if I could save it by freeing some and leaving others alone I would also do that." Stuart reported that if one could believe Senator Charles Sumner, who supported abolition and chaired the Foreign Relations Committee, most of the president's cabinet favored a proclamation of emancipation that, the British chargé declared, served as both a political weapon at home and a scheme designed to deter outside interference. Argyll soon received a letter from Sumner, declaring that both Lincoln and his cabinet were ready to engage in a struggle for emancipation. Congress had made progress against slavery, but only the war itself, Sumner insisted, would end the institution. If Lincoln also intended to use emancipation to fend off foreign intervention, his effort had a convincing effect on Argyll, who recognized that Union supporters would not accept mediation. For Unionists it was a "Life or Death" struggle, with no conceivable terms of compromise.[28]

ARGYLL, however, did not speak for the majority, either in or out of office. A great number of European commentators seemed certain that Lincoln's emancipation proposal demonstrated the Union's desperation and that the war would determine any decision regarding intervention. To the displeasure of Confederate leaders, French opinion seemed to be taking the same course. From Paris, Slidell reported to Richmond that Thouvenel had advised him against requesting recognition. The South needed a victory on the battlefield, Slidell declared. France would not act without England, and England would not move until North and South had disabled each other. From Washington Stuart assured Russell that only "another Bull Run" would enhance the prospects for peace. Hammond was torn between his anti-Union feelings and his concern about England's relations with America after the war. He joined his countrymen in considering the Union cause desperate, but unlike them he argued that a continuation of the struggle would benefit England. The more damage sustained by North and South, "the less likely will they be to court a quarrel with us or to prove formidable antagonists if they do so."[29]

The Palmerston ministry continued to receive signs that pointed to intervention, albeit at some yet undetermined time. In late August Cobden expressed concern about Lancashire's growing need for cotton and joined Argyll in writing Sumner regarding the matter. Bright did not favor a British diplomatic initiative and advocated continued neutrality. British workers seemed calm, which suggested that the American war could go on for another year without unsettling British society. He complained that the government and press "had done all they can, short of direct interference by force of arms, to sustain the hopes of the Southern conspirators" who sought to force England "to spill her blood & treasure in [their] Godless cause!" Gladstone cautioned that even though the present situation was not favorable to mediation, Europe should not "stand silent without limit of time and witness these horrors and absurdities, which will soon have consumed more men, and done ten times more mischief than the Crimean War." In the Crimea, the fighting had been warranted because of the uncertain outcome. The war in America was not defensible because the outcome was "certain in the opinion of the whole world except one of the parties." Now, in the autumn of 1862, Gladstone felt mediation was justified because of the "frightful misery which this civil conflict has brought upon other countries, and because of the unanimity with which it is condemned by the civilised world."[30]

A major factor offsetting the popular pressure for intervention was the support the Union received from numerous British textile workers. Admittedly, the textile industry was in trouble, even though Britain's overall industrial productivity and shipping remained on the rise throughout the American Civil War. Indeed, hardships in the cotton industry had forced nearly 75 percent of the mill workers into unemployment or on short time. Henry Adams felt that the suffering in Lancashire and in France had grown to alarming levels. Gladstone feared riots, and Lyons believed that the distress in the manufacturing areas might exert enough pressure on the government to force an intervention. But Gladstone and Lyons misread the economic situation and underestimated the workers' antislavery sentiment. Even though a third of the mills had closed, they were small in size and employed less than a third of the country's cotton operatives. Further, the British would soon receive more cotton from blockade runners and from sources in India, Egypt, China, and Brazil. Hotze had tried to win over the workers, but his warnings of economic losses failed to pull them into the Confederate camp. As he explained to Benjamin, the supply of manufactured goods had neared depletion and prices now approximated the level of raw materials, thereby allowing many mills to reopen a few days a week. Another factor was the public and private charity provided the unemployed. Indeed,

Hotze thought, the Palmerston ministry would probably propose that Parliament establish a national loan for relief and that such a measure would hurt chances for recognition. The "Lancashire operatives," Hotze lamented, were the only "class which as a class continues actively inimical to us. . . . With them the unreasoning . . . aversion to our institutions is as firmly rooted as in any part of New England. . . . They look upon us, and . . . upon slavery as the author and source of their present miseries." [31]

No one can be certain about the direction mill workers' sentiment was taking because the question was complicated by the existence of several industries in England that profited from wartime commerce. But evidence suggests that many British workers viewed the North as the advocate of democracy and the South as the defender of slavery. Had not Lincoln called this "a People's contest"? The Union, he had told Congress on July 4, 1861, sought equal opportunity for all mankind. The avowed spokesman of the working class, Karl Marx, asserted from his place of exile in England that Lincoln, "the single-minded son of the working class," headed a "world-transforming . . . revolutionary movement" against the "slave oligarchy." Events in America were earthshaking, Marx declared. "As the American War of Independence initiated a new era of ascendancy for the middle class, so the American anti-slavery war will do for the working classes." [32]

If the economic situation in England did not yet demand some form of intervention in the American contest, the same did not hold true in France. Overall industrial production and shipping might not have dropped to crisis proportions during the American Civil War, but neither index of economic well-being suggested a healthy situation. Working-class discontent put great pressure on the Paris government, which had paralleled the British in moving toward mediation but was willing to take the next step toward recognition. At a reception in Paris in April 1862, Thouvenel told the Union minister in Brussels, Henry Sanford, "We are nearly out of cotton, and cotton we *must have*." Later that evening the French foreign secretary emphasized to his guest that "we are going to have cotton even if we are compelled to do something ourselves to obtain it." Stuart reported from Washington that Mercier wanted to postpone mediation until after the November congressional elections. If the returns demonstrated a desire for peace, the European powers should make a joint offer of mediation. Mercier did not consider mediation the first and only step in intervention. So certain was he of the election outcome that he wanted the European powers to prepare a "Manifesto" granting recognition of the South, which their representatives could implement at the time they thought appropriate. Stuart still preferred recognition, but he did not want representatives in the United States empowered to decide when that step should take place. Recognition should come from the home governments if either North or South refused mediation. Mercier did not support Stuart's suggestion that recognition alone be accorded. Such an approach would upset the North while "playing away one of our best cards without doing us any good."[33]

Like those in England, French movements toward intervention took a circuitous and uncertain course that led to mediation; but unlike the British, the French seemed susceptible to regarding mediation as the initial step in a process that could culminate in recognition. Mercier wrote the Paris government that the time had come for mediation and urged Thouvenel to reach an understanding with Russell. England and France must make the offer known to the entire Union, for Seward would interpret the move in accordance with his own ends. A public offer might arouse the Peace Democrats. It must be made in a friendly manner but with the assurance that, if rejected, the powers would recognize the South. Mercier first wanted the North to have the chance to accept Europe's mediation in an effort to stop the bloodshed. If Russia participated, the Union would probably accept, but if offered when the Lincoln administration was staggering both on the battlefield and at the polls, it would have to accept the proposal even if it came only from England and France. Stuart considered Mercier's arguments persuasive and believed that Lyons's return to Washington on the eve of the November elections would be an opportune time to make a mediation offer. Stuart believed that Russia would privately encourage Union acceptance of British mediation but would not publicly take part in any move calling for a separation. If England refused to act, Stuart warned Russell, it would be criticized for having "some ulterior object in continuing to look quietly on."[34]

In England, Argyll continued his attempt to halt the move

toward intervention by arguing that the war was over slavery and that the fighting itself should be the crucible for ending that system. Argyll, whose mother-in-law was the well-known opponent of slavery the Duchess of Sutherland, wrote Gladstone that the American conflict did not divide into "independence" on one side and "Empire" on the other. The contest arose from "one great cause, in respect to which both parties have been deeply guilty, but in respect to which, on the whole, the revolt of the South represents all that is bad, and wrong." Slavery was the central issue, and neither the North nor the South could disclaim responsibility for permitting a system of human bondage to continue well into the nineteenth century. Gladstone and others were wrong, Argyll insisted, in claiming that Southern separation offered the best guarantee for abolition. Even if the establishment of a slave nation assured the collapse of its own edifice, that same assurance would not justify intervention. The South personified all that was corrupt in the war. Argyll feared that the English people were not aware of the debilitating effect of slavery on the American character. Slavery was "rotting the very heart & conscience of the Whites— all over the Union—in direct proportion to their complicity with it." Consequently, the more intense the war became, the better. The war was not England's concern, nor was it in England's interest. No one wanted to restore the South's control over cotton and again make Lancashire dependent on that supply. When the war had resolved the issues that brought it on, "*then* I shd not object to *help* in the terms of peace."[35]

England's apprehensions regarding the American conflict had increased, but the timing and nature of an intervention remained unsure. Some observers urged the ministry to regard the approaching cutoff of cotton as a godsend and called on British businessmen to turn to other sources of supply in an effort to avoid future dependence on the South. By early September the Foreign Office was under great pressure from investors to stimulate the cultivation of cotton in Morocco, Turkey, China, Egypt, and India. Stuart meanwhile thought that a Confederate drive northward would take the fighting to the doorsteps of Northerners and encourage them to ask for peace. Bright noted that private sources in New York claimed an imminent Union triumph. Gladstone tended to agree with Stuart's prognosis and thought that an alternative to a friendly offer to end the war might be a proposal for recognition. "It is our absolute duty to recognise, when it has become sufficiently plain to mankind in general that Southern independence is established, i.e. that the South cannot be conquered." European intervention would be "an act of charity." Gladstone did not think the powers needed to warn the North against "resorting in [its] extremity to a proclamation of Emancipation for that I cannot think Lincoln would do."[36]

Henry Adams insisted that the Union would resort to any expedient to prevent foreign involvement in the war. Peace was not possible in the United States, he declared in early September, "so long as the southern people exist." To his brother he wrote: "I don't much care whether they are destroyed by emancipation, or in other words a vigorous system of guerilla war carried on by negroes on our side, or by the slower and more doubtful measures of choaking [sic] them with their own cotton." The Union "must exterminate them in the end, be it long or be it short, for it is a battle between us and slavery."[37]

European mediation—and perhaps recognition—seemed imminent in mid-September, when news arrived in London of another resounding Union defeat—again at Bull Run. The elder Adams became nearly despondent as the war took an alarming twist with the Union once more on the defensive. With undisguised relief, Russell told Palmerston that the Confederacy's victory in Virginia meant the end of the war was near. In Washington, the administration's distress gave way to anger when it learned that McClellan, who had been encamped near Bull Run, had refused to assist fellow Union soldiers. Stanton joined Chase, Secretary of the Interior Caleb Smith, and Attorney General Edward Bates in handing President Lincoln a letter calling for McClellan's removal from command. According to Bates, the capital appeared certain to fall and Lincoln "seemed wrung by the bitterest anguish," even muttering that he felt "almost ready to hang himself." Lincoln resisted the cabinet's pressure to change the army's command. If McClellan could not himself fight, the president explained, "he excels in making others ready to fight." Lincoln had good reason for his deep melancholy. Not only had McClellan repeatedly failed to deliver the long-promised conquest of the South, but his defeats encouraged European interest in intervention. Most ominous for the Union, Russell now seemed interested in extending recognition to the South. Just before applauding the Southern victory, he asked Thouvenel about a joint intervention aimed at an armistice that, if rejected, might be followed by British, French, Austrian, Prussian, and Italian recognition of the South as "Independent Confederate States." Perhaps the step would "dispose the North to Peace."[38]

The British and French must have experienced a feeling of déjà vu upon receiving word of the second major engagement at Bull Run. At long last the Union stood on the brink of a convincing defeat that would force it to give up the ill-conceived attempt to subjugate the South. And how bittersweet that fate had cast its judgment for Northern humiliation again at Bull Run. Had not Stuart proved prophetic in declaring that only "another Bull Run" would bring an end to the war? Surely, British observers noted with impatience, the Union would not tempt fate again. In France, Thouvenel observed that no reasonable leader on the Continent thought the Union could win.[39]

But again European hopes turned into exasperation. In a reaction similar to that after First Bull Run, the Lincoln administration lost neither its resolve to win the war nor its resistance to intervention. Union spirits soared even as disaster threatened to follow a trail northward.

If Seward considered recognition probable, he refused to reveal that concern to Mercier. When the French minister approached Seward about mediation in the aftermath of Second Bull Run, the latter allowed that recent battle news had raised interest in European intervention: "I have noticed it," he sternly replied, "but as for us it would be a great misfortune if the powers should wish to intervene in our affairs. There is no possible compromise, tell Mr. Thouvenel, and at any price, we will not admit the division of the Union." To Mercier's assurances of goodwill, Seward declared that "we do not doubt your sentiments but the best testimony that you are able to give us of it is that you will stay out of our affairs." When Mercier recommended the establishment of two "confederated Confederacies," Seward abruptly cut him off and repeated the impossibility of separation. "Do not believe for a moment," he exclaimed, "that either the Federal Congress, myself or any person connected with this government will in any case entertain any proposition or suggestion or arrangement or accommodation or adjustment from within or without upon the basis of a surrender of the Federal Union." Peace would not come until the South laid down its arms.[40]

BY THE END of the summer of 1862 the Union and British governments had taken mutually antagonistic positions on the war. The Lincoln administration hoped that emancipation would promote victory and deter intervention. The British regarded the Union's stand against slavery as a desperate effort to stir up a black rebellion that would spread destruction throughout the South and necessitate the very intervention the Union sought to prevent. From England's perspective, its appeals to humanitarian and economic considerations remained unheeded because the Union had adopted a new wartime aim that intensified the fighting. Emancipation, many in the Union now firmly believed, would undermine the South and assure ultimate victory.

Let us do something,

as we are Christian men.

—London Morning Herald,

September 16, 1862

Antietam and the Move toward Mediation

To many British observers, both inside and outside the government, the second Union defeat at Bull Run had underlined the North's inability to subjugate the South and, by mid-September, justified a move toward ending the war on the basis of a separation. The *Times* and the *Morning Post* (both usually expressing Palmerston's views) leaned heavily toward recognition, whereas the *London Morning Herald* made a broader appeal: "Let us do something, as we are Christian men." Whether "arbitration, intervention, diplomatic action, recognition of the South, remonstrance with the North, friendly interference or forcible pressure of some sort . . . , let us do something to stop this carnage." Palmerston thought the time for intervention was nigh. "The Federals . . . got a very complete smashing," he wrote Russell on Sep-

PUNCH, OR THE LONDON CHARIVARI.—September 13, 1862.

"Don't you think we ought to fetch the Police?"

"NOT UP TO TIME;"

Or, Interference would be very Welcome.

"Not up to Time" (London Punch, Sept. 13, 1862)

tember 14, "and it seems not altogether unlikely that still greater disasters await them, and that even Washington or Baltimore may fall into the hands of the Confederates. If this should happen, would it not be time for us to consider whether . . . England and France might not address the contending parties and recommend an arrangement upon the basis of separation?" If the mediation offer were refused, Palmerston declared, the two European nations should "acknowledge the independence of the South as an established fact." Three days later, Russell proclaimed his support. If the mediation proposal were rejected, he insisted, "we ought ourselves to recognise the Southern States as an independent State." A cabinet meeting to discuss the matter in late October would be advisable.[1]

The South's second victory at Bull Run had started a move toward British intervention, a mediation that was premised on a division of the United States and one that, if rejected, would be followed by recognition. From the Union's perspective, however, the distinction between mediation and recognition might well not have existed, for either action would constitute interference in American domestic affairs and encourage the South to maintain its resistance. In all probability, mediation would serve as a practical prelude to recognition, assuring British acknowledgment of Southern independence as an accomplished fact. But before the ministry could begin the diplomatic procedure that would lead to mediation, word arrived that General Robert E. Lee's Confederate forces had launched a daring raid into Maryland.

T H E   M O V E toward British intervention had approached a climactic point by the late summer of 1862. Indeed, if Lee had not followed his army's success at Bull Run with an immediate march north, the South might have won a mediation followed by recognition. But before the full impact of Second Bull Run had settled on London, Lee took the war into Maryland, inspiring hope among Southern strategists of bringing about the intervention that was, perhaps, already in their grasp.

Both Palmerston and Russell had turned to mediation after Second Bull Run, although the prime minister still was concerned about Union refusal to cooperate. Now, with news of the Southern advance northward, Palmerston hoped that Lee might win again, thereby increasing the chances for Union acquiescence in mediation. Another series of Confederate victories, particularly in Union territory, would further persuade the North to realize the war's futility and to accept peace. Palmerston seemed relieved when he wrote Russell on September 22: "Though the time for making a communication to the United States is evidently coming, yet perhaps it is partly actually come." The two armies were nearing each other north of Washington, and "another great conflict is about to take place." Its outcome should place us "in a better State than we now are in, to determine as to our course." The "northern Fury has not as yet sufficiently spent itself," and the Union might adopt "a more reasonable state of mind" if it were soundly beaten north of Washington. Russell concurred. He also agreed with the queen's recommendation to consult Austria, Prussia, and Russia, although he thought France should be first. The government in Paris provided support for intervention. Russell enclosed a recent letter from Stuart containing Mercier's warning that if the British did not act now, Europe would have to await the Union's "complete exhaustion."[2]

Palmerston foresaw difficulties in mediation. Even if both North and South accepted the offer, a question would develop whether "the fact of our meddling would not of itself be tantamount to an acknowledgement of the Confederate as an independent State." More explosive were the ramifications of a mediation that the South accepted and the North did not. For at least that reason alone, Palmerston believed, England and France would have to invite Russia to participate. If Russia were involved, the North would be more likely to go along. Even if the Russians declined, as was probable, England would have established credibility with them by extending the invitation. Admittedly, it was better not to have the Russians involved because of their avowed favor for the North. But in the interests of peace, he hoped that they would set aside the bitterness still lingering over the recent conflict with England and France in the Crimea and realize that the North's welfare (and that of everyone else) lay in calling off the war. As for the other European powers, Palmerston agreed with the queen that England should communicate with them, but he feared that any additional participants would be too many.[3]

Only the certainty of a major battle held off an immediate offer of mediation. In view of Lee's advances, Palmerston deemed it advisable to postpone action until the South had time to inflict a mortal wound inside the Union that would assure its consent to mediation. "It is evident," he wrote Russell, "that a great conflict is taking place to the north-west of Washington, and its issue must have a great effect on the state of affairs. If the Federals sustain a great defeat they may be at once ready for mediation, and the Iron should be struck while it is hot. If, on the other hand, they should have the best of it, we may wait awhile and see what may follow."[4]

On the eve of what was shaping up to be a major military encounter in Maryland, the British government had advanced toward a mediation that rested on the assumption of another Union defeat and that, for the first time, was accompanied by proposed terms of settlement. On September 24 Palmerston notified Gladstone of Russell's support for a mediation proposal that the ministry, with cabinet approval, should invite France and Russia to join. The terms should be an armistice followed by the Union's lifting the blockade and entering negotiations based on Southern separation. Gladstone learned two days later from Russell that he advocated an "offer of mediation to both parties in the first place, and in the case of refusal by the North, to recognition of the South." A safeguard seemed necessary. Russell would support mediation "on the basis of separation and recognition accompanied by a [renewed] declaration of neutrality." A cabinet meeting as early as October 16 would be suitable if he could communicate his and Palmerston's views to France and Russia in the interim. To his ambassador in Paris that same day, Russell wrote that England and France should invite Russia to participate. If the Union rejected a mediation offer, England should extend recognition to the South while reaffirming neutrality. "Palmerston agrees entirely in this course," he added.[5]

Despite Russell's precautions, the ministry's mediation proposal would heighten the danger of war with the Union. His deliberations rested on two questionable assumptions: that Lee would win in the North and that the Union would capitulate. And even if the first did take place, there was no guarantee that the second would also. Mediation might begin as a mere search for peace, but the monumental nature of any form of intervention had the potential of carrying the involvement beyond England's reassurances of continued neutrality. Doubtless Russell counted heavily—too heavily—on the North's inability to rebound from Second Bull Run and certain other losses that would stem from Lee's assaults. Clearly Russell did not appreciate the significance of the Union's ongoing military successes in the West. The foreign secretary also relied on Stuart's ill-informed assurances from Washington that the South would never relent and that the Peace Democrats in the North would win in the November congressional elections. But Russell felt confident that the weight of world opinion—even without Russian participation—would rest on the side of the peacemakers. Would not England and others who joined in the mediation erase suspicions of self-interest by reaffirming neutrality while extending recognition? And even if the Lincoln administration considered waging a war against the outsiders, the imminence of winter would force Washington's policy makers to give the matter more thought than if mediation came during the warm months. A reasonable man, Russell assumed the rationality of the leaders in the White House. They would accept a separation.

Gladstone was pleased that the time had come for the European powers to end the American war. If the Confederates made additional military gains, they would themselves pose problems in the negotiations. He agreed that England should first make "a friendly effort" to convince the North to quit the war before Lee's advancing forces aroused strong Southern sentiment and complicated the task of securing peace. If Europe failed to act, the South would conquer too much territory and want to hold on to its new possessions. Gladstone had another reason for immediate intervention. His native Lancashire had been suffering "with a fortitude and patience exceeding all example, and almost all belief." If the workers' forbearance should break and violence erupt, the government would seem to be interested only in cotton and lose its claim to being an "influence for good." Americans would complain that England was interfering out of self-interest rather than for the general good of humanity. The United States would regard British (and French) intervention as an effort to expand their American holdings. Russian involvement would give the move "moral authority."[6]

While the Palmerston ministry prepared for mediation, Confederate and Union forces confronted each other on September 17 at Antietam, a creek lying outside the small village of Sharpsburg in Maryland that would become the scene of the bloodiest single day's fighting in the war. The South's first major effort to take the war into the North came to a sudden and brutal end in the course of a few hours as tens of thousands of soldiers engaged in mortal combat. By early evening, more than twenty-four thousand Union and Confederate soldiers had been wounded or killed. Lee's army had sustained such heavy casualties that it limped back into Virginia on the evening of the following day, leaving McClellan's battered legions in possession of the battlefield.[7]

News of Antietam reached London in late September, at first disappointing the ministry by demonstrating again the North's stubborn determination to win and yet, paradoxically, lending more support to mediation to stop the bloodbath. Given the heightened British interest in some course of action, it seems more than coincidental that the Earl of Shaftesbury, who was the son-in-law of Lady Palmerston and widely known to be under the prime minister's influence, should pass through Paris about September 23 (before news of Antietam had reached Europe) to offer assurances, according to Slidell, that British recognition was no more than a few weeks away. The South's drive for independence and self-government, Shaftesbury explained, had won the support of Englishmen who opposed the North's imperial interests. Indeed, on September 30 (after the news of Antietam reached Europe) Shaftesbury assured Slidell that the British attitude had not changed: "There is every reason to believe that the event so strongly desired of which we talked when I had the pleasure of seeing you in Paris is very close at hand." If Charles Francis Adams was correct—that Shaftesbury was a "good key" to understanding British policy—the battle of Antietam had *not* put the quietus on intervention. British observers were shocked by the South's poor showing, for they had hoped for another military success that would have compelled the North to accept mediation. Instead, the Union claimed victory and hardened its resolution. Although Antietam proved indecisive from a tactical point of view, it restored Union morale that had been severely shaken at Second Bull Run. More than that, news of the battle in Maryland had caused the Palmerston ministry to pause and reevaluate the timing of an intervention that some said was needed now more badly than before.[8]

The first accounts of Antietam drew a mixed appraisal. From Richmond came a positive view of the South's performance. Benjamin boasted that McClellan's inability to destroy Lee put the South in a good position to safeguard the entire area from the Atlantic to the Mississippi. Lewis remarked that the North had found out what it meant to be governed by a "village attorney appointed Prime Minister for 4 years certain, during a period of civil war." Hammond asserted (perhaps more correctly than he knew) that the Confederate crossing of the Potomac was "more in the nature of a feeler" than an actual offensive. Others interpreted the outcome as a Union success. Moran rejoiced that McClellan's victory was "a bitter draught and a stunning blow" to the British. "They express as much chagrin as if they themselves had been defeated." Gladstone found satisfaction with the South's reversal. "I am not sorry for the apparent ill success of the Confederates as invaders," he wrote Argyll. "They might have become intoxicated, & entangled, by good Fortune." After the fighting in Maryland, the war's outcome remained unresolved, even though in retrospect it seems that the balance had tipped toward the Union.[9]

Antietam confirmed the contemporary view that the American antagonists had become locked in a death grip that could be broken only by outside assistance. In Washington Stuart interpreted the results at Antietam as a lethal stalemate. After the battle, he wrote Russell, McClellan had wanted to rest his army and, like the Southern commander, did not want the Potomac River behind him during this season of rain and swollen waters. The general had failed to achieve a victory because he refused to pursue the enemy. Antietam was therefore "as near a drawn Battle as could be, only that the Federals have since held the ground." Stuart persisted in his optimism. A revolution appeared to be brewing in the North that would push the peace advocates to the front. Palmerston likewise thought the war had deadlocked, which was, he told Russell with some relief, "just the case for the stepping in of friends." Each side had satisfied honor and might listen to reason. "One thing must be admitted and that is that both sides have fought like bull dogs." North and South were "pretty equally balanced," and neither antagonist was able to subjugate the other.[10]

England also came under pressure from France to move toward mediation. Within a week of the battle, Stuart prepared a dispatch containing Mercier's proposal that he and Lyons jointly declare their desire for an armistice that would enable North and South to discuss peace terms. The two ministers would be ready with their good offices if wanted, but England and France should consider themselves free to act according to their own interests. For strategic reasons, Mercier recommended avoiding the word *separation*. He felt confident that an armistice would be accepted because, after the grisly outcome at Antietam, neither North nor South would want to resume hostilities. Stuart thought Mercier's approach could be pursued with "perfect safety." It would have a favorable impact on the United States because, Stuart believed, most Northerners now wanted peace.[11]

Not everyone in the British cabinet favored intervention; Argyll and Granville admitted to a humanitarian need for mediation, but they also feared a war of retaliation by the North. Argyll assured Gladstone that he had never objected to a mediation offer as long as it had a "reasonable chance" of acceptance. The Union, however, first had to realize the impossibility of subjugating the South. Argyll believed that the Confederacy had not yet proved itself a nation and did not deserve recognition, but if the present military course continued, it would establish its claim to nationhood. Granville preferred continued inaction because the British did not understand American politics well enough to mediate the dispute. A former foreign minister and now a cabinet member sitting in the Lords, Granville was a Liberal who advocated free trade and opposed foreign entanglements. Mediation carried numerous problems because the mediators bore the nearly impossible task of suggesting terms for settlement. British public opinion, Granville warned Russell, opposed both Northern and Southern views on slavery; boundary questions were important to the West as well as to the North and South; negotiations must include the French, who sorely needed cotton. Recognition, he assured the foreign secretary, would not end the blockade and ensure the importation of cotton. Instead, recognition would stir up Northern patriotism and guarantee the Union more men and money for the war. And if the war continued long afterward, England would drift into it and Napoleon would be free to carry out his designs in Europe. England must avoid the war while helping distressed cotton workers. A change in policy would be "premature." England's neutrality, Granville reminded Russell, had the approval of Parliament, the press, and the people.[12]

British mill workers, wanting to see the end of the war and a revived cotton industry, did not welcome the initial news erroneously calling Antietam a Southern victory. The Earl of Clarendon, a former foreign secretary under Palmerston, sympathized with the workers but did not like either North or South and thought that a continuation of the war would exhaust both antagonists and prevent them from turning against England. Clarendon's interest in the workers' plight received encouragement from his brother Charles P. Villiers, who sat in Palmerston's cabinet and presided over the Poor Law Board. But another consideration had become preponderant. Clarendon complained to another relative of his in the cabinet, Secretary for War Lewis, that the mill owners had profited from the war. If the war had not occurred, they would have been forced to close their mills because of massive overproduction. The war had enabled them to sell their stocks at high prices. And that was not all. "They have sold their raw cotton at 50% profit. They have shut up every mill that could not be worked at a profit & they have contributed little or nothing to their starving work people. In the worship of the almighty dollar they have acted exactly in accordance with their hard & grinding instincts." [13]

Clarendon's analysis of both mill owners and mill workers seems arguable. Evidence now shows that the South's bountiful harvest years of 1858 to 1861 had led to an overabundance of raw cotton in England and that numerous textile firms found it unprofitable in 1862 to engage in cotton manufacturing because of the glut of finished goods on the European market caused by British and French overproduction in 1860 and 1861. Contemporary observations support that conclusion. An influential mill owner in Clitheroe perceived the approaching end of the war but was not pleased. At the outset of the fighting, James Garnett had profited from the reduced influx of cotton because he had been able to sell his surplus manufactured goods at higher prices. He had then become concerned that Lee's push into Maryland might force the North into an armistice. Indeed, impending battle news had brought business in Manchester to a standstill. A Southern victory, Garnett knew, would drive prices down, whereas Northern success would push them up by extending the war. When the long-feared and so-called cotton famine actually came during the winter of 1862–63, mill owners took advantage of the economic slowdown to rebuild their plants and install new capital-saving machinery. The mill workers were already hurting from the war— and increasingly so. John O'Neil, a leader in the trade union movement, let his diary lapse for two years after early June 1862 because he was "too sad and weary" to write. Not until April 1864 did he return to his desk: "It has been a very poor time for me all the time owing to the American war, which seems as far of being settled as ever." [14]

Thus was the Union victory at Antietam replete with ironies. At least in part to win foreign involvement in the war, Lee had sought a victory in the North that failed on the battlefield but, by reverse logic, heightened British interest in mediation. In the aftermath of the Union's narrow victory, Adams in London joined Seward in happily—and mistakenly—noting the declining British interest in intervention.[15] Lincoln also misread the situation. He thought that Antietam had dealt a crippling blow to foreign intervention and prepared to play his trump card—a proclamation of emancipation that would, he felt certain, constitute the death knell to outside involvement. But unknown to both the American embassy in London and the highest governing circles in Washington, Lee's defeat at Antietam and rumors of Lincoln's decision for emancipation had already combined with the growing horror of the war to intensify British interest in mediation.

SINCE FIRST RAISING the issue of emancipation before his cabinet in July, Lincoln, for both domestic and foreign reasons, had been undergoing greater pressure to turn the war into an antislavery crusade. On September 13 a group called Chicago Christians of All Denominations presented him with a memorial insisting that emancipation would win the favor of all civilized countries that saw the higher purpose in the war. "No other step," Lincoln replied, "would be so potent to prevent foreign intervention." Emancipation would also give Northerners a "glorious principle" for which to fight. Further, the proclamation would attract the slaves from the plantations, leaving Southerners without workers and providing the Union with both a work force and additional soldiers. The delegation urged Union leaders to instill in the blacks a reason to fight for freedom. Lincoln concurred: "What the rebels most fear is what we should be most prompt to do; and what they most fear is evident from the hot haste with which, on the first day of the present session of the Rebel Congress, bills were introduced threatening terrible vengeance if we used the blacks in the war." [16]

In late September the *Chicago Tribune* led other papers in printing Lincoln's reply to the delegation, which pinpointed slavery as the basis of the war. He revealed that he had been considering the matter for months. "I do not want to issue a document that the whole world will see must necessarily be inoperative, like the Pope's bull against the comet! Would *my word* free the slaves, when I cannot even enforce the Constitution in the rebel States? . . . And what reason is there to think it would have any greater effect upon the slaves than the late law of Congress, which I approved, and which offers protection and freedom to the slaves of rebel masters who come within our lines?" If the slaves did come over, "*what should we do with them?*" How would the United States feed and care for so many? "Nor do I urge objections of a moral nature, in view of possible consequences of insurrection and massacre of the South. I view the matter as a practical war measure, to be decided upon according to the advantages or disadvantages it may offer to the suppression of the rebellion." Lincoln insisted that slavery was "the root of the rebellion, or at least its *sine qua non*." Emancipation would convince Europe that "we are incited by something more than ambition." [17]

Shortly after the battle of Antietam the president released his preliminary proclamation of emancipation. On September 22, timed as Seward had counseled—in the immediate aftermath of a Union military victory—Lincoln prepared to issue his announcement by calling a cabinet meeting at noon. "Gentlemen," he declared to his advisers, "I have, as you are aware, thought a great deal about the relation of this war to Slavery." The time had come for action. He wished that the Union army were in a better position. But it had secured the North by pushing the enemy out of Maryland. When the rebels were at Frederick and threatening Washington, Baltimore, and Harrisburg, he had decided that upon their retreat from Maryland, he would issue a proclamation of emancipation. "I said nothing to anyone; but I made the promise to myself, and (hesitating a little)—to my Maker. The rebel army is now driven out, and I am going to fulfill that promise." He wanted them only to hear what he had written. "I do not wish your advice about the main matter—for that I have determined for myself." He read the preliminary emancipation proclamation and made pertinent comments. As of January 1, 1863, Lincoln made clear in the document, all slaves in states still in rebellion were "forever free." [18]

If Lincoln had moral objectives in mind, he had formulated an ingenious plan that could be all things to all people. Domestically, the proclamation promised great social, political, and economic changes—if only by implication. Although abolitionists were unhappy that the president had not declared all slaves free, they joined black leaders in recognizing that the proclamation would begin the momentum in that direction. Lincoln had acted constitutionally. Emancipation was an act of "military necessity," he insisted, permissible under his powers as commander in chief to take whatever steps were necessary to win the war. The action was legal; it did not affect the slaves in areas loyal to the Union and did not violate the due process guarantee in the Constitution. Politically, the move averted confrontations with the border states, the Southern Unionists, and conservative Northerners who had no interest in blacks. Finally, the proclamation had diplomatic implications that would undermine the South's professed claim of fighting oppression by converting the war into a humanitarian crusade.[19]

British suspicions of the Union's ulterior motives in emancipation were exaggerated but not entirely off the mark: Lincoln intended that this wartime measure would undermine slavery and thus tear down the South from within. But no evidence suggests that he envisioned a Nat Turner style of revolt. He talked only of black service in the Union army, mass flight from the plantations, and, to those slaves who remained, encouragement not to work. Emancipation, however, was certain to raise the slaves' cry for freedom while intensifying Southern resistance to the Union and thereby necessitating a war of subjugation. The South, as it had made clear at the start of the war, denounced emancipation as an effort to stir up the slaves in rebellion. Just as certainly, residents of the border states were apprehensive about the loss of their slaves.

McClellan was embittered about the new dimension of the war, especially because the measure had come from the president whom the general loved to hate. Lincoln had not been pleased with McClellan's leadership during the early stages of the Peninsular Campaign, and later, McClellan grumbled, the president expressed displeasure with what he mistakenly called a partial victory at Antietam. How could a civilian understand what McClellan, a professional soldier and officer, knew both by instinct and training—that his men had been too few in number and too lacking in organization to pursue Lee's retreating army into Virginia? McClellan was convinced that Lincoln was now interfering with the war effort by trying to create racial problems for the South. Wars took place between soldiers and not civilians. McClellan wrote his wife that he could not "fight for such an accursed doctrine as that of a servile insurrection."[20]

The general was partly correct. Lincoln did not want a racial upheaval, but he admitted to an official in the Department of Interior that "the character of the war will be changed. It will be one of subjugation. . . . The [old] South is to be destroyed and replaced by new propositions and ideas."[21]

The Union population at first only moderately favored the proclamation, despite the Lincoln administration's efforts to alleviate concern that the measure would foment unrest among the slaves. Lincoln made two additions to the proclamation at Seward's request—that freedmen be urged "to abstain from all violence, unless in necessary self-defense," and that, "in all cases, when allowed, they labor faithfully for reasonable wages." Further, in the hundred days between the preliminary and final proclamations, Lincoln agreed to delete passages misinterpreted by many as a call for insurrection—those declaring that the executive would not restrict blacks in their attempt to secure freedom and those referring to colonization and compensated emancipation. After a serenade of the president on the evening of the public pronouncement some friends gathered at Chase's home to celebrate. The secretary of the treasury satirically praised the South for helping to bring on the proclamation: "This was a most wonderful history of an insanity of a class that the world had ever seen. If the slaveholders had staid [sic] in the Union they might have kept the life in their institution for many years to come. That what no party and no public feeling in the North could ever have hoped to touch they had madly placed in the very path of destruction." From New Orleans a Union official wrote Chase, albeit with exaggeration, that the proclamation had resulted in "the organizing and arming of the colored population throughout the South."[22]

Stuart reacted to the proclamation with disgust, followed by a fevered warning of slave revolts. The British chargé derisively wrote Russell that the decree applied only to areas still in rebellion, where the Union had no "*de facto*" jurisdiction." One of Lincoln's chief motives, Stuart complained, was to "render intervention impossible." The move demonstrated no "pretext of humanity" and was "cold, vindictive, and entirely political." It offered "direct encouragement to servile Insurrections."[23]

News of the president's proclamation reached England in early October, causing British spokesmen on both sides of the American issue to fear additional atrocities. Emancipation, Russell learned from Stuart, had infuriated the Confederate Congress and caused "threats of raising the Black Flag and other measures of retaliation." A Northern governor had called for the importation of the French guillotine, and if Lincoln and the Republicans stayed in power, Stuart warned, "we may see reenacted some of the worst excesses of the French Revolution." Hammond likewise regarded the proclamation with disdain. Even Cobden had reservations about using emancipation as a military weapon. Rather than curtail the South's resistance, he declared, the measure would bring on a fiercer war. In attempting to prevent separation and the establishment of a slave nation, the North would "half ruin itself in the process of wholly ruining the South." To seek victory with black cooperation would lead to "one of the most bloody & horrible episodes in history." The English view drew support from across the Channel. That same month the French informed the Palmerston ministry that the threat of a slave uprising was another reason for their willingness to work with England in ending the American war.[24]

The British press reacted to the proclamation with uniform hostility. The *Times* of London sarcastically remarked that Lincoln considered himself "a sort of moral American Pope." He intended to incite a "servile war" in those states that the Union had failed to occupy by encouraging the blacks to "murder the families of their masters" while they were away at war. "Where he has no power Mr. LINCOLN will set the negroes free; where he retains power he will consider them as slaves." The announcement was "more like a Chinaman beating his two swords together to frighten his enemy than like an earnest man pressing on his cause." The *Spectator* of London sympathized with the Union but was befuddled by its declaration regarding slavery: "The principle is not that a human being cannot justly own another, but that he cannot own him unless he is loyal to the United States." The *Bee-Hive* of London, which remained pro-South until a change in editors in January 1863, criticized the proclamation for attempting to free slaves in the South, where Lincoln had no authority, and leaving those in bondage where he did. In an editorial, the *Times* asked whether "the reign of the last PRESIDENT [was] to go out amid horrible massacres of white women and children, to be followed by the extermination of the black race in the South? Is LINCOLN yet a name not known to us as it will be known to posterity, and is it ultimately to be classed among that catalogue of monsters, the wholesale assassins and butchers of their kind?" *Blackwood's Edinburgh Magazine* called the proclamation "monstrous, reckless, devilish." To win the war "the North would league itself with Beelzebub, and seek to make a hell of half a continent." [25]

Palmerston, of course, was the central figure in a mediation decision, and if he had moved closer to taking such an action before Antietam, in early October he moved just as cautiously farther away. He remained confident that the South would accept mediation "upon the Basis of Separation," but, he assured Russell, the North would reject the offer because Antietam had deluded the Lincoln administration into believing that its war aims were attainable. The South had still not achieved a major battlefield success that would compel the North to accept mediation without demanding a war of revenge against England. The mediation offer "has been lately checked" by the battle at Antietam, and England might have to wait another ten days for "future prospects." If the Union insisted upon war with the mediating nation (or nations), it might be advisable to delay the offer until spring weather opened British communications to Canada and permitted the Royal Navy to operate along the Atlantic coast. Perhaps the only way to avert an Anglo-American conflict resulting from mediation would be to arrange a multilateral recognition of the South. "If the acknowledgement were made at one and the same time by England, France and some other Powers, the Yankee would probably not seek a quarrel with us alone, and would not like one against a European Confederation." [26]

To circumvent the dangers of mediation, Palmerston devised a seemingly less provocative plan that would highlight Antietam's atrocities as a reason for peace while delaying any formal interventionist move until the South achieved a decisive victory on the battlefield. Before making an actual proposal of mediation, he wrote Russell, the British government should offer the North a "friendly suggestion" to accept a separation "which must apparently be the inevitable result of the contest, however long it may last." Admittedly, armistice terms would be difficult to arrange. A cease-fire accompanied by the end of the blockade would help the South; one without the end of the blockade would favor the North. But no matter how rancorous the armistice discussions might become, the North and South themselves must resolve the details.

Any quarrels that developed during the negotiation, Palmerston declared, "would do us no harm if they did not lead to a renewal of war." At present, inaction continued to be the best policy because neither side seemed ready for a cease-fire. "The whole matter is full of difficulty, and can only be cleared up by some more decided events between the contending armies."[27]

Russell, however, had become dissatisfied with Palmerston's reluctance to act and wanted to forge ahead. "This American question," he admitted to the prime minister, "must be well sifted." Lewis was also "against moving," but Russell argued that the moment for action had come: "I think unless some miracle takes place this will be the very time for offering mediation, or as you suggest, proposing to North and South to come to terms." A British proposal must make two points: that England recommended separation and that it "shall take no part in the war unless attacked." Russell did not share Palmerston's concern that British acknowledgment of Southern separation necessarily meant war with the Union. "My only doubt," he declared, "[was] whether we and France should stir if Russia holds back. Her separation from our move would ensure the rejection of our proposals." Yet he appeared willing to go ahead with France and without the Russians. Further, he suddenly became amenable to avoiding any mention of separation. He referred to Stuart's letter of September 23 expressing his and Mercier's call for an armistice proposal containing no reference to a separation. "If no fresh battles occur," Russell declared, "I think the suggestion might be adopted, tho' I am far from thinking with Mercier that the North would accept it. But it would be a fair and defensible course, leaving it open to us to hasten or defer recognition if the proposal is declined."[28]

Thus did the battle of Antietam join with the preliminary proclamation of emancipation to encourage British intervention. In addition to humanitarian concerns, Russell feared that the endless fighting, compounded by a certain slave insurrection, might spread beyond the United States to involve other nations. Further, the war's continuance would soon cause an economic crisis in England stemming from an eventually depleted cotton supply. Of more immediate importance was his concern that the war would become racial as well as sectional. For months resentment had

ABE LINCOLN'S LAST CARD; OR, ROUGE-ET-NOIR.

"Abe Lincoln's Last Card; or, Rouge-et-Noir"
(London Punch, *Oct. 18, 1862)*

been growing in England over a suspected White House maneuver to steer the war into an antislavery channel for reasons having little or nothing to do with moral purpose. Since the president had waited so long to make a stand against slavery, Russell and many British observers believed that his decision grew out of a desperate attempt to avert defeat by stirring up a slave rebellion. Lincoln and the Republican party, it appeared to many Englishmen, had mouthed empty statements about containing the spread of slavery and achieving its "ultimate extinction." Now they were prepared to capitalize on human bondage in seeking to destroy the South.

Seward had been correct: the British would regard emancipation as the dying gasp of the Union unless the proclamation followed a decisive Union victory in the field. But because the Union victory at Antietam was so thin, the British bitterly denounced the proclamation as an exploitative move against slavery that would escalate the war. Lincoln had played "his last card," according to the *Times.* "He will appeal to the black blood of the African; he will whisper of the pleasures of spoil and of the gratification of yet fiercer instincts; and when blood begins to flow and shrieks come piercing through the darkness, Mr. LINCOLN will wait till the rising flames tell that all is consummated, and then he will rub his hands and think that revenge is sweet."[29]

DESPITE THE long-standing belief that the Union victory at Antietam, followed by the preliminary proclamation of emancipation, had halted a move toward British intervention, the truth is that the coming of the battle only put on hold a mediation procedure that was well matured and then, when the results of the battle became known, encouraged Russell to depart from Palmerston's cautionary strictures to begin the move again. Union forces had turned back Lee's first major thrust into the North and earned the right to claim a strategic victory. The administration in Washington had tried to take advantage of that outcome to announce emancipation in an effort to preempt British intervention. But the battle and proclamation did not shake the interest of Russell, Gladstone, and numerous others outside the ministry in mediation. Antietam and the proclamation combined to raise the specter of a war of subjugation made more horrible by a certain slave uprising.[30]

To Russell the proclamation intensified his felt need to act. He had made clear to Mason that recognition was an unlikely first step in intervention, and now Russell led the way toward a mediation based on an armistice that he knew would, as a matter of course, culminate in recognition. The difference between his position and that of Palmerston had become crucial: the former wanted to move now, the latter at some future and more propitious moment—if it ever came. Russell had emerged as the chief advocate for stopping the war in the name of peace.

Prelude to
Intervention

By the autumn of 1862 the division within the Palmerston ministry over the intervention issue had intensified. Russell
had become the leading proponent of intervention, whereas Palmerston showed increasing reluctance to act. Gladstone's advocacy
of intervention was well known. The sticking point was timing.
Russell and Gladstone wanted an immediate move based on a
mixture of humanitarian and economic considerations; Palmerston remained the pragmatic realist, preferring to wait until the
South proved itself on the battlefield and thereby convinced the
North to accept mediation without seeking revenge against the in-
truding powers. Even though Russell and Gladstone won support
from Westbury (the lord chancellor), they faced substantial opposition within the cabinet. Lewis and Argyll were the most outspoken and influential, counting among their following the Duke
of Newcastle from the Colonial Office, Earl Granville sitting in

the Lords, Charles P. Villiers as president of the Poor Law Board, Sir George Grey from the Home Office, and Thomas Milner-Gibson from the Board of Trade. Lewis expressed skepticism that any form of intervention could bring the war to a close, whereas Argyll thought the South had established its claim to independence but feared that the North would refuse mediation and turn on the outsider. England, Lewis insisted, had no practical solution to the war and should maintain neutrality. Yet the central figure in the controversy remained Palmerston, and he had moved farther from intervention.[1]

ON OCTOBER 7, 1862, Gladstone delivered a stirring speech before a large audience in Newcastle that left the mistaken impression that the ministry was ready to recognize the Confederacy and further solidified the cabinet's division over the American question. Amid loud cheering, he declared: "We may have our own opinions about slavery, we may be for or against the South; but there is no doubt that Jefferson Davis and other leaders of the South have made an army; they are making, it appears, a navy; and they have made what is more than either—they have made a nation." In a dramatic conclusion, he proclaimed: "We may anticipate with certainty the success of the Southern States so far as regards their separation from the North." The South entertained no doubt about Gladstone's meaning. Its former commissioner and now minister in Belgium, Ambrose D. Mann, exulted over impending recognition and noted that the news had caused a sensation in Europe. Over two months later, excitement remained high as Francis Lawley, a special correspondent of the *Times* who was in Richmond and who was heavily pro-South and had strong connections with its leaders, wrote Gladstone that the Confederacy welcomed the opportunity of "establishing hereafter mutually beneficial relations between the two countries." Forster, who had become Adams's confidant, urged him to inform Russell of Seward's instructions to sever relations if the British extended recognition. Adams feared the worst but preferred to wait until he could determine whether the ministry supported Gladstone. The chancellor, Adams told Seward, favored the South, and the speech appeared to signal the policy that the government would pursue once Parliament assembled. "We are now passing through the very crisis of our fate," Adams recorded in his diary.[2]

Gladstone was a Liberal, but his speech failed to attract the support of fellow Liberals Cobden and Bright, both of whom favored the North and opposed intervention. Cobden complained that Gladstone should not have made a public statement on American affairs: "I could not help wishing that Cabinet Ministers would apply to their tongues the principle of non-intervention which they profess to adopt in their diplomacy." Bright was embittered. Gladstone had expressed no concern over the black man in America and now held the dubious distinction of being "the first public man who has complimented Jeff Davis." Indeed, Gladstone had come from a slaveowning family in the West Indies and, though professing to hate the principle of slavery, favored only gradual emancipation and had not joined the abolition movement in 1833. The chancellor, Bright remarked, claims that he "pities the North—bears with it in its trials—& unduly believes in & hopes for the success of its deadly enemies!" The "taint" of slavery seemed "ineradicable."[3]

Gladstone's speech likewise unsettled Argyll, who also believed that the North was unable to subjugate the South but nonetheless insisted upon the maintenance of neutrality. He agreed with Cobden that interference of any sort would be dangerous. The North might cut off exports of corn and flour and add to England's economic problems. Workers realized this and had defeated every resolution for intervention brought before meetings in the depressed mill areas. Argyll complained to Russell that Gladstone's phrase "made a nation" had embarrassed the ministry. "Whatever you may do—He, at least, has 'recognised' the South!" Argyll wanted to wait. The South, he felt confident, would establish independence and in the coming winter the North might admit as much. Recognition would be "wholly premature." It would be "followed up by other measures; and in this case, wd probably involve us in a war."[4]

Gladstone's pronouncements had encouraged the common belief that the Palmerston ministry tended to meddle in other countries' internal affairs, and it now threatened to set off a massive protest based on an alliance between Conservatives and Liberals.

The leader of the Conservative opposition, Lord Derby, favored private charity to relieve Lancashire's distressed workers rather than British intervention in the American war and feared that the Newcastle speech heralded immediate recognition of the South. Gladstone "must be considered as speaking in the name of his colleagues & it will be awkward if they don't agree with him, & even if they do I think it is a strong measure to say what he did." Clarendon agreed with his political opponent and regretted that Gladstone had taken such a hazardous course, especially if Palmerston and Russell had not asked him to do so. The American war, Clarendon told Palmerston, "had not yet marked out the stipulations of a Treaty of Peace."[5]

In vain did Gladstone deny that he was pro-South and insist that he was and always had been neutral. Both in public declarations and in private letters, he maintained that his only purpose at Newcastle had been to drive home the point that the Confederacy had proved its mettle and, in the name of peace, deserved independence. Gladstone regretted that the speech, according to the newspapers, had assumed a broader meaning than intended. He assured Russell that he had not meant to leave the impression that recognition of the Confederacy was forthcoming. Yet the chancellor admitted that this feeling had become so intense among his countrymen that one result had been the creation in Liverpool of a society on behalf of the Confederacy.[6]

Palmerston attempted to distance himself from the incident. He at first admitted that the chancellor was "not far wrong in pronouncing by anticipation the National independence of the South." Within a week, however, Palmerston had become alarmed by the mounting furor and told Russell that Gladstone should have "steer[ed] clear of the Future unless authorized by his colleagues to become . . . the organ of the Govt. for announcing Decisions come to upon suitable Deliberation." Two months later, Palmerston declared that "Gladstone ought not to have launched into Confederate acknowledgement." In fairness to Gladstone, he had been making these arguments since the early days of the American war. During a speech in Manchester the previous April and in a personal letter just three weeks before his appearance at Newcastle, he had expressed the same ideas. To his correspondent, Gladstone had argued that "it has long been (I think) clear that

Secession is virtually an established fact & that Jeff. Davis & his comrades have made a nation." But by the autumn of 1862 the situation had worsened. In addition to the growing horror of the war, England's cotton supply was dangerously low and the country's economic picture was threatening. Not only were the British people more aware of the issues in the American conflict, but they understood how those issues affected them. They also knew that the public declarations of a cabinet member—particularly one of Gladstone's stature—automatically took on the nature of an official communiqué. His speech had seemingly increased pressure on the cabinet to intervene in the American war.[7]

Hammond enjoyed Gladstone's discomfort, for even though the permanent under secretary favored the South, he opposed recognition and apparently thought that the chancellor's indiscretion might disable the government's major advocate of recognition—Russell himself. To Layard in the Foreign Office, Hammond remarked: "You will be amused by Gladstone's attempts to write himself out of the scrape which his tongue brought him into." What could be expected from recognition, "heaven only knows: good cannot come of it." Still under the illusion that the South had performed well at Antietam, Hammond insisted that Lee's withdrawal into Virginia had provided the North with a pretext for claiming victory. The proclamation of emancipation had been "a great mistake." It would not only alienate the border states and divide the North, but it would encourage the South to retaliate and thereby cause a race war.[8]

Like Gladstone, Russell supported an intervention aimed at ending the war for humanitarian and economic reasons, but he had wanted to bring it about with as little popular excitement as possible. Russell had been among the first to admit that recognition would follow mediation. Gladstone's impropriety, Russell feared, had ensured a public debate that would intrude in cabinet affairs. In declaring that Davis had made a nation, Russell complained to Gladstone, he had gone "beyond the latitude which all speakers must be allowed." His statements made it appear that the British were ready to extend recognition. "Negotiations would seem to follow, and for that step I think the Cabinet is not prepared."[9]

Agreeing with Gladstone's premise though not with his tactics, Russell had to convince Adams that there was no cause for alarm. "If Gladstone be any exponent at all of the views of the cabinet," the American minister confided in his diary, "then is my term likely to be very short." Americans in the London legation regarded Gladstone's statements as proof of the Palmerston ministry's support of the South. Moran noted the widespread feeling that the speech was the preliminary step to recognition. To quiet the uproar, Russell truthfully told Adams that Palmerston and other members of the government "regretted the speech" and that Gladstone "was not disinclined to correct, so far as he could, the misinterpretation which had been made of it." Russell also assured Adams that Britain's policy had not changed and then, not so truthfully, claimed that no change was under consideration. Did that mean that the British intended to maintain neutrality? Yes, Russell responded.[10]

RUSSELL HAD meanwhile moved away from more direct forms of intervention—mediation and recognition—to the seemingly less dangerous measure suggested earlier by Palmerston: an armistice followed by a negotiation. Russell's growing interest in this approach (also advocated by Mercier) came under close scrutiny by Palmerston. The prime minister emphasized in early October that any communication to North and South must be by England *and* France and in identical terms. It should first urge the antagonists to reach some basis of agreement. If North and South were unable to do this beforehand, Palmerston warned, they would probably refuse the proposal—particularly if either side held a military advantage at the time of the offer. The success of an armistice rested on neither belligerent benefiting from it. The danger was that both sides might use the cease-fire to enlarge their armies. An "armistice without some agreement as to a Basis of negotiation, and that Basis can be none other than separation, would only be like breathing Time allowed to Boxers between Rounds of a Fight, to enable them to get fresh wind." The North would not approve a separation without "a good deal more pummelling by the South." Yet Palmerston thought the armistice idea worth a cabinet discussion. The next ten days would tell.[11]

Russell persisted in his drive for an armistice, but he moved closer to Palmerston's watch-and-wait position while seeking to ease the North's suspicions of England by urging France to take the lead and making a greater effort to persuade Russia to participate. He recognized, as did Palmerston, the difficulty in preventing the antagonists from exploiting a cease-fire to prepare for a renewed war. But Russell also knew that the first step toward a long truce was to secure a short one. He wrote his ambassador Lord Cowley in Paris that the initial contact with the Union government should be "the most confidential kind, & yet certain & official enough to enable me to lay something tangible before the Cabt." The French government, Russell thought, should make the "first overture" in "so easy and plausible a course." Russell recommended that Mercier's dispatches be sent to London along with Napoleon's views. Russell was as anxious as the French ambassador to London, Count Charles de Flahault, to act in concert regarding the American question. Russell preferred that Russia join England and France in making the proposal. Most important, the British must "remain neutral, even were we to recognise the South & acknowledge that Jeff. Davis has made a 'Nation.' "[12]

In preparation for the cabinet meeting, Russell wrote a memorandum to his colleagues urging support for an armistice. Emancipation, he argued, had authorized Union armies to commit "acts of plunder, of incendiarism, and of revenge" that would destroy the South. The war must stop, but the British decision to bring this about through an intervention depended upon support from across the English Channel. Europe's Great Powers had to decide whether intervention was justified on the basis of present conditions in America—the balance of military forces, indecisive battles, heightened political hatreds, and a society enraged by Lincoln's effort to excite "the passions of the slave to aid the destructive progress of armies." Europe's duty was "to ask both parties, in the most friendly and conciliatory terms, to agree to a suspension of arms for the purpose of weighing calmly the advantages of peace against the contingent gain of further bloodshed and the protraction of so calamitous a war." [13]

Argyll reacted favorably to Russell's memo but noted pitfalls in the plan. He accepted Russell's argument that the European powers (including England) should jointly recommend an arms suspension aimed at negotiations leading to peace. He agreed that they must present the proposal in a "friendly & conciliatory spirit." But Argyll warned that England must not commit to "any farther

George Cornewall Lewis, British secretary for war
(Gilbert F. Lewis, ed., Letters of the Right Hon.
Sir George Cornewall Lewis
[London: Longmans, Green, 1870], frontis.)

step, tending to direct interference." A simple armistice proposal would not be provocative—or so Argyll thought. Anything beyond would lead to difficulties. And yet, he admitted, suggestion of an armistice alone did not guarantee success. On the slavery question, Argyll declared that the Lincoln administration had never supported abolition: "I have always looked to the irresistable [sic] tendency of events, rather than to the *intentions* of the North, for the AntiSlavery effects of the War."[14]

Russell's most formidable opponent was Lewis. The secretary for war had long been convinced that any form of British intervention would be a mistake. A gentle and unpretentious man, he was a philosopher and scholar of unquestionable integrity who commanded widespread respect because of his wisdom and devotion to justice and country. The American war had disturbed him from the beginning. He had never believed that military force could keep the Union intact. To a friend in January 1861 he had declared: "You may conquer an insurgent province, but you cannot conquer a seceding State." Secession, he confided to another friend, would lead to "arbitration of the sword." The North would seek "to gratify passion or pride" in punishing its enemy, whereas the South would strive for independence. England must stay out of the war.[15]

Lewis responded to Russell's memorandum with a speech in Hereford followed three days later by a memo to the cabinet, both arguing against intervention. In Hereford he insisted that the South had not yet established independence. Support for this view came from Clarendon (Lewis's brother-in-law) and Derby. Recognition, Derby insisted, would not benefit England if it challenged the blockade and thereby committed "an act of hostility towards the North." Mediation would not work because a North-South reconciliation was impossible. Knowing that Clarendon had notified Palmerston of Derby's views, Lewis warned that Russell's armistice proposal would not go to a "conclave of philosophers" but to the great mass of "heated and violent partizans" on both sides who bitterly opposed compromise. The effect of an armistice would be the same as that of a mediation: both measures implied the existence of, at least, two belligerents and, at most, two nations. The North would reject either proposal. And even if the antagonists accepted a temporary arms suspension, they would not feel the results equally. One or the other would lose its military advantage. The only way both North and South might accept an armistice was if they expected the war to end. But in a declaration demonstrating his understanding of the conflict, he insisted that neither side had retreated from its wartime objective: the South for independence, the North for restoration of the Union. No compromise was possible.[16]

Even if intervention was wise, Lewis wrote, the time had not arrived. He agreed with Russell that Lincoln intended for emancipation to cause a slave uprising in the South. But for the same reason that Russell justified intervention, Lewis stood in opposition. The war had reached such a "moment of peculiar bitterness and exasperation" that the North would "resent" an armistice proposal as a virtual concession of Southern independence. Any proposal at this point, Lewis warned, could cause trouble with the Union that would put England in the difficult position of having to reinforce Canada during the winter. The ministry should wait for the November congressional elections to see if sufficient sentiment existed in the North for a peace with the South based on independence.[17]

Lewis asked what peace terms England could recommend as mediator. If any plan sanctioned slavery, the ministry would become its guarantor but would alienate the North. If England called for abolition, the South would resist. Where would the boundary lie between North and South? How would England deal with the border states and with the territories? "The sword has not yet traced the conditions of a treaty recognizing the independence of the South." In "looking to the probable consequences of this philanthropic proposition, we may doubt whether the chances of evil do not preponderate over the chances of good, and whether it is not—

> 'Better to endure the ills we have,
> Than fly to others which we know not of.' "[18]

In light of the lack of ministerial support for an armistice along with additional difficulties caused by events in France, Russell decided to delay his call for intervention. He informed Stuart that the cabinet would meet within a week and that Lyons would return to Washington on October 25. "But I do not expect to have any decisive instructions to give him." That same day Russell expressed displeasure with Napoleon's silence on the question along with a recent ministerial crisis in France that had led to the dismissals of Thouvenel and Flahault: "The moral of the late events at Paris is that it is dangerous to trust a man [Napoleon] whose counsels are so very secret, whose professions are so little to be trusted, & whose actions are so little to be foreseen." Russell regretted the loss of Thouvenel—"a true European statesman"—but the new foreign minister, Edouard Drouyn de Lhuys, was an "old friend" who would surely want to maintain Anglo-French cooperation. Russell conceded with regret that now was not the time to act. He assured Palmerston that recognition would be premature and, because Russia's stand remained uncertain, agreed that "we ought not to move *at present* without Russia." [19]

Lewis's memo, combined with the negative response to Gladstone's speech in Newcastle, confirmed Palmerston's desire to postpone intervention until the war itself had convinced the antagonists to lay down their arms. The prime minister noted that in any attempt to formulate peace terms, slavery was England's "great difficulty." Could the ministry, he asked Russell, "without offence to many People here[,] recommend to the North to sanction Slavery and to undertake to give back Runaways, and yet would not the South insist upon some such Conditions[,] especially after Lincoln's Emancipation Decree[?]" Further, winter was approaching and political and military considerations were so indecisive in the United States that a delay was unavoidable. Palmerston emphasized the necessity of having a basis for negotiation and repeated that neither side would accept an armistice if the other side had something to gain. All England could do was suggest to North and South that they make "an arrangement between themselves." The outcome was predictable. The North's only condition would be reunion, whereas the South's would be independence. "I am therefore inclined to change the opinion on which I wrote to you when the Confederates seemed to be carrying all before them, and I am very much come back to our original view of the matter." The British must remain "lookers on till the war shall have taken a more decided turn." [20]

After receiving Palmerston's message, Russell postponed the cabinet meeting scheduled for October 23. But Russell's notification did not reach all members in time, and some of them appeared that day and insisted upon an informal discussion in which they could express opposition to his armistice idea. Palmerston had stayed at his Broadlands retreat in the south, but Lewis led those present—including Newcastle and Grey—in attacking Russell's interventionist stand. With the prime minister absent, however, the cabinet members could take no official action, and Russell's hopes for intervention remained alive. Lewis thought that he and his cohorts had killed the plan. He felt "greatly relieved" by Russell's "voluntary abandonment of the scheme of interfering in the American quarrel, which could only have led to mischief." Later that afternoon Russell assured Adams that the ministry's neutrality policy remained intact.[21]

RUSSELL HAD NOT been dissuaded from his interventionist course. He remained determined to pursue an armistice as the measure least conducive to trouble with the Union and most likely to succeed. How could anyone question the motives of a nation (or nations) that merely asked two belligerents to lay down their arms and explore the possibilities of negotiating a peace? An armistice, he believed, was less provocative than a mediation, for it carried no connotations of imminent recognition. The foreign secretary hoped that saner heads would prevail after a respite in the fighting. Any peace was preferable to a resumption of war.

When Russell returned to his office after the cabinet encounter to prepare a response to Lewis's memo, a note arrived from a British special agent in America that lent support to the foreign secretary's fear of an intensified war. H. Percy Anderson reported a strong war sentiment in those states dependent upon the Atlantic trade and a weaker feeling in those reliant on the Mississippi River. Many of the latter wanted peace as the first step toward resuming trade with the South. No unanimity existed regarding emancipation, although some westerners considered the president's policy to be confiscatory and purposefully destructive to the South. Those Americans who sought subjugation of the South welcomed emancipation; the measure encountered opposition in areas where peace was once thought possible but now were torn apart by abolition. No one showed concern for freed blacks. The only point of unanimous agreement was opposition to their migration into the free states. Freedom was acceptable in America, Anderson derisively remarked—as long as blacks were kept at a distance. He concluded that the war was far from over. The dominant group in the North wanted to destroy the South, which meant that to prevent ruin the South would resist to the end. Nothing made sense. Americans were still irritated with England, although most of them wanted only one war at a time.[22]

Lewis's memo, Russell wrote after he had finished studying the missive from America, had misrepresented his views. Russell denied having made an actual interventionist proposal and insisted that he would never take such action without a cabinet meeting. Further, he had not called for unilateral intervention. In one instance, he had said, "It has now become a question for the *Great Powers of Europe.*" And in another instance, he had declared: "It has become a question, in the sight of these afflictions, and the prospect of more and worse, whether it is not a duty *for Europe.*" But whereas Russell had earlier advocated French and Russian participation, he now contemplated "a step" by the combined powers of England, France, Russia, Austria, and Prussia. "In this shape, I think, the recommendation would be accepted." Without Russia's cooperation, however, the measure would fail. An armistice proposal was the only correct approach. And he still insisted that no time was more opportune than the present to begin the process. The period of negotiations needed among the European powers to put the plan in motion would allow the armies of both North and South to settle into winter quarters. The proposal would come when the men were not engaged in battle and "it can hardly be said that either side will be a loser by an armistice." When the British cabinet debated the question, he would clarify his views.[23]

Palmerston approved Russell's decision to delay the meeting. He did not consider "Lewis's Doctrine"—which the prime minister defined as opposition to recognition until the North admitted to Southern independence—either "sound in Theory, [or] consistent with historical events; But the Pugilists must fight a few more Rounds before the Bystanders can decide that the State Should be divided between them." The proclamation of emancipation and the coming elections had caused so much bitterness on both sides that any attempt to talk about peace "would be as useless as asking the winds during the last week to let the waters remain calm."[24]

Despite Lewis's belief that the threat of intervention had subsided, the question remained as unsettled as before the rump meeting of the cabinet. In a note praising Lewis's memo for opposing intervention and causing cancellation of the meeting, Clarendon wryly commented that "Johnny [Russell] always loves to do something when to do nothing is prudent, and I have no doubt that he hoped to get support in his meddling proclivities when he called a Cabinet for yesterday." But Lewis had exposed the "idiotic position" that England would have taken, "either in having presented our face gratuitously to the Yankee slap we should receive, or in being asked what practical solution we had to propose after an armistice had been agreed to at our suggestion." England would have had no terms to suggest, which forced Russell "to draw in his horns."[25]

But Clarendon was wrong: the same day he congratulated Lewis, Russell reiterated his position to Palmerston. "As no good could come of a Cabinet," the foreign secretary explained, "I put it off." But he declared that even though he was willing to accept Palmerston's restraint "for the present," he intended to set Lewis straight. The secretary for war, Russell complained, had "made a proposition for me which I never thought of making." The foreign secretary denied ever having made a proposal calling on just England and France to join Russia in asking the Americans to suspend their war. "Less than the whole five [England, France, Russia, Austria, and Prussia] would not do." He was "not at all inclined to adopt G. Lewis' invention." Russell had not given up his plan. All five powers must combine in urging an armistice.[26]

In the meantime, Gladstone expressed disappointment with the decision to postpone the cabinet meeting and circulated a memo of his own entitled "The War in America." On the same day that Russell confirmed his unchanged stance to Palmerston, Gladstone argued that England's choice was either inaction or an "interference limited to moral means" that emphasized good offices, mediation, an armistice, or recognition. To do nothing was to shirk the duties of a civilized state. The main question, Gladstone insisted, was whether interference would "do good or harm." Such an action would be unnecessary if England could detect an approaching end to the war as a result of exhaustion on either side or if the North was willing to negotiate on the basis of a separation. But the end of the war was not in sight, and the North would not forgo its aim of subjugating the South. Like Russell, Gladstone was convinced that only a concert of powers would suggest "the prevailing judgment of the civilized world" and thereby put sufficient pressure on North and South to call off the war. Most important, Russia furnished "the one vital element" in a peacemaking venture—friendship with the Union. "Again, if we desire the war to continue, either with a view to the possible success of the North, or to the extinction of slavery through a servile war or otherwise, or on any other ground, then of course all room for argument is gone. But I assume that we wish the war to end, and that we see no early probability of its ending if left to itself." The Lincoln administration could not ignore a step resting on "the common interests of humanity." [27]

Lewis and Russell exchanged one more volley before laying down their pens. Lewis apologized for having misunderstood Russell's argument to have been a formal proposal but agreed that no intervention could succeed without European collaboration. Yet the secretary for war expressed doubt that Russia, Austria, and Prussia would participate. Even if all five powers acted in concert, he warned, their interference in American affairs must involve "some element of dictation, either in form or substance." If they acted together "cordially in the event of hostilities becoming necessary, the intervention would doubtless be effectual." But at what cost? Many feared that the war would not end with the mere separation of North and South, "but that the disintegration will go still further." The only certainty was that "*some* separation is inevitable." Russell assured Lewis that France favored recognition even though Russia, admittedly, had not yet revealed its position. Like other Englishmen, Russell added, he too opposed the use of arms to settle the American war. But if the North rejected the European powers' offer to intercede, those same powers would be justified under international law in recognizing the Confederacy. Russell thought the "most suitable" time was in the spring, when the next military campaign began and while Parliament was in session. [28]

Russell saved one parting shot for Grey, who advocated the maintenance of neutrality. An armistice was dangerous, the home secretary had warned; it was "not a separate form of proceeding, as it could only be proposed with a view to mediation." Intervention would heighten the chances of a British quarrel with America. Russell responded the next day that England must act. Lewis "sprang a mine upon me," Russell complained, "but I cannot agree with any part of what he said. No country has ever waited to make peace till it was unable to carry on war." If England and France invited Russia to participate in an armistice proposal, Russell argued, "the Emperor of Russia would not like to say that he preferred war and desolation." If Russia were involved, both North and South would accept an armistice. Failure in negotiations was not certain. "If a friend were to cut his throat, you would hardly like to confess, 'he told me he was going to do it, but I said nothing as I thought he would not take my advice.' "[29]

ALTHOUGH Gladstone's speech had heated up the interventionist controversy, it had also compelled Russell and his supporters to confront the three greatest obstacles to such a move: how to step in without becoming involved in the war and how to present a workable solution to the problem while securing Russian participation. For the South, then, Gladstone's declarations had offered only the illusion of encouragement; the real importance of his words at Newcastle was that they caused a closer examination of the complexities involved in the American war and, in doing so, mobilized more Englishmen against intervention.

If Granville had been correct on the first day of October in his belief that most of the cabinet favored mediation, Gladstone's speech and Lewis's memo take on great importance in undercutting that support. When Palmerston, Russell, and Gladstone months earlier made the decision to intervene at some propitious time, they thought they had moved toward a mediation that would end the American war. But now they realized that mediation was deceptively simple. Besides France and perhaps the European governments, England had to secure Russian cooperation while devising peace terms that would resolve the war without providing a breather for both sides to regroup and resume the fighting on a higher level of ferocity. The humanitarian and economic objectives of Russell and Gladstone were understandable; but more so were the practical considerations posed by Palmerston and Lewis. On only one point did Russell win Palmerston's support.

"I believe you are right," the prime minister wrote Russell, "in fixing next Spring for the period for the acknowledgement of the Confederate States." But Palmerston still insisted that Southern "independence can be converted into an Established Fact by the Course of Events alone." [30]

10

Denouement: The November Decision in London

Although the October events seemed to have eased the pressure for British intervention, Napoleon III raised Russell's hopes a few days later by proposing a joint interventionist plan that doubtless grew out of the British foreign secretary's own overtures to Paris the previous September. The emperor had delayed a response to Russell's entreaties because of concurrent unification problems in Italy, but that situation had calmed and Napoleon now faced serious economic unrest at home and growing public sympathy for what was perceived as a Southern struggle against Northern oppression. Consequently, he revealed a plan of his own that carried grave risks but still attracted Russell's support.[1]

EVEN BEFORE the autumn crisis, Stuart and Mercier in Washington had intensified their support for intervention. In the middle of October Stuart raised the question with Stoeckl, who considered Mercier "too anxious to precipitate matters" but then surprisingly admitted that an involvement might soon become "useful." Such a step, however, should not take place until after the congressional elections of early November had yielded the expected Democratic victories. Stuart felt elated over Stoeckl's response—so much so that he told Russell that recognition of the South would hurry the end of the war. Mercier likewise expressed optimism. He had recently returned from New York, where members of both political parties had assured him of their desire for peace. Even the Republican moderates, Mercier noted, wanted to know whether the powers could persuade the South to approve gradual emancipation. Stuart concluded that Lincoln and his cabinet were "merely fighting to cover a retreat." Only the Democratic party and an enraged public could force the administration to give up the war. A gubernatorial victory for Horatio Seymour in New York, Stuart jubilantly declared, could provide the lever for a mediation offer that would lead to Southern independence. "If independence has ever been nobly fought for and deserved, it has been so in the case of the Confederacy." Mercier agreed but noted strong anti-English feeling in the United States and suspected that Stoeckl sought an exclusive Franco-Russian mediation in an effort to divide England and France. The best approach, Mercier insisted, would include all three powers.[2]

Meanwhile, the French government followed Mercier's advice and made its first overtures to England regarding a joint intervention. British ambassador Lord Cowley met on October 27 with Napoleon III, who expressed interest in the British, French, and Russian governments making a joint mediation offer to the Americans. Although Cowley responded that he had no directives on such a matter, the emperor recommended a jointly proposed six-month armistice, accompanied by a suspension of the blockade, that would "give time for the present excitement to calm down." He admitted to Cowley, however, that the plan had no chance without Russia's involvement.[3]

The next day Napoleon privately revealed his intentions to Slidell. "What do you think," the emperor asked, "of the joint

Napoleon III, emperor of France (A. R. Tyrner-Tyrnauer, Lincoln and the Emperors *[New York: Harcourt Brace, 1962], opposite 96)*

mediation of France, England, and Russia? Would it, if proposed, be accepted by the two parties?" Slidell had heard this proposal before and saw no reason for optimism. He did not trust England and knew the Russians favored the North. In such a mediation, Slidell warned, "France could be outvoted." Although hoping that France would act alone, he assured Southern support for Napoleon's "umpirage," though accepting his argument that European affairs precluded any move without British cooperation. Napoleon then shifted the thrust of his suggestion. He preferred a six-month armistice proposal, accompanied by the opening of Southern ports for the same period. "This would put a stop to the effusion of blood, and hostilities would probably never be resumed." The powers could make this proposal on humanitarian grounds. Slidell was receptive. Had he not made the same proposal to Thouvenel the previous February? But rather than stop with an armistice proposal (as Russell had in mind), Napoleon, or so Slidell thought, went farther. The emperor noted that Union rejection of the offer would provide "good reason for recognition" and, in a veiled but unmistakable reference to the use of force, "perhaps for more active intervention."[4]

Slidell needed assurances from Napoleon that such an ambitious project might work. The minister expressed doubt that Palmerston would participate in any venture that might lead to recognition. Napoleon did not consider this a problem, for he had not mentioned to Cowley the possibility of further steps in the event of the Union's rejection of an armistice. If Slidell was aware of this omission, his report of the meeting with Napoleon did not say so. Instead, Napoleon referred to a letter written by King Leopold of Belgium while the British queen was in Brussels, in which he exhorted the French to intervene in the American war and bring relief to distressed mill workers throughout Europe. Slidell understood the importance of the queen's presence at the time the letter was written. "It is universally believed," he observed to Benjamin, that "King Leopold's counsels have more influence with Queen Victoria than those of any other living man." As a final boost, Napoleon encouraged the South to build a navy in France. Slidell explained that efforts were under way in England but that its neutrality legislation had caused difficulties. "If the Emperor," Slidell declared, "would give only some kind of verbal assurance that his police would not observe too closely when we wished to put on board guns and men we would gladly avail ourselves of it." To this Napoleon replied: "Why could you not have them built as for the Italian Government? I do not think it would be difficult, but will consult the minister of marine about it."[5]

The Southern reaction to Napoleon's proposal was mixed because it hinged on British involvement. Slidell thought the offer sincere. He had also received private assurances from others close to the emperor that there would be no official interference with the South's efforts to build warships in France and had invited Confederate naval agent James Bulloch to join him in Paris to pursue the matter. Benjamin first heard of the proposal through Mason and in his elation responded that the news confirmed Confederate officials' optimism about winning the war. He was struck by Napoleon's willingness to pursue an "ulterior action which would probably follow the offer of mediation." Recognition was imminent, he assured Mason, and would be followed by a quick end to the fighting. Indeed, Benjamin proceeded into a lengthy discussion of problems that the Confederacy would face during the postwar period. Much of the economic hardship the South would suffer after the war, he complained, would be attributable to England's refusal to abide by international law regarding the blockade. The North had won economic advantages at Southern expense. The only way to prevent a Northern monopoly of the Southern economy was for the Confederacy to regain its preblockade economic position in regard to foreign trade. The French idea would allow Europe to transport goods to the Confederacy that it would have acquired if the Union had not violated neutral rights with the blockade. Mason remained skeptical about an imminent intervention because of the emperor's insistence on working with England. His views "lose their value to us, as his purpose not to act independently seems unaltered."[6]

The Confederate government was not aware of Russell's interest in intervention and had become upset with England's refusal to grant recognition. Before news of the French proposal reached Richmond, Benjamin wrote Mason that the British were "unfriendly to this government." They first violated the Declaration of Paris in submitting to a paper blockade that hurt the Confederacy. Then Russell exhibited a "rude incivility" in refusing to meet with the Confederate minister in London. Finally, he resorted to the unorthodox procedure of quoting from Seward's dispatch warning of slave revolts if the British intervened and prolonged the war. These allegations were "derogatory to the government and without foundation in fact." To Benjamin, Russell's tactics demonstrated his inability to provide a "well-founded reason" for withholding recognition. Benjamin felt confident that the Palmerston ministry would not remain in office long because the British people, he was convinced, favored recognition. He directed Mason to lodge a protest over the blockade and wait for Russell to make an overture regarding recognition.[7]

Southern denunciations of Russell were misguided, for he was so distraught over the lack of progress in ending the American war that, after an initial expression of skepticism, he decided to support the French project. Upon learning unofficially of the French proposal on November 1, Russell sarcastically wrote Lyons (then en route back to the United States) that the emperor wanted to offer peace to North and South and that both would accept, "the one on the ground of Union, & the other on the ground of separation!" The two antagonists were not close to peace. The "most horrible thing" he had heard was Seward's boast to Stuart that restoration of the Union would take place after the South's "extermination." Russell agreed with Cobden that "to preach peace" to Northerners was "like speaking to mad dogs." But the war's atrocities led Russell to change his initial reaction. Any peace proposal was better than turning his back on the American problem. To Cowley, Russell moaned that Seward intended to "wear out the South by mutual slaughter. Was there ever any war so horrible?"[8]

Even without references either to recognition or to an additional though unspecified form of intervention, Napoleon's proposal carried dangerous implications. In the talks with Slidell the emperor first spoke of a joint mediation, which, Russell knew, implied the existence of two belligerents and would have aroused Union opposition. Then Napoleon appeared to drop the mediation approach in favor of an armistice offer (Russell's position) along with the end of the blockade.[9] Russell knew that the proposal had little chance for success in the North and that the emperor's statements did not always coincide with his intentions. The foreign secretary could not have forgotten how, just a little more than a year before, Napoleon had worked with England and Spain in trying to collect debts in Mexico, only to expand his operations into a full-scale interventionist scheme that his two European allies had abandoned. Russell realized the hazards in joining another French project in the New World, and he knew that most cabinet members would object. But the American war threatened serious economic harm to neutrals and, on the basis of international law, justified European intervention. Further, a French commitment might lead Russia to participate.

Russell claimed to remain pro-Union, but his strongest desire was for peace. A continuation of the war between North and South was more dangerous to European stability than the chance (albeit a good one) of hostilities between England and the Union. Russell was prepared to argue that an armistice proposal, unlike a mediation, did not carry the connotation of an impending recognition. If the Lincoln administration rejected an armistice, the growing pressure from the Peace Democrats would force it to relent. After the Union had a respite from combat, it would surely come to its senses and realize that war with neither the South nor England was worth pursuing. France's proposal might get the two American belligerents to the peace table.

The risks of a European intervention—particularly under Napoleon's lead—remained high. The Lincoln administration could not forgo one of its most effective weapons, the blockade, and allow the South six months to trade cotton for supplies. Even if both North and South agreed to a cease-fire for that period, nothing could keep them from reloading during the interim. If mediation suggested the imminence of recognition, an armistice did the same. No one could guarantee that the process of intervention would come to a halt if one of the American antagonists refused an armistice proposal. Acceptance by the North of a mediation or an armistice would have constituted a virtual surrender of its wartime objective of preserving the Union. If the Lincoln administration turned down the armistice offer, would England extend recognition and accept the possibility of war with the Union? In the unlikely event of a cease-fire, what terms of settlement could the British suggest that would lessen the chances of a renewed war? What indication was there of Russian cooperation? With or without Russia's involvement, how could England be certain that the powers would not fall out among themselves over competing interests in the New World? Until those questions had satisfactory answers, the powers would either have to allow the war to proceed or embark on a highly dangerous venture.

Russell deluded himself into believing that the French proposal might work. As a by-product of any effort to intervene, he believed, England would maintain its leadership position alongside France in international affairs. Even if there was "little chance of our good offices being accepted in America," he explained to Palmerston, "we should make them such as would be creditable to us in Europe." The British should suggest to France that "in offering our good offices we ought to require both parties to consent to examine, first, whether there are any terms upon which North and South would consent to restore the Union; and secondly, failing any such terms, whether there are any terms upon which both would consent to separate." Russell did not suggest how the intervening powers might "require" North and South to discuss terms. If the antagonists consented to talk, he did not indicate what would happen when the North rejected any arrangement leading to a Southern separation and the South rejected anything less than independence. And he still had no reason to count on Russian participation, which both he and Napoleon considered essential to success. At this point in Russell's note to Palmerston, he admitted that this was a "rough sketch" but promised to elaborate on his views at the cabinet meeting. It would be an "honourable proposal," Russell concluded, although he added, quizzically, "the North and probably the South will refuse it." [10]

Palmerston remained certain that mediation was a good idea even though he believed the timing still was bad. He had asked the Belgian king if "the time had come to offer a mediation and to recognize the Southern States." In response, Leopold assured Russell that a refusal of Napoleon's offer would encourage those among the French who wanted to see the North succeed as "future enemies of England." Palmerston instructed Russell to put off the "French Scheme" until the cabinet met. The prime minister doubted more strongly than did his foreign secretary that the North would approve an armistice accompanied by a cessation of the blockade. He also opposed any program engineered by Napoleon. The North, Palmerston allowed, might agree to lift the blockade on all but contraband goods; but the Washington government realized that if the South sent cotton to Europe, it would "contrive somehow or other to get the value back in muskets & warlike Stores." Palmerston also emphasized that the powers would be unable to formulate a policy on slavery that would be acceptable to the South, the North, and the English people. The French, he remarked, could make any number of interventionist proposals because they were freer from the "Shackles of Principle and of Right & Wrong on these Matters, as on all others than we are." England, Palmerston concluded, should await the elections in the North before doing anything.[11]

Palmerston's stand seemed justified, for reports from Washington continued to predict a Democratic landslide in the congressional elections that would guarantee Union compliance in a mediation. Stuart and Mercier repeated that a victory by Horatio Seymour in the New York gubernatorial election would provide the occasion for either a mediation offer or an armistice proposal. Although Stoeckl recommended waiting a while longer, he also thought "the time may be very near." He had talked with Seward, who no longer warned of a war arising from a mediation followed by recognition. But unknown to Stoeckl, Stuart explained to Russell, Seward relied on faulty information alleging that the British and French were unable to agree on mediation. Stuart agreed that now was the time to take action. Seward considered mediation inevitable, Stuart argued. "We might now recognize the South without much risk to ourselves."[12]

The outcome of the elections afforded enough of a Democratic victory to keep interventionist hopes alive but not enough to substantiate Stuart's optimistic predictions. He nonetheless assured Russell that the time had arrived for mediation or recognition. The Democrats' successes, he declared without a careful examination of the returns, were greater than anticipated. Russell felt uplifted. He had told fellow cabinet member Sir George Grey that only the election of new Democratic leaders would prevent the revival of war in spring. "I heartily wish them success." Now, it appeared, the Democrats had achieved that victory. In truth, however, they had not done well. Admittedly, they made big advances, winning thirty-four additional congressional seats along with the governorships of New York and New Jersey and control over the legislatures in Indiana, Illinois, and New Jersey. But the Republicans held on to seventeen of the nineteen free state governors' houses and sixteen of the legislatures. They also gained five seats in the Senate and kept a twenty-five-vote majority in the House during the smallest overall loss of congressional seats in an off-year election for two decades. Moreover, the Democratic leads in six states were so narrow that had the Union soldiers (who were primarily Republican among the enlistees) been home to vote, they would probably have overturned the results. When it eventually became clear that the Peace Democrats had failed to seize control, Stuart's ardor for intervention cooled.[13]

The chaotic atmosphere in Washington seemed to call for desperate measures. Only a few days after the elections, on November 5, Lincoln had relieved McClellan (regarded as the Democrats' spokesman in the army) of his command and seemed to tighten the relationship between the presidency and what the British referred to as the Radicals or the war party. Lyons thus returned to Washington in the midst of the great public uproar over McClellan's removal and the Democrats' bold claims that they would soon bring the president under control. Some party spokesmen called for an armistice in the war followed by a convention authorized to make modifications in the Constitution that would induce the South "to return to the Union." But the British minister thought that most Democrats regarded the Union's restoration as impossible and would consider an armistice to be a "preliminary to peace—and for the sake of peace would be willing to let the Cotton States at least depart." If so, the Democrats could not declare this publicly. They called instead for a more vigorous pursuit of the war to embarrass the administration, put the North in a favorable position for an armistice, and gain a sound frontier if an armistice ended in a separation. The Democrats would accept mediation if the moderates controlled the president and if "*all* the Powers of Europe" were supportive—which Lyons assumed to mean "principally *Russia* in addition to England and France, and perhaps 'Prussia.'" The Democrats were wary of foreign intervention, and the South had not a "shadow of a desire to return to the Union." At present, Lyons observed, "foreign intervention, short of the use of force, could only make matters worse here."[14]

Mercier now recommended that France act alone and that it

employ threats to achieve Northern compliance. Intervention remained the central theme in Mercier's thoughts, Lyons remarked. The French minister at first hesitated because the Republicans still controlled the cabinet and Congress. Recognition after a refusal of mediation, he feared, would cause a quarrel with the North and fail to benefit either the South or Europe unless the intervening powers forced open the blockade. Mercier had lost patience with the Democrats. Like Stuart, Mercier had misinterpreted the election results and now termed the Democrats "timid" for not taking advantage of their successes. He urged his home government, with the public approval of England, to offer to mediate the war on a unilateral basis. This approach would reduce Northerners' irritation against England, he argued. Further, England's consent would give France the weight of European support. Then, whatever stand the Russians took would help the effort. If they joined France in the mediation offer, it would not matter if they had done so out of a desire to split England and France. If Russia refused to go along, Mercier declared, the plan might have a better chance for success. Russian participation, he argued, would remove "the element of *intimidation*, which though kept in the background, must be felt by the United States to exist." Mercier allowed that joint mediation by all the European powers "might have the effect of reconciling the pride of the United States to negotiation with the South." But he thought the United States would find it difficult to reject an offer made by France and England or by France alone. England and France had an "obvious and pressing interest" in ending the war and would have their navies ready to satisfy that interest. Russia, Mercier concluded, did not share these concerns and, in view of its friendship with the Union, would not become a party to the use of force.[15]

Lyons agreed that no form of intervention could work unless accompanied by the threat of force, but he insisted that the American situation was not conducive to outside involvement and that no European powers would take stern measures. The Democrats had not swept the congressional elections, and the president's dismissal of McClellan had solidified a vague political alignment between the moderate Republicans and the Radicals. Further, several Democrats privately told Lyons that a mediation offer at this time would be premature and provide the Radicals with a rallying cry for continuing the war. The powers must wait until the Democrats controlled the presidency and the North was in a position to seek an armistice with honor. In any event, the Democrats favored a mediation involving several European powers but one that played down the British role. Lyons warned that Lincoln and the Radicals would capitalize on a mediation attempt to warn against outside interference and whip up support for the war effort. Recognition was unwise: "I do not clearly understand what advantage is expected to result from a simple recognition of the Southern Government." Nor could he believe that the European powers would "contemplate breaking up the blockade by force of arms, or engaging in hostilities with the United States in support of the independence of the South." Lyons saw no chance for a compromise. "All hope of the re-construction of the Union appears to be fading away, even from the minds of those who most ardently desire it." [16]

England, Lyons noted, could offer a mediation with Russian participation, but the North would probably reject it. And, he added, "if nothing followed, we should have played out a good card without making a trick." French mediation alone was better than France and England acting together without Russia. To make intervention palatable to Americans, the English role would have to be downplayed. "The bitter portion of the draft which the Americans would have to swallow in a case of joint mediation would be the English portion, and the more it is diluted by the mixture of foreign elements the better." Mercier insisted upon intervention, even without the Russians. Europe must prevent a resurgence of war in the spring of 1863 that would, of course, block a renewed flow of cotton. The choices were mediation, recognition, or inaction. In either of the first two cases, Mercier warned, the intervening powers should make clear that a refusal "would be followed by something more in favour of the South than naked recognition." Lyons considered Russian involvement "essential" but feared that Stoeckl seemed ready to declare that his country would refuse to follow "in the wake of the French and English governments." Lyons agreed with Mercier that an "element of intimidation" must be clear. The blockade was the "critical point." The North believed that to give up the blockade was "to give up the war for ever," whereas the South would reject an armistice without an end to the blockade. If England and France issued threats and did nothing, they would be "crying out Wolf now, when there is no Wolf." [17]

Napoleon's scheme fomented a second and more serious phase of the intervention crisis for the Union. Russell's October proposal had been an armistice with recognition possibly to follow; Napoleon's involvement made the interventionist approach more dangerous, particularly in light of his call for forcibly lifting the blockade and his private intimation to the Confederacy that some measure beyond recognition was possible. Although Russell was not aware of Napoleon's duplicity, the revelation of such behavior would not have been a surprise. The joint intervention in Mexico sent a warning to any nation that collaboration with the French emperor carried great risks. But the November plan might be the European powers' last chance at halting the American war, and Russell was not going to let that chance pass by.

EARLY NOVEMBER 1862 marked the Union's time of greatest crisis in foreign affairs. Unknown to all save a tiny circle of top government figures in Paris, London, and St. Petersburg, the three European powers were secretly contemplating a dangerous interventionist proposal made by France. The numerous flirtations, the countless discussions, the many warnings and counterwarnings—all had come together during the autumn in an armistice plan devised by Napoleon that, carried to its logical conclusion, might have guaranteed a war with the Union and permanent division of the United States. What made the drama more complete was that the dispatches between Adams and Seward during this period did not reveal any awareness of the peril then confronting the Union.

One major figure in England recognized the threat to international peace contained in the French proposal and, as he had with Russell's interventionist attempt in October, Secretary for War George Cornewall Lewis again rose to the challenge. On November 7 he circulated a fifteen-thousand-word memorandum among cabinet members that highlighted the pitfalls inherent in intervention and argued that the South had not earned a right to recognition under international law. His treatise, entitled "Recognition of the Independence of the Southern States of the North American Union," was actually written in part by his stepson-in-law, William Vernon Harcourt, who later became the first person to hold the Whewell Chair of International Law at Cambridge University. The *Spectator* of London exposed Harcourt's identity and praised his use of history and international law in showing that it was realistically impossible to conduct an intervention that was idealistically desirable.[18]

Added emphasis to the argument against intervention came from a series of letters in the *Times* of London, one of which appeared on the same day that Lewis's memorandum made the cabinet circuit. This letter to the editor, signed by "Historicus" (a pseudonym for Harcourt) and focusing on "The International Doctrine of Recognition," presented the same ideas contained in Lewis's essay. Historicus trenchantly reminded readers: "Rebellion, until it has succeeded, is Treason; when it is successful, it becomes independence. And thus the only real test of independence is final success." A joint mediation, he added in another letter to the *Times*, "would practically place our honour in the hands of our copartners in the intervention." Such a venture was not "child's play." The mere announcement of a European involvement would not bring peace. "To interpose without the means or the intention to carry into effect a permanent pacification is not to intervene, but to intermeddle." Though the proposal might be "wise," "right," and "necessary," it could never be "short, simple, or peaceable." History shows that even under the best circumstances, an intervention "almost inevitably . . . results in war." Historicus insisted that the intervening powers could not bring peace "except by recourse to arms; it may be by making war upon the North, it may be by making war upon the South, or, what is still more probable, it may be by making war upon both in turns." The belief that an armistice could end an "irrepressible conflict" was "childish in the extreme." Neutrality was the only safe policy. "We are asked to go we know not whither, in order to do we know not what." Intervention with no plan of settlement and no expectation of using force would prove to the world that the European powers lived in a "Paradise of fools."[19]

In the memorandum, Lewis first agreed with Russell's observation that the American Civil War had endangered the welfare of neutrals and was the most signal event in history since Waterloo. The results could be a "complete territorial re-arrangement of the

Union," as well as basic changes in the American Constitution regarding federal and state relations. The brief time span of the war was deceiving: "events of many years" had transpired in eighteen months. Both sides had fought with greater ferocity and at higher costs than had the antagonists in the Napoleonic Wars—and with no verdict yet in sight. The war had settled into a bloody stalemate in which the North had failed to force the South's submission, and the South had not substantiated its claim to independence. And all the while the Union blockade had inflicted "greater loss, privation, and suffering to England and France, than was ever produced to neutral nations by a war." [20]

For several reasons large numbers of people in England preferred that the American war end with Southern separation. They wanted the blockade removed and the cotton flow restored to Lancashire. They sympathized with the South's efforts to resist Northern coercion. They were shocked by the war's savagery and felt a "rational and laudable desire" to see the British government recognize the South and bring a close to the fighting. The British people realized, however, that an intervention between "two angry belligerents, at the moment of their greatest exasperation, [was] playing with edge tools." The outcome of the war remained uncertain, and any interventionist attempt at this point would actually promote Southern independence and cause war between England and the North. Despite this danger, the supporters of intervention insisted upon immediate action. Indeed, Lewis allowed, the civilized world would thank England if it could, "without unduly sacrificing or imperilling her own interests," achieve peace.[21]

The central question in the interventionist controversy, Lewis declared, was whether the South had established independence and deserved recognition. The deceptively simple act of extending recognition bore an awesome responsibility that needed careful study. The intervening nations must distinguish between recognition by a former sovereign and that by a third state, as explained by Sir James Mackintosh and agreed to by Foreign Secretary George Canning in a June 1824 debate in the Commons regarding the independence of Spanish colonies. Recognition of the first class involved the issue of which belligerent was in the right because it necessitated "Renunciations of sovereignty"—"a surrender of the power or of the claim to govern." But recognition of the second class—by a third state—did not involve renunciation of sovereignty, abdication of power, or conferral of legal rights. Lewis emphasized the realistic nature of the second type of recognition: "A state whose independence is recognized by a third state is an independent without that recognition as with it." Mackintosh had declared that the only action involved in a "practical recognition" was to send diplomatic representatives. "It implies no guarantee, no alliance, no aid, no approbation of the successful revolt; no intimation of an opinion concerning the justice or injustice of the means by which it has been accomplished." The first form of recognition sought to benefit the state acknowledged as independent; the second attempted to benefit the state acknowledging the independence. The first waived a "legal pretension," whereas the second was "only the acknowledgment of a fact, together with a policy required by that acknowledgment."[22]

Even if outside powers decided upon recognition, Lewis argued, they would not be justified in doing so unless the South had established independence. A nation had no right to extend recognition to subjects of another nation in revolt against their government until they were "virtually an independent community according to the principles of international law." Recognition of independence by a foreign government was "recognition of a fact." If not a fact, the North would have ground for protest and war. There must be *some* test for the independence of an insurgent community." Indeed, Lewis insisted, two "marks of independence" were incontestable: one positive, the other negative. First, the "community claiming to be independent should have a Government of its own, receiving the habitual obedience of its people." Second, the insurgents' "habit of obedience" to the old government must have ceased and the relationship between that government and subjects must have been broken. At this point, according to international law, neutrals might extend recognition.[23]

Lewis tied the controversy to international law and historical precedent. No one could doubt that the South had a governing body that commanded the obedience of its people. Each state in the Confederacy had a legislature and executive as well as a militia and could perform government functions. The Northern experience in occupying New Orleans had disproved the claim that substantial Union sentiment existed in the South. But, Lewis declared, doubt remained about whether the split between North and South was total and irrevocable. When people in revolt reached the level of independence, neutrals had the moral and legal authority to extend recognition. But when did this moment of maturity arrive? "It is easy to distinguish between day and night; but it is impossible to fix the precise moment when day ends and night begins." Even the great English legal theorist John Austin admitted that "it was impossible for neutral nations to hit that juncture with precision." Lewis supported his argument by referring to seven historical examples, including that of the American colonies and England. After the British defeat at Saratoga in October 1777, he explained, France told the American commissioners of the king's intention to recognize the independence of the colonies. The United States, "as an independent nation," signed two treaties with France in February of the following year. Then, in March 1778, the French minister in London notified England of America's independence as proclaimed by the declaration in Philadelphia of July 4, 1776. England, however, did not consider colonial independence a fait accompli. It regarded the French note as a declaration of war and broke diplomatic relations. Lewis agreed with Canning's exhortation in 1823 relating to the Spanish colonies then in revolt: England must not extend recognition if there was any "reasonable chance of an accommodation."[24]

Lewis charted two courses open to England if it intervened and, in so doing, helped bring about Southern independence. First, it could extend a "simple recognition" by signing a commercial treaty or by sending diplomatic agents. Second, it could use "negotiation or arms" in an act of "interference for establishing [the South's] independence." Lewis admitted that England had extended simple recognition by designating the South as a belligerent. But recognition of belligerency was not the same as recognition of independence. The Swiss expert on international law Emmerich de Vattel declared that when a nation was so deeply divided by internal conflict that neither side obeyed a common authority, the state was dissolved and the fighting between them became that between nations—a public war. Under these conditions, only a resort to arms could determine which party was right. But Lewis argued that these conditions did not exist in the

American conflict and that England should maintain neutrality until they did. If England intervened now, it would become a virtual ally of the South in achieving its independence. War with the Union would be certain. England must not take action while the outcome in America remained in doubt.[25]

Lewis had brought focus to the toughest single problem in the recognition crisis: deciding when a people in revolt had achieved independence. Proponents of intervention had presented two arguments for recognition of Southern independence: that the move would be in accordance with international law and that it would be conducive to a North-South settlement. Lewis pointed out that neither argument was valid. On the first, he insisted that England had always abided by international law in refusing to recognize the independence of subjects in revolt while a "*bona fide* struggle with the legitimate sovereign was pending." The well-known American theorist on international law Henry Wheaton admitted that French recognition of the United States in 1778 had been unjustifiable because the Americans had not yet established their independence and the outcome remained uncertain. England's past record was different. When the Spanish colonies revolted in 1808, the government in London did not recognize them until 1825, when no struggle was going on and, as Lord Lansdowne said then, when they were "*de facto*, independent" and Spain had no chance of reestablishing control. On the second argument, Lewis declared, there was no indication that recognition would promote an agreement between the antagonists. The central fact in the American war, he emphasized, was that neither side had lost its determination to win.[26]

The proclamation of emancipation and the Southern pleas for recognition constituted evidence of the ongoing nature of the war. Lincoln, Lewis insisted, did not support emancipation on humanitarian grounds. Seward called the proclamation "a just and proper military act." Emancipation, Lewis declared, was "intended to impoverish and distress the Southern planters, possibly even to provoke a slave insurrection." That document alone proved that a "*bona fide* struggle" was still under way. Further, the South's repeated appeals for recognition were an admission that the outcome was in doubt. "If the independence of the seceding States was equally clear," Lewis concluded, "they and their English advocates would not be so eager to secure their recognition by European Governments." [27]

Lewis appeared to leave no argument for intervention. Not only would recognition of the South encourage a war with the North, but the action would violate international law by constituting an interference in a war whose verdict remained unsettled. History showed that new states were rarely created out of existing states except by force. "If the Great European Powers are not contented to wait until the American conflagration has burned itself out, they must not expect to extinguish the flames with rose-water." [28]

Yet Lewis admitted to one avenue of intervention that the neutral nations might examine: under certain conditions, international law condoned "an avowed armed interference in a war already existing." Lewis suspected that the "Southern champion" (Napoleon) supported "armed mediation" or "dictation." In fact, Lewis later admitted to Harcourt, this step might have been "very desirable—but it is not what the French despatch professed to mean—and it is not what is meant by the advocates of *moral force*." Lewis added: "Nothing was said about *coercing* the North a few weeks ago." No one, he now declared in his memorandum, disputed the claim that the American war had hurt neutrals economically and might draw them into the conflict. If the European powers (assuming they could cooperate) resorted to force, they could appeal to the law of nature in using their good offices to achieve peace. If mediation failed, they might help the party they believed to be in the right—if that party either asked for assistance or agreed to accept it. The situation would be the same as if two countries were at war and another helped one of them.[29]

But, Lewis asked, would this approach be expedient and wise? The North remained powerful despite secession, and the European powers would have great difficulty in sending fleets and armies to the Potomac. How would they transport large armies across the Atlantic? How would Europe's wooden vessels fare against the North's ironclads? And even if Europe's Great Powers (England, France, Russia, Austria, and Prussia) succeeded in forcing the North to recognize the South, new problems would arise at the peace table. The intervening nations would have to establish in Washington a "Conference of Plenipotentiaries of the Five Great

Powers." What would be its makeup? If comprised of their five foreign ministers then in Washington, it would not have enough weight. If Europe sent over new plenipotentiaries, they would have no intimate knowledge of American politics. "What would an eminent diplomatist from Vienna, or Berlin, or St. Petersburg, know of the Chicago platform or the Crittenden compromise?" Distance would also pose a problem. Would the plenipotentiaries act on their own, or would they have to refer back to their home governments for instructions on every issue? It was dangerous to grant unlimited powers of negotiation, but if not done, long delays would make matters worse.[30]

Many times in history, Lewis knew, one nation had intervened in another nation's affairs without exploring potential difficulties; England must not make that mistake. The questions he had raised about Russell's October interventionist attempt remained unresolved. If the European powers used force to end the war, the ensuing "Washington Conference" (as Lewis called it) would have to formulate peace terms. What would be the boundaries of the two new American nations? How would the powers partition the western territories? Who would control river navigation—especially that of the Mississippi? Who would handle the national debt? What would be the status of slavery? Abolition in the Gulf areas would hurt cotton production for years. Yet England could not approve the continuation of slavery. "These and other thorny questions would have to be settled by a Conference of five foreigners, acting under the daily fire of the American press." And even if the five powers intervened in concert, how long would that concert last? "In the same proportion that, by increasing the number of the intervening powers, you increase the military or moral force of the intervention, you also multiply the chances of disagreement." A conference of the five powers would be "an imposing force," Lewis admitted, "but it [was] a dangerous body to set in motion." The powers would not only have to satisfy the North and South but themselves as well. As in Belgium's recent trouble, Austria, Prussia, and Russia might take one side and England and France the other. "England might stand alone."[31]

Lewis's lengthy memorandum greatly influenced the outcome of the cabinet meeting that Russell convened on November 11. By no stretch of the imagination could Russell formulate a policy capable of dispensing with the problems presented by Lewis. That Russell did not try to do so was a testament to their force. The foreign secretary had had no success in October, and this new proposal carried the added burden of Napoleon's imprimatur. As Russell called the meeting to order, rumors were widespread in London of a French proposed intervention with England and Russia. The day before, Russell announced, the French ambassador in London had officially presented him with a proposal to join France and Russia in asking North and South to agree to a six-month armistice, accompanied by a suspension of the blockade for the same period. Russell was willing to go ahead with France alone, for he informed his colleagues that the British ambassador in St. Petersburg had notified the Foreign Office that even though Russia would not participate, it would informally support any Anglo-French effort that did not alienate the Union. Russell argued that such outside encouragement would strengthen the peace advocates in the North and promote an end to the war. He also warned that British refusal might lead Russia to reconsider and move ahead with France, thereby accomplishing the Russian aim of dividing France and England. England should join France in the armistice offer.[32]

Russell threw open the matter for discussion. Palmerston spoke briefly on its behalf but with a notable lack of enthusiasm. Acceptance of the proposal, he argued, would demonstrate the British government's sympathy with Lancashire's workers. Lewis countered that British participation in an American venture might have the opposite effect of causing the workers to accuse the ministry of "indifference" to their plight. After the prime minister completed his argument, the proposal went before the cabinet which, according to Lewis, "proceeded to pick it to pieces." Everyone "threw a stone at it" except Gladstone and Westbury. The main complaint was that a six-month suspension of the blockade was "so grossly unequal, so decidedly in favour of the South," that even Russell admitted that the North would not accept it. According to Lewis's account, Palmerston realized that the cabinet would not bend and switched sides. Though Lewis had not grasped his superior's strong aversion to intervention, he observed that the prime minister's support had not been "very sincere" and "certainly was not hearty." Gladstone felt bitter. Russell had "turned tail . . . without resolutely fighting out his battle," whereas Palmerston had given him only "a feeble and half-hearted support."[33]

The cabinet episode took on the nature of a poorly written play in which the plot unraveled in the opening scene and the actors continued playing their parts out of professional obligation. Since the fate of France's offer seemed certain even to its supporters, Lewis concluded that Russell's "principal motive was a fear of displeasing France, & that Palmer[ston's] principal motive was a wish to seem to support *him*." The cabinet voted against Napoleon's proposal and recommended sending a note of refusal to France, which Russell ("under protest," Lewis declared) agreed to prepare. The cabinet would meet the following day to study the draft.[34]

Russell's note to France declining the offer managed to maintain a good relationship between the countries while keeping his flickering hopes for intervention alive. Europe had watched the bloodshed in America for over a year, he wrote, and now the threat of a servile war had developed. Both America and Europe suffered from the fighting. The purpose of the French proposal, Russell remained convinced, had been to "smooth obstacles, and only within limits which the two interested parties would prescribe." Even if unsuccessful, the move might persuade the antagonists to think about peace. Despite rejecting the proposal, Russell continued, the British government sought continued cooperation with France on international issues. Neither the queen nor her people would forget France's support during the *Trent* affair. But the ministry concluded that there was "no ground at the present moment to hope that the Federal Government would accept the proposal suggested, and a refusal from Washington at present would prevent any speedy renewal of the offer." It was best to watch American public opinion to determine any change that might someday offer hope for a three-power "friendly counsel."[35]

At least four times—in a note approved by the cabinet—Russell implied the possibility of intervention at a later time. Gladstone thought so. The British reply, he told his wife, was "put upon grounds and in terms which leave the matter very open for the future." From Washington, Lyons thought the cabinet decision correct and assured Russell that the Union would have rejected the French proposal.[36] Russell held on to the prospect of intervention even though he had no choice but to return to the stand advocated by Palmerston during the early stages of the war: events on the American battlefield would have to convince the North that subjugation of the South was impossible.

The Americans in London were not aware of these secret deliberations within the Palmerston ministry that could have had a serious impact on the outcome of the Civil War. Indeed, rumors of a French interventionist suggestion to England and Russia had not caused much concern at the American legation even as late as November 11, the day the cabinet talks began; Russell had recently reassured Adams that England would take no action without first consulting him. On November 13, the day after the cabinet had adjourned, the *Times* of London published the French note to England and France and declared that "the present is not the moment for these strong measures." It would be "cheaper to keep all Lancashire on turtle and venison than to plunge into a desperate war with the Northern States of America, even with all Europe at our back." To dispel American alarm, Russell two days later assured Adams that the cabinet "never intended agreeing to the mediation." That same day, November 15, word publicly arrived from St. Petersburg that the Russians had declined the offer. And yet, Stoeckl in Washington had also received instructions that if France and England went ahead, he was "to lend to both his colleagues, if not official aid, at least moral support." Adams had not been worried about either British or Russian participation. He trusted Russell and cited assurances of goodwill from the Russian ambassador in London, Baron Philip Brunow, along with a favorable article in the government's semiofficial *Journal of St. Petersburg.* Moran dismissed the French proposition as "a piece of weak insolence" that had come from that "prince of intriguers Slidell."[37]

The controversy was not over, for news of the French proposal soon reached Washington and set off several bitter exchanges. The Lincoln administration was stung by the realization that the European powers had discussed intervention. In a heated conversation with Lyons, Seward expressed dissatisfaction and asked the British minister to relay this sentiment to Mercier. Seward praised the Russian response before focusing his wrath on France and England. Their joint actions, he wrote Adams, had convinced

ONE HEAD BETTER THAN TWO.

Louis Napoleon. "I SAY, HADN'T WE BETTER TELL OUR FRIEND THERE TO LEAVE OFF MAKING A FOOL OF HIMSELF?"

Lord Pam. "H'M, WELL, SUPPOSE YOU TALK TO HIM YOURSELF. HE'S A GREAT ADMIRER OF YOURS, YOU KNOW."

"One Head Better Than Two" (London Punch, *Nov. 22, 1862)*

Americans of Napoleon's "aggressive designs," even though Lincoln had wisely chosen to regard the proposal as the result of a "mistaken desire to counsel in a case where all foreign counsel excites distrust." Seward nonetheless complained that the French proposal had raised the South's hopes and prolonged the war. "This Government will in all cases," he emphasized to his minister in Paris, "seasonably warn foreign Powers of the injurious effect of any apprehended interference on their part." After the war, "the whole American people will for ever afterwards be asking who among the foreign nations were the most just and the most forbearing to their country in its hour of trial."[38]

The South's reaction to the failed interventionist project was likewise bitter. Francis Lawley, the *Times*'s correspondent in Richmond, who was intensely partisan toward the Confederacy, tried to express the depth of Southern disappointment with England. In a statement that revealed both his and the South's shallow understanding of the complexities involved in the British government's attitude toward the war, he lamented that slavery alone had obstructed good relations. The solution to the problem of slavery had a better chance when the South was independent than when it had to be "on the defensive" in opposing abolitionists. The *Index* challenged the British: "Has it come to this? Is England, or the English Cabinet, afraid of the Northern States?"[39]

Most observers attributed the defeat of intervention to Russell. The *Index* and Slidell, not knowing the foreign secretary's real feelings, blamed him for undermining Napoleon's proposal. Adams remained convinced years afterward that Russell had been the chief stalwart against British intervention. According to Adams's biographer, the American minister never realized that Russell had initiated the interventionist discussions. As a result, Adams had waited until mid-November 1862 (after the crisis had passed) to reveal to Russell the instructions from Seward to break diplomatic relations if the British recognized the Confederacy. Adams was so taken by Russell's assurances that he recorded in his diary in 1868 that the foreign secretary had submitted the French proposal to the cabinet "with his own opinion adverse to it. It had then been declined without dissent." The *Richmond Whig* spread the blame. It denounced both Palmerston and Russell as "two old painted mummies" who wanted the war to continue until both North and South had collapsed.[40]

Not everyone held Russell accountable. Charles Francis Adams, Jr., who wrote numerous published accounts of this period, believed that Palmerston had orchestrated the cabinet rejection because he thought the Union was dissolved. Slidell later learned about Palmerston's reluctance to intervene and asked Mason: "Who would have believed that Earl Russell would have been the only member of the Cabinet besides Gladstone in favor of accepting the Emperor's proposition?" Harcourt thought it a "little amusing that the whole wrath of the South and the imputation of being the real obstacle to Intervention should fall on Lord John. It only shows how little is known of the real history of affairs. Probably when the history of 1862 is written," he noted with pungent humor, "it will be apparent that Ld. Palmerston and Russell were the two men who decided the question against interference. It reminds me of what Sir R.[obert] Walpole said[:] 'don't tell me of History[;] I know that *can't* be true.' "[41]

M O S T   O B S E R V E R S believed that the intervention crisis had passed; a few thought it had only dissipated in intensity and would erupt again as the American war followed its brutal course. Adams noted a diminished tendency to meddle in American affairs, and Palmerston admitted that England would have "great difficulty . . . at any time" in persuading North and South to negotiate. But the prime minister held out the possibility, slim though it was. England, he declared to Russell in mid-December, could extend recognition "with less Risk in the Spring" because it could send reinforcements to Canada. George Grote, a well-known British jurist who favored the North, nonetheless approved Lewis's remarks about America's unfounded criticisms of England and praised the ministry's neutrality as a model for history. Gladstone still believed in intervention. He wrote New York financier Cyrus Field that "this destructive and hopeless war" had to end. So many killed and so much destroyed: "Is not this enough?"[42]

Conclusion

Lewis's memorandum and Palmerston's reluctance to act provide the final denouement to the question of why the British government refused to intervene in the Civil War.[1] Lewis knew that the key person he had to dissuade from intervention was Russell. He also knew that the foreign secretary relied on history and international law to justify his stand and that the only way to undermine his argument for intervention was to appeal to that same history and international law. This Lewis did with his November 7 memorandum. In arguing against intervention, he included references to history and citations and quotes from Austin, Vattel, and Wheaton, knowing that Russell had relied on these writers in justifying his call for intervention. Lewis lauded the interventionist move as humanitarian in nature—thereby praising Russell—and then, after complimenting the foreign secretary's use of history and international law to promote an intervention, raised the practical and legal obstacles to such a move. Lewis's tactics made it impossible for Russell to sustain his argument. Russell returned to the camp of the prime minister, who had already confirmed his own hesitation after Antietam.

As time approached for implementing the Emancipation Proclamation, the chances for intervention disappeared as British indignation over Lincoln's move eased with the growing realization that slavery's end was in sight. Argyll, Bright, Cobden, and others had discerned the long-range implications of the document. To the north of London, workers likewise grasped its ramifications. Ignoring the man-made boundaries of the new freedom, they gathered in huge rallies beginning in December, cheering the North and proclaiming the rights of workers everywhere. For weeks Adams was besieged with petitions, resolutions, and letters from working groups (and emancipation societies), all supporting the president's action.[2] The North's heightened morale stemming from Antietam and the imminent Emancipation Proclamation, or so the workers believed, would sweep away the South's resistance and bring a peace that, not coincidentally, would reopen the cotton flow and permit a return to normal work time.

England's move both toward and away from intervention had little to do with moral sentiments about slavery. Without question, Lincoln's call for emancipation made it difficult for the British to take any action that might place them on the side of the Confederacy. But slavery existed in the South at the beginning of the war, and the Palmerston ministry considered intervention anyway. If one is skeptical about Russell's claims to favor the Union, no doubt can exist that he and his colleagues were neutral and wanted peace as integral to their own nation's best interests. If anything, the attacks by both North and South on the ministry provided evidence of its neutrality. More than a few British spokesmen remained infuriated with what they regarded as the Union's hypocrisy concerning slavery and only reluctantly joined the swelling flood of pro-North support. The Emancipation Proclamation made that task easier. In that sense Lincoln's move against slavery had the impact on England that he mistakenly thought it was having some months earlier. Despite the oft-claimed argument that the Emancipation Proclamation helped to prevent outside interference in the war, the pattern of events in the period before the autumn crisis of 1862 shows that the dec-

SCENE FROM THE AMERICAN "TEMPEST."
Caliban (Sambo). " *YOU* BEAT HIM 'NOUGH, MASSA! BERRY LITTLE TIME, I 'LL *BEAT HIM TOO.*"—Shakspeare. (*Nigger Translation.*)

"Scene from the American 'Tempest' "
(London Punch, Jan. 24, 1863)

laration actually encouraged talk of intervention because of the widespread fear of slave revolts and ultimate race war.[3]

Other divisive issues irritated Anglo-American relations throughout the remainder of the war and into the postwar period, but none were as explosive as the crisis over intervention. The South continued its efforts to build a navy in England, and more than once the murmurs of war resumed. In early January 1863, after the Southern victory at Fredericksburg of the previous month, Napoleon III made a unilateral and informal offer of mediation, which the Union promptly rejected. Finally, Southern sympathizers John Roebuck and William Lindsay tried one more time in Parliament during the summer of 1863 to arrange an Anglo-French recognition of the Confederacy, but their poorly managed plan collapsed under the weight of its own intrigues, betrayed confidences, and exaggerated claims. British business interests continued to profit from wartime trade with the Union, and the cotton famine in England (and on the Continent) came to an end in 1863 as increased supplies came from blockade runners and from sources other than the American South. And from 1863 on, England became increasingly preoccupied with prob-

VERY PROBABLE.

Lord Punch. "THAT WAS JEFF DAVIS, PAM! DON'T YOU RECOGNISE HIM?"
Lord Pam. "HM! WELL, NOT EXACTLY—MAY HAVE TO DO SO SOME OF THESE DAYS."

"Very Probable" (London Punch, *Aug. 27, 1864)*

lems in Europe. Though the Palmerston ministry had repeatedly threatened to deviate from its course, it remained true to its initial decision not to intervene until the North had learned on the battlefield that subjugation of the South was impossible. In an ironic twist, however, the Union itself sealed the fate of foreign intervention (and that of the Confederacy) with pathbreaking victories at Vicksburg and Gettysburg in July of that same year. A month later, Benjamin directed Mason to leave London.[4]

THE LAST SUGGESTION FROM RICHMOND.

GHOST OF THE CONFEDERACY—"*I propose to throw myself under your protection—either joint-ly or separately.*"

BOTH—"*We don't see it. While you were a live person we might—but now you are a mere skeleton—nary—no—no.*"

"The Last Suggestion from Richmond": Napoleon III and John Bull reject the Confederacy (Frank Leslie's Illustrated Newspaper, *Jan. 28, 1865)*

The British had found themselves caught in an unparalleled dilemma. Humanitarian, economic, political, and strategic interests were at stake, and yet the government in London could do nothing to stop the fighting in America. Although the responsibilities of civilization and self-interest rested on the Palmerston ministry, it had no remedy to the American problem and could take no action either with or without allies. The likelihood of conflict with the North outweighed the attraction of intervention. Not only was Canada indefensible, but Palmerston feared an outbreak of war in Europe caused by its own set of problems. French aggressions had already alienated the Union, and Russia's pro-Union sentiment prevented participation in any policy alien to the Lincoln administration's wishes. Finally, Palmerston and others believed that the Union navy and army had grown to alarming proportions. Lewis's arguments and Palmerston's reluctance led to London's rejection of Napoleon's project, which killed the last major effort at joint intervention. To his consul general in Paris, Seward offered a requiem for the intervention crisis: "We are no longer to be disturbed by Secession intrigues in Europe. They have had their day. We propose to forget them." [5]

The British decision to stay out of the war proved crucial to the collapse of the Confederacy. Before 1863, when talk of intervention was at its highest, the verdict of the war hung in the balance. Had the British chosen to intervene, the South would doubtless have won recognition and dissident groups in the North would have been strengthened in their opposition to the war. The British would then have felt called upon to challenge the blockade, assuring confrontations with Union vessels and a virtual certainty of war. In the meantime, the Confederacy would have secured enough outside military and commercial aid to have prolonged its resistance and perhaps to have won independence. One cannot conclude that recognition would have changed the war's ultimate judgment. And yet, recognition would have provided a morale boost to the South at a pivotal time, heightened its chances for floating loans abroad and raising more money at home, furnished a powerful impetus for war between the Union and England, opened the possibility of the South's signing military alliances, forced the North to dig deeper into its will to maintain the Union, and damaged Anglo-American relations for years to come.

Adams was correct in declaring that the Union was passing through the crisis of its fate during the late autumn of 1862. Mediation, however well-intentioned, would undoubtedly have gone beyond a mere push for peace into the next step of recognition and then to an outbreak of hostilities fostered by the North's unyielding opposition to foreign involvement. Even without British intervention, Americans harbored ill feelings toward the Palmerston ministry that were still in evidence years afterward. In 1871 an arbitral commission in Geneva awarded the United States $15 million in damage claims arising from the blockade-running activities of the *Alabama* and other vessels built in England. But running beneath these complaints was the Union's bitter belief that England's refusal to renounce any intention to recognize the South had prolonged the war. To make such an admission, the British claimed, would bolster Seward's unfounded attempt to hold them liable for all losses stemming from the Civil War. A little over a year after the war, Seward had complained to Adams that England's premature recognition of Southern belligerency had approved "British sympathy, aid, and assistance," making them "active allies" of the Confederacy. England's meddling in America's domestic affairs, Seward insisted, had threatened "the life of the nation itself."[6]

Fortunately, in 1862, Lewis emerged as the voice of reason and supported Palmerston's hesitancy to become involved in a war in which the intervening power possessed no remedy other than the use of force. Given the other issues that threatened the midcentury Anglo-American rapprochement both during the Civil War and afterward, British intervention would almost certainly have led to a third war between the Atlantic nations with repercussions reaching well into the twentieth century.[7] Once the British refused to intervene, the French followed suit, and this most horrible of wars, as the Palmerston ministry regarded the American conflict, would have to grind on to its end at Appomattox Courthouse in April 1865.

NOTES

AR: Duke of Argyll
BFSP: *British and Foreign State Papers*
BPP: *British Parliamentary Papers*
Brit. Lib., Add. Mss.: British Library,
Additional Manuscripts, London,
England
CFA: Charles Francis Adams
CFA Diary, Letterbook: Adams Family
Papers, Massachusetts Historical
Society, Boston, Massachusetts
CFA, Jr.: Charles Francis Adams, Jr.
CL: Fourth Earl of Clarendon
CWL: Roy P. Basler, ed., *Collected
Works of Abraham Lincoln*
Disp., GB (NA): Department of State,
Diplomatic Dispatches, Great
Britain (National Archives),
Washington, D.C.
DS: Department of State, United
States
FO: Foreign Office, Great Britain
FRUS: United States, Department of
State, *Papers Relating to Foreign Affairs*
GB: Great Britain

GC: General Correspondence
NA: National Archives, Washington,
D.C.
NFBL (NA): DS, Notes from the
British Legation in the United States
to the Department of State, 1791–
1906 (National Archives),
Washington, D.C.
NTFL, GB (NA): Department of
State, Notes to Foreign Legations in
the United States, from the
Department of State, 1834–1906,
Great Britain (National Archives),
Washington, D.C.
ORN: *Official Records of the Union and
Confederate Navies in the War of the
Rebellion*
Parl. Debates: Thomas C. Hansard, ed.,
Hansard's Parliamentary Debates
PM/J: Prime Minister/Journal
PRO: Public Record Office, Kew,
England
RU: Lord John Russell

1. See Blumenthal, "Confederate Diplomacy"; Davis, *Rise and Fall of the Confederate Government*, 2:368–70. Not until the early twentieth century did nations distinguish between de facto and de jure recognition. See Lauterpacht, *Recognition in International Law*, 332. A de facto government is in control, regardless of questions of its legality. A de jure government is considered lawful even though it may not be in actual control.

2. Russell to Lyons, Mar. 21, 1861, no. 69, Gladstone Papers, Brit. Lib., Add. Mss., 44,593, vol. 508. Palmerston was Henry John Temple, Third Viscount.

3. Lyons to Russell, Feb. 4, 1861, Russell Papers, PRO 30/22/35. In April 1861 Stoeckl tried to arrange negotiations between Seward and Southern representatives, but the secretary of state at the last minute decided

against the meeting and staunchly opposed compromise. See Saul, *Distant Friends*, 323; Wheaton, *Elements of International Law* (1866 ed.), pt. 2, sect. 73, 101 n.; Woldman, *Lincoln and the Russians*, chap. 3. Lyons was Richard Bickerton Pemell Lyons, Second Baron. Everett was minister to London from 1841 to 1845.

4. Seward to Bremen's minister Rudolph Schleiden, quoted in Wheaton, *Elements of International Law* (1866 ed.), pt. 2, sect. 73, 101 n.; ibid., pt. 3, sect. 288; Lyons to Russell, Jan. 7, 1861, quoted in Newton, *Lyons*, 1:30. One writer, Stanley Gallas, argues that Lyons's dispatches were "always informative and marked with clarity." But if, as Gallas argues, Lyons had come to realize after 1861 that Seward was not a warmonger, most of the damage had already been done. The London ministry acted throughout the intervention crisis largely on the basis of Lyons's often wrongly premised assessments of Seward's behavior. See Gallas, "Lyons and Civil War," 149, 153–56. For a defense of Seward's aggressive tactics, see Ferris, *Desperate Diplomacy*, and Ferris, "Seward and Faith of a Nation," 160–69.

5. Beale, ed., *Diary of Welles*, 1:37 (Mar. [?], 1861).

6. Much of any historian's work, of course, is necessarily derivative from that of predecessors in the field, and this study is no different. Where it follows or breaks with conventional accounts should become clear in the text and in the notes.

7. Brauer, "British Mediation and Civil War," 50–51; Robert H. Jones, "Anglo-American Relations," 38, 40. Derby was Edward George Geoffrey Smith, the Fourteenth Earl of Derby.

8. Historians who have referred to Lewis's role in countering the interventionists are E. D. Adams, *GB and Civil War*, 2:44–46, 52–58, 62–63, 73–74; Ellsworth, "Anglo-American Affairs," 94–95; Merli and Wilson, "British Cabinet and Confederacy," 254, 256, 258; Merli, *GB and Confederate Navy*, 109–15; Crook, *North, South, and Powers*, 233–36, 240–41, 251; Jenkins, *Britain and War for Union*, 2:169–70, 173–76, 179.

CHAPTER ONE

1. Kenneth Bourne calls the period of British neutrality during the Civil War "the most menacing phase of Anglo-American relations since 1814" ("Foreign Secretaryship of Lord Stanley," 343–45). See also Bourne, *Britain and Balance of Power*, 210, 252–53. Making good offices available generally meant offering any assistance toward encouraging the antagonists to resolve their differences. Mediation could result from this offer. See Wheaton, *Elements of International Law* (1836 ed.), pt. 3, sect. 288.

2. Seward's view on "counter-revolution" in Brauer, "Slavery Problem," 445; contemporary's quote in Graebner, "Northern Diplomacy and European Neutrality," 59; Berwanger, ed., Russell, *Diary*, 60 (Apr. 4, 1861);

Ferris, *Desperate Diplomacy*, 8; Lyons to Russell, Mar. 26, 1861, Russell Papers, PRO 30/22/35.

3. Lyons to Russell, Mar. 26, 1861, Russell Papers, PRO 30/22/35. Norman B. Ferris raises serious doubt about whether Seward was more challenging than Lyons in the brief confrontation. According to the Belgian envoy's account, Lyons warned Seward that "we must have cotton and we shall have it!" (quoted in Ferris, *Desperate Diplomacy*, 214 n. 26).

4. Russell to Lyons, Feb. 20, 1861, *BFSP 1860–1861*, 51:175–76; Lyons to Russell, Feb. 12, Mar. 26, 29, May 6, June 18, 1861, Russell Papers, PRO 30/22/35.

5. Lincoln to Seward, Apr. 1, 1861, *CWL*, 4:316–17; Seward's memo, "Some thoughts for the President's consideration," Apr. 1, 1861, ibid., 317–18. See Brauer, "Seward's 'Foreign War Panacea,'" 136–37, 153–55. For a defense of Seward's strategy, see Ferris, *Desperate Diplomacy*.

6. Lincoln to Seward, Apr. 1, 1861, *CWL*, 4:317; Brauer, "Seward's 'Foreign War Panacea,'" 156–57.

7. Brauer, "Slavery Problem," 441, 443–45.

8. St. Clair, "Slavery as Diplomatic Factor," 262; Charles Greville (the Englishman) to Earl of Clarendon (former foreign secretary), Jan. 26, 1861, in Maxwell, *Clarendon*, 2:237. See also E. D. Adams, *GB and Civil War*, 1:35.

9. Brauer, "Slavery Problem," 450; Beale, ed., *Diary of Bates*, 179 (Mar. 31, 1861); Dennett, ed., *Lincoln and Civil War*, 22 (May 10, 1861); Russell to Lyons, Dec. 29, 1860, Russell Papers, PRO 30/22/96; Berwanger, ed., Russell, *Diary*, 51 (Mar. 28, 1861). Actually, the number of slaves freed by the war would be in excess of 4 million because more than 430,000 slaves in the border states would also go free.

10. The president reaffirmed his views on slavery in a message to Congress on July 4, 1861. Less than three weeks later, Congress passed resolutions offering the same assurances of noninterference in Southern rights and declaring that the Washington government sought only to defend the Constitution and save the Union. See *CWL*, 4:263, 439; *Congressional Globe*, 37th Cong., 1st sess., 222–23 (House, July 22, 1861), 258–65 (Senate, July 25, 1861); CFA to CFA, Jr., June 21, 1861, in Ford, ed., *Adams Letters*, 1:14. For Lincoln's racial views, see Fredrickson, "Man but Not Brother," 39–58, and Oates, "'Man of Our Redemption,'" 15–25.

11. Seward to CFA, Apr. 10, 1861, no. 2, *FRUS 1861*, 72–79.

12. Ridley, *Palmerston*, 549; Bell, *Palmerston*, 2:274–75; Bourne, *Foreign Policy of Victorian England*, 90; Bourne, *Britain and Balance of Power*, 252–53; Jenkins, *Britain and War for Union*, 1:82. Wilbur D. Jones convincingly argues that, despite the claim that the British Conservative party wanted a breakup of the Union, both public and private evidence fails to substantiate this allegation as well as the related charge that the Conservatives sympathized with the South as a means for undermining republicanism. Conservatives, Jones declares, were preoccupied with numerous other concerns

unrelated to the American conflict. See his article "British Conservatives and Civil War." Another writer disagrees and not so convincingly argues that British upper-class hatred of democracy was the biggest reason for Southern sentiment. See Hernon, "British Sympathies in Civil War." For the McLeod affair, see Howard Jones, *To the Webster-Ashburton Treaty*, chap. 4, and Stevens, *Border Diplomacy*. Seward was governor of New York during the McLeod crisis. For an excellent discussion by a British historian of the confused and divided British reaction to the war, see Parish, *Civil War*, 383–89.

13. Palmerston to Russell, Dec. 30, 1860, Apr. 14, 1861, Russell Papers, PRO 30/22/21; Bell, *Palmerston*, 2:276–77, 291.

14. Russell to Lyons, Mar. 22, 1861, *BFSP 1860–1861*, 51:177; Dallas to Seward, Apr. 9, 1861, no. 330, *FRUS 1861*, 81; miscellaneous draft in unidentified hand and undated, Russell Papers, PRO 30/22/118A; Tilby, *Russell*, 19–20, 72, 156; Russell to queen quoted ibid., 73. For a contemporary argument about recognition, of which Russell was certainly aware, see Wheaton, *Elements of International Law* (1836 ed.), pt. 1, sect. 26.

15. Merli, *GB and Confederate Navy*. Russell's dispatch regarding the Italian crisis, Oct. 27, 1860, quoted in Tilby, *Russell*, 185; ibid., 189, 193, 197, 211–13; Russell to Lyons, Apr. 12, 1861, no. 89, Gladstone Papers, Brit. Lib., Add. Mss., 44,593, vol. 508; Dallas to Seward, Apr. 9, 1861, no. 330, *FRUS 1861*, 82. British Conservatives, as one writer demonstrates, did not believe the American Union perpetual. An example was Thomas C. Grattan, the British consul in Boston from 1839 to 1846, who condoned secession as constitutional. See Bellows, "British Conservative Reaction to Civil War," 514.

16. Seward to CFA, Apr. 27, 1861, no. 4, *FRUS 1861*, 83; Palmerston to Queen Victoria, Jan. 1, 1861, in Ridley, *Palmerston*, 548; Russell to Lyons, Jan. 10, 1861, Russell Papers, PRO 30/22/96.

17. Pratt, ed., Russell, *Diary*, pp. vii–ix; Berwanger, ed., Russell, *Diary*, pp. 7–8, 37 (Mar. 25, 1861), 65–66 (Apr. 8), 77 (Apr. 15), 79 (Apr. 16), 90 (Apr. 18), 110 (Apr. 30), 131–32 (May 8), 138 (May 12), 206 (June 18); Seward's statement to William H. Russell, Mar. 26, 1861, in Atkins, *William Howard Russell*, 2:11; CFA, Jr., *Autobiography*, 112.

18. Russell to Lyons, Apr. 6, 1861, Russell Papers, PRO 30/22/96; Russell to Cowley, May 21, 1861, ibid., PRO 30/22/104; Dallas to Seward, May 2, 1861, no. 333, *FRUS 1861*, 84. On May 22, the Union's minister in Paris, William Dayton, wrote Seward after a meeting with Thouvenel, the foreign secretary, six days earlier, "You will not fail to have observed that the action of France and England upon this question of belligerent rights has been upon a mutual understanding and agreement" (Dayton to Seward, May 22, 1861, *BFSP 1860–1861*, 51:85).

19. Palmerston to Russell, May 5, 1861, GC/RU/1138, Palmerston Papers; Palmerston to Edward Ellice (member of Parliament), May 5, 1861, enclosed ibid.; *Times* (London), May 3, 1861, p. 9; *Parl. Debates*, 167:1378–79 (Commons, May 2, 1861).

20. Russell to Lyons, May 6, 1861, no. 121, Gladstone Papers, Brit. Lib.,

Add. Mss., 44,593, vol. 508. Russell was familiar with Vattel's definition of a civil war: "When a party is formed in a state, who no longer obey the sovereign, and are possessed of sufficient strength to oppose him,—or when, in a republic, the nation is divided into two opposite factions, and both sides take up arms,—this is called a *civil war*." According to Vattel, some referred to a civil war as a "just insurrection of the subjects against their sovereign, to distinguish that lawful resistance from *rebellion*, which is an open and unjust resistance." The term *rebellion* was applicable "only to such an insurrection against lawful authority, as is void of all appearance of justice." But when the rebels "have acquired sufficient strength to give [the sovereign] effectual opposition, and to oblige him to carry on the war against them according to the established rules, he must necessarily submit to the use of the term 'civil war'" (Vattel, *Law of Nations*, bk. 3, chap. 18, sect. 292). See also Wheaton, *Elements of International Law* (1836 ed.), pt. 1, sect. 23. For the Anglo-American rapprochement, see Thistlethwaite, *Anglo-American Connection*; Fladeland, *Men and Brothers*; Crook, *North, South, and Powers*, 4–9; Howard Jones, *To the Webster-Ashburton Treaty*; Bourne, *Foreign Policy of Victorian England*, 89. For the importance of wheat to England, see Eaton, *History of Confederacy*, 68–69, and Emory Thomas, *Confederate Nation*, 172. Wheat was important to Anglo-American relations during the war, as the following studies show: Ginzberg, "Economics of British Neutrality"; Robert H. Jones, "Long Live the King?"; and E. D. Adams, *GB and Civil War*, 2:13–14 n. 2.

21. See "British Proclamation for the Observance of Neutrality in the contest between the United States and the Confederate States of America, May 13, 1861," *BFSP 1860–1861*, 51:165–69. France and Spain likewise declared neutrality in June 1861. See Wheaton, *Elements of International Law* (1866 ed.), Dana's notes, 167 n. 84; Sumner quoted and Seward cited in Graebner, "Northern Diplomacy and European Neutrality," 60–61. See also CFA, Jr., "British Proclamation."

22. Lyons to Seward, Apr. 29, 1861, NFBL (NA); Lyons to Russell, May 2, 1861, *BPP: Civil War*, 16:22. Vattel argued that neutral countries were to remain "common friends to both parties" and thus maintain "strict impartiality towards the belligerent powers." In a civil war, he continued, the opposing sides were "two separate bodies, two distinctive societies," who "stand therefore in precisely the same predicament as two nations, who engage in a contest, and, being unable to come to an agreement, have recourse to arms." The "common laws of war" apply to civil wars (Vattel, *Law of Nations*, bk. 3, chap. 7, sects. 103–4; see also ibid., chap. 18, sects. 293–94; Wheaton, *Elements of International Law* (1836 ed.), pt. 1, sects. 23, 26; Bourne, *Foreign Policy of Victorian England*, 92). See also Johnson, "Investment by Sea," 45–46. For an incisive contemporary defense of British neutrality, see Bernard, *Historical Account of Neutrality*, 166–70. Bernard was Chichele Professor of International Law and Diplomacy at Oxford University.

23. "British Proclamation of Neutrality," *BFSP 1860–1861*, 51:165–69.

24. Wheaton, *Elements of International Law* (1836 ed.), pt. 1, sects. 21, 23.

See also Dana's extensive notes, ibid. (1866 ed.), 31 n. 15. Blockades had been implemented as early as the 1720s without recognition of a state of war (Johnson, "Investment by Sea," 46). No evidence suggests that the Lincoln administration was aware of this fact. For the argument that British neutrality worked to the North's advantage, see Baxter, "British Government and Neutral Rights," 29, and his "Some British Opinions," 518.

25. See Claussen, "Peace Factors in Anglo-American Relations," 512; Merli, *GB and Confederate Navy*, 58–59; Spencer, *Confederate Navy in Europe*, 9–10. See also Duberman, *CFA*, 259–60; CFA, Jr., *Before and After Treaty of Washington*, 15–18.

26. Duberman, *CFA*, 261. For Forster's pro-Union stance, see Reid, *Forster*, 1:337–39. For the *Prize Cases*, see *U.S. Supreme Court Reports, 17 Law. Ed.*, 2 Black [U.S. 67], sects. 665–74. See also Bernath, *Squall Across Atlantic*, 25; Kelly, Harbison, and Belz, *American Constitution*, 304; Randall, *Constitutional Problems under Lincoln*, 51 n. 2, 53–54; Merli, "American Way with Blockades."

27. CFA, Jr., *Autobiography*, 107–8, 111–13; E.D. Adams, *GB and Civil War*, 1:111–12; Merli, *GB and Confederate Navy*, 42; Jenkins, *Britain and War for Union*, 1:33.

28. CFA Diary, Mar. 10, 1861; CFA to Russell, Sept. 18, 1865, CFA Letterbook; CFA to Seward, May 17, 1861, ibid.; Russell to Lyons, May 21, 1861, Russell Papers, PRO 30/22/96; Russell to Lord Cowley (British ambassador in Paris), July 13, 1861, ibid., PRO 30/22/104; Jenkins, *Britain and War for Union*, 1:33.

29. Hammond quoted in E.D. Adams, *GB and Civil War*, 2:2; CFA to Seward, May 17, 1861, no. 1, *FRUS 1861*, 85–86; CFA to Seward, May 17, 1861, CFA Letterbook.

30. Seward quoted in Donald, *Sumner and Rights of Man*, 21.

31. *Richmond Whig*, May 18, 1861, quoted in Jenkins, *Britain and War for Union*, 1:109; Seward to CFA, May 21, 1861, no. 10, *FRUS 1861*, 87–90.

32. Yancey quoted in E.D. Adams, *GB and Civil War*, 2:5 n. 3. Numerous times the South naively referred to justice and divine intervention in securing diplomatic recognition instead of seeking a foreign alliance. See Blumenthal, "Confederate Diplomacy," 151–52, 155, 162–64, 169.

33. Russell to Lyons, May 11, 1861, *BFSP 1860–1861*, 51:186–87. Russell met with the Southern commissioners on May 3 and 9.

34. Berwanger, ed., Russell, *Diary*, 126 (May 7, 1861). Benjamin was then attorney general but soon became secretary of state.

35. Yancey and Ambrose D. Mann to Robert Toombs, May 21, 1861, in Richardson, ed., *Messages and Papers of Confederacy*, 2:37. See also Yancey's diary, which is shallow and disappointing, in Hoole, ed., "Notes and Documents."

36. Duberman, *CFA*, 265–66; CFA to Seward, May 17, 21, 1861, CFA Letterbook; CFA Diary, May 18, 1861; CFA to Seward, May 21, 1861, no. 2, *FRUS 1861*, 91.

37. CFA to Seward, May 21, 1861, no. 2, *FRUS 1861*, 91.

38. Russell to Lyons, May 21, 1861, no. 140, Gladstone Papers, Brit. Lib., Add. Mss., 44,593, vol. 508; CFA to Seward, May 21, 1861, no. 2, *FRUS 1861*, 92; CFA to Seward, May 21, 1861, CFA Letterbook. The lord chancellor was Baron Westbury (Richard Bethell).

39. Russell to Lyons, Dec. 19, 1860, Russell Papers, PRO 30/22/96; Clarendon to Secretary for War George Cornewall Lewis, Jan. 24, 1861, Clarendon Papers; Clarendon was George William Frederick Villiers, the Fourth Earl of Clarendon.

40. Lyons to Russell, May 6, 1861, Russell Papers, PRO 30/22/35; Lyons to Russell, May 12, 1861, *BPP: Civil War*, 16:79.

41. Russell to Lyons, May 18, 1861, no. 136, Gladstone Papers, Brit. Lib., Add. Mss., 44,593, vol. 508. For the bases of Russell's observations on international law, see Vattel, *Law of Nations*, bk. 2, chap. 18, sect. 328; ibid., bk. 3, chap. 18, sect. 296; and Wheaton, *Elements of International Law* (1836 ed.), pt. 2, sect. 73.

42. Lyons to Russell, Apr. 27, 1861, Russell Papers, PRO 30/22/35; Berwanger, ed., Russell, *Diary*, 108–9 (Apr. 29, 1861).

43. *Times* (London), Nov. 7, 1861, p. 6.

44. *Economist* (London), May 18, 1861, quoted in E. D. Adams, *GB and Civil War*, 1:174. Charles Francis Adams believed that most English observers considered America's division into two republics an irrevocable fact (CFA Diary, May 26, 1861).

CHAPTER TWO

1. See Vattel, *Law of Nations*; Wheaton, *Elements of International Law* (1836 ed.); Austin, *Province of Jurisprudence Determined*; Bernard, *Historical Account of Neutrality*, 166.

2. Russell to Lyons, May 18, 1861, no. 136, Gladstone Papers, Brit. Lib., Add. Mss., 44,593, vol. 508; Russell to Lyons, May 25, 1861, Russell Papers, PRO 30/22/96; Wheaton, *Elements of International Law* (1866 ed.), Dana's notes, 381–82 n. 173; Case and Spencer, *U.S. and France*, 77–78.

3. Russell to Lyons, July 6, 1861, Russell Papers, PRO 30/22/96; Russell to Lyons, May 18, 1861, no. 136, Gladstone Papers, Brit. Lib., Add. Mss., 44,593, vol. 508.

4. Lyons to Russell, Apr. 27, 1861, Russell Papers, PRO 30/22/35; Russell to Lyons, May 18, 1861, no. 139, Gladstone Papers, Brit. Lib., Add. Mss., 44,593, vol. 508; Case and Spencer, *U.S. and France*, 122.

5. Russell to William Grey (chargé in Paris), June 12, 1861, *BFSP 1864–1865*, 55:555–56; Case and Spencer, *U.S. and France*, 78, 91–92.

6. Grey to Russell, June 14, 1861, *BFSP 1864–1865*, 55:556–57; Case and Spencer, *U.S. and France*, 92–93, 97.

7. Meeting between William H. Russell and Judah P. Benjamin, May 7,

1861, in Berwanger, ed., Russell, *Diary*, 126 (May 7, 1861); CFA to Seward, June 7, 1861, no. 5, *FRUS 1861*, 98–99.

8. CFA to Seward, June 14, 1861, no. 8, *FRUS 1861*, 103–4; CFA Diary, July 13, 1861.

9. Russell to Lyons, June 1, 1861—enclosure: Russell to Lords Commissioners of Admiralty, June 1, 1861, *BPP: Civil War*, 16:80; Lyons to Russell, June 14, 1861, Russell Papers, PRO 30/22/35; CFA to Seward, June 14, 1861, no. 8, *FRUS 1861*, 105.

10. Vattel defined rebellion as "an open and unjust resistance" and civil war as "a just insurrection of the subjects against their sovereign." The Union, not surprisingly, preferred the term *rebellion* in talking about the South's resistance but rejected the precept in international law that a rebellion bestowed belligerent status. See Vattel, *Law of Nations*, bk. 3, chap. 18, sect. 292k; Kelly, Harbison, and Belz, *American Constitution*, 306–7; Randall, *Constitutional Problems under Lincoln*, 60–65.

11. Kelly, Harbison, and Belz, *American Constitution*, 307–8. Justice Robert Grier would proclaim in the *Prize Cases* of March 1863 that a civil war was "never solemnly declared; it becomes such by its accidents—the number, power, and organization of the persons who originate and carry it on. . . . It is not the less a civil war, with belligerent parties in hostile array, because it may be called an 'insurrection' by one side, and the insurgents be considered as rebels and traitors" (*U.S. Supreme Court Reports, 17 Law. Ed.*, 2 Black [U.S. 67], sects. 666–69). See also Randall, *Constitutional Problems under Lincoln*, 53–54, 65–69, 71–73; Bernath, *Squall Across Atlantic*, 29–33.

12. CFA to Seward, May 21, 1861, no. 2, *FRUS 1861*, 92–94. In this same conversation of May 18, Russell recalled that the United States itself had once acted hastily—when Louis Kossuth led an insurrection in Hungary and the administration in Washington, against the Hungarian government's protests, sent an agent authorized to extend recognition. Adams was not persuaded. He thought (correctly) his country's intention regarding Hungary had been only to acquire information and that, once done, it had taken no action toward recognition. Besides, in the Hungarian example, there was strong feeling in the United States for the insurgents. "Are we therefore to infer a similar impulse to actuate the precipitate measure now taken here?" (ibid).

13. Ibid., 93–95.

14. Ibid.

15. "Act passed by the Confederate Congress, prohibiting the Exportation of Cotton except through Southern Seaports, May 21, 1861," quoted *BFSP 1860–1861*, 51:200; Bourne, *Foreign Policy of Victorian England*, 90; Crook, *North, South, and Powers*, 20.

16. CFA to Seward, June 14, 1861, no. 8, *FRUS 1861*, 104–5.

17. Lyons to Russell, May 6, June 10, 1861, Russell Papers, PRO 30/22/35; Russell's comments on need for strengthening British North America, May 21, 1861, ibid., PRO 30/22/35; Palmerston's comments on same,

May 23, 1861, ibid.; Bourne, *Britain and Balance of Power*, 212–15; CFA to Seward, June 14, 1861, no. 8, *FRUS 1861*, 105; Seward to CFA, July 1, 1861, no. 32, ibid., 111; CFA to Seward, June 28, 1861, CFA Letterbook.

18. Lyons to Russell, June 14, 1861, Russell Papers, PRO 30/22/35; Russell to Lyons, June 21, 1861, no. 185, Gladstone Papers, Brit. Lib., Add. Mss., 44,593, vol. 508; Russell to Lyons, July 19, 1861, *BFSP 1860–1861*, 51:205–11. The Union had seized the *Tropic Wind* for violating the blockade in Richmond. The decision came on June 13, 1861. For the case, see 28 Federal Cases 218–22 (case no. 16,541a). Dunlop cited Story's decision of 1822 in the case *The Santissima Trinidad and the St. Ander*, found in *U.S. Supreme Court Reports, 5 Law. Ed.*, 7 Wheaton [U.S. 20], sects. 337–38. Russell often used history to substantiate his position. See Fitzmaurice, *Granville*, 1:441.

19. Lincoln's quote in Wheaton, *Elements of International Law* (1866 ed.), 570 n. 235; Lyons to Russell, May 2, 1861, *BPP: Civil War*, 16:23; Lyons to Russell, May 4, 1861, *BFSP 1864–1865*, 55:664; Lyons to Russell, May 25, 1861, ibid., 670–71; Lyons to Seward, May 11, 1861, NFBL (NA); Seward to CFA, May 21, 1861, no. 10, *FRUS 1861*, 89; CFA to Seward, May 21, 1861, no. 2, ibid., 95. The question of the blockade's effectiveness remains the subject of debate. For a recent account that highlights the South's successes in running the Union blockade, see Wise, *Lifeline of Confederacy*. Especially vital in assessing the impact of the blockade, according to historian James M. McPherson, is the question of how many more vessels would have aided the Confederacy had not the Union navy patrolled the Southern coasts. See his magisterial study, *Battle Cry of Freedom*, 381–82. For the argument that the blockade played no significant role, see Beringer, Hattaway, Jones, and Still, *Why the South Lost the Civil War*, 56, 63.

20. Wallace and Gillespie, eds., *Journal of Moran*, 2:820 (May 28, 1861); CFA Diary, May 27, 1861; *Parl. Debates*, 168:134 (Commons, May 27, 1861); CFA to Seward, May 31, 1861, no. 4, *FRUS 1861*, 96; Russell quoted in Tilby, *Russell*, 196–97.

21. Seward to CFA, June 8, 1861, no. 15, *FRUS 1861*, 102–3. On the port closings issue, see Brauer, "Seward's 'Foreign War Panacea,'" 147–48. For the relevant constitutional provision, see art. I, sect. 9. As will become clear in this chapter, the Palmerston ministry considered port closings to be unconstitutional.

22. Lyons to Russell, Apr. 15, June 14, 24, 1861, Russell Papers, PRO 30/22/35; Russell to Lyons, July 6, 1861, *BPP: Civil War*, 16:89.

23. Bernath, *Squall Across Atlantic*, 12; *Charleston Mercury*, June 4, 1861, quoted in Owsley, *King Cotton Diplomacy*, 24; Berwanger, ed., Russell, *Diary*, 79, 82 (both Apr. 16, 1861), 92 (Apr. 18), 95 (Apr. 20), 107 (Apr. 28), 112 (May 2), 130 (May 7).

24. Russell to Lyons, June 27, 1861, Russell Papers, PRO 30/22/96; Berwanger, ed., Russell, *Diary*, 218–19 (June 25–30, 1861). Confederate commanders continued to raid commerce vessels but now, denied access

to British prize courts, they simply threw captured goods overboard. See Wheaton, *Elements of International Law* (1866 ed.), pt. 4, sect. 521, and Dana's notes, 30–31 n. 15.

25. Palmerston to Russell, Dec. 11, 30, 1860, Russell Papers, PRO 30/22/21; CFA to Seward, June 14, 1861, no. 8, *FRUS 1861*, 106; Russell to Lyons, June 21, 1861, no. 185, Gladstone Papers, Brit. Lib., Add. Mss., 44,593, vol. 508; Russell to Lyons, July 19, 1861, *BPP: Civil War*, 16:91–92. For *Tropic Wind*, see 28 Federal Cases 218–22. The *Prize Cases* of 1863 confirmed Dunlop's decision in the *Tropic Wind* by declaring the blockade proclamation a belligerent act of war and finding no distinction between a civil war and a public (foreign) war. For *Prize Cases*, see *U.S. Supreme Court Reports, 17 Law. Ed.*, 2 Black [U.S. 67]. sects. 635–99.

26. Seward to CFA, June 3, 1861, no. 14, *FRUS 1861*, 97–98; Seward to CFA, June 8, 1861, no. 15, ibid., 100–101; Sumner to Duchess of Argyll, June 4, 1861, in Palmer, ed., *Letters of Sumner*, 2:69.

27. For this meeting, see Frederick Seward, *Reminiscences*, 179–80; quotations in the following paragraphs are from this source. See also Lyons to Russell, June 17, 1861, *BFSP 1864–1865*, 55:558–61; Case and Spencer, *U.S. and France*, 69–71; Blumenthal, *Reappraisal of Franco-American Relations*, 127.

28. Seward to CFA, June 19, 1861, no. 21, *FRUS 1861*, 106–9; Seward quote to Lyons in Carroll, *Mercier and Civil War*, 78–79.

29. Seward to CFA, June 19, 1861, no. 21, *FRUS 1861*, 107, 109; Seward to CFA, July 1, 1861, no. 32, ibid., 112; Berwanger, ed., Russell, *Diary*, 227–28 (July 4, 1861); Seward to CFA, July 21, 1861, no. 42, *FRUS 1861*, 117–21.

30. Russell to Cowley, June 12, July 13, 1861, Russell Papers, PRO 30/22/104.

31. CFA to Seward, Aug. 16, 1861, no. 29, *FRUS 1861*, 128. See also CFA to CFA, Jr., July 18, 1861, in Ford, ed., *Adams Letters*, 1:19–20.

32. CFA to Seward, June 21, 1861, CFA Letterbook; Henry Adams to CFA, Jr., June 10, 1861, in Levenson et al., eds., *Letters of Henry Adams*, 1:238. For Henry Adams's account of his stay in England, see his *Education of Henry Adams*, chaps. 8–10.

33. Henry Adams to CFA, Jr., July 4, 1861, in Levenson et al., eds., *Letters of Henry Adams*, 1:243; CFA to Seward, June 21, 1861, CFA Letterbook; William H. Russell to Lyons, May 21, 1861, Russell Papers, PRO 30/22/35; Yancey and Root to Toombs, June 10, 1861, *ORN*, 2d ser., 3:221; Bourne, *Foreign Policy of Victorian England*, 95; Bourne, *Britain and Balance of Power*, 210–93.

34. Wheaton, *Elements of International Law* (1866 ed.), Dana's notes, 575 n. 239; Seward to CFA, July 21, 1861, no. 42, *FRUS 1861*, 120–21; Lyons to Russell, July 8, 19, 20, Aug. 23, 1861, Russell Papers, PRO 30/22/35; Russell to Lyons, July 6, 1861, ibid., PRO 30/22/96; Lyons to Russell,

July 12, 1861, *BPP: Civil War*, 16:97–98; Pease and Randall, eds., *Diary of Browning*, 1:489 (July 28, 1861).

35. CFA to Richard Henry Dana, Jr., June 14, 1861, CFA Letterbook; CFA to Everett, July 26, 1861, ibid.; CFA Diary, July 25, 1861; CFA to Seward, June 21, 1861, no. 9, *FRUS 1861*, 109–10; CFA to Seward, June 28, 1861, no. 10, ibid., 110–11. Among numerous writers who insist that no chance ever existed for British intervention because it was never in England's interest to do so, see Beloff, "Historical Revision no. CXVIII," 43. Henry Blumenthal argues that the South failed to realize that Europe would act only out of self-interest ("Confederate Diplomacy," 170). For the role of commerce in discouraging British involvement, see Claussen, "Peace Factors in Anglo-American Relations," 516, 522.

36. Lyons to Russell, July 8, 1861, *BPP: Civil War*, 16:96.

CHAPTER THREE

1. McPherson, *Battle Cry of Freedom*, 334–47; Catton, *Coming Fury*, 439–69. For contemporary British interest in recognition of the Confederacy, see Argyll, ed., *Argyll, Autobiography and Memoirs*, 2:171.

2. Duberman, *CFA*, 272; Lyons to Russell, July 22, 1861, *BPP: Civil War*, 16:102–3; Palmerston quoted in Ridley, *Palmerston*, 551; Bell, *Palmerston*, 2:292; minutes of Palmerston, Aug. 15, 1861, in Newton, *Lyons*, 1:48.

3. Russell to Lyons, Aug. 16, 1861, quoted in E. D. Adams, *GB and Civil War*, 1:179 n. 1; CFA to Richard Henry Dana, Jr., Aug. 28, 1861, CFA Letterbook; CFA Diary, Aug. 6, Sept. 10, 1861.

4. Berwanger, ed., Russell, *Diary*, 279 (July 22, 1861), 282 (July 23), 304 (Aug. 31); *Times* (London), Aug. 20, p. 7, Aug. 24, 1861, p. 10; E. D. Adams, *GB and Civil War* 1:177–78; *New York Herald*, July 22, 26, 1861, quoted ibid., 178 n. 2.

5. William L. Yancey, Pierre A. Rost, and Ambrose D. Mann to Russell, Aug. 14, 1861, *BFSP 1860–1861*, 51:219–28.

6. Russell to Yancey, Rost, and Mann, Aug. 24, 1861, *ORN*, 2d ser., 3:248.

7. Henry Adams to CFA, Jr., Aug. 26, 1861, in Ford, ed., *Adams Letters*, 1:26; CFA, Jr., to Henry Adams, Aug. 25, 1861, ibid., 33, 36; Beale, ed., *Diary of Bates*, 190 (Aug. 27, 1861); Seward to CFA, no. 74, Aug. 27, 1861, *FRUS 1861*, 134–35.

8. Lyons to Russell, July 30, 1861, Russell Papers, PRO 30/22/35. Seward also apologized to Lyons for the delay in sending Adams the administration's views. Because of work demands, he explained, the White House had been "unable to keep abreast of foreign questions or of their impact & relationship to domestic events" (ibid).

9. Russell to Lyons, Aug. 8, 1861, *BFSP 1860–1861*, 51:217–18; Russell

memo of July 30, 1861, Russell Papers, PRO 30/22/27; Russell to Cowley, July 31, 1861, ibid., PRO 30/22/104.

10. Russell to Lyons, Aug. 16, 24, 1861, Russell Papers, PRO 30/22/96; Westbury to Russell, June [?] 1861, ibid., PRO 30/22/27. On Westbury's attitude, see Tilby, *Russell*, 219–20, 224.

11. Lyons to Russell, Aug. 16, 23, 30, 1861, Russell Papers, PRO 30/22/35.

12. Seward to CFA, Aug. 17, 1861, no. 63, *FRUS 1861*, 131. See also Ferris, *Desperate Diplomacy*, 99–116; E. D. Adams, *GB and Civil War*, 1:184–96; Jenkins, *Britain and War for Union*, 1:136–39, 157; Case and Spencer, *U.S. and France*, 116–17.

13. Seward to CFA, Aug. 17, 1861, no. 63, *FRUS 1861*, 131–32. Seward also argued that consuls did not have the authority to issue passports—that this was a diplomatic function. Foreign consuls in the United States once had the power to grant passports. But after the insurrection broke out, the State Department notified the British consul in Charleston that the United States would no longer honor a diplomatic or consular passport that allowed the bearer to move through national lines or out of the United States unless that passport bore the counter signatures of the secretary of state and the U.S. Army's commanding general (ibid., 131).

14. Ibid., 132–33; Seward to CFA, Aug. 17, 1861, no. 64, ibid., 133; CFA Diary, Sept. 2, 1861.

15. CFA to Seward, Sept. 9, 1861, no. 41, *FRUS 1861*, 149–50; CFA to Russell, Sept. 3, 1861, enclosed ibid., 151–53; CFA to Seward, Sept. 14, 1861, no. 44, ibid., 155–57; Case and Spencer, *U.S. and France*, 117–18. Russell's refusal to recall Bunch caused some to believe that the Union would send Lyons home (Bell, *Palmerston*, 2:293). Palmerston thought that Lyons should relocate in Canada until Seward calmed down (ibid.). See also Palmerston to Russell, Sept. 9, 1861, Russell Papers, PRO 30/22/31.

16. Bunch to Lyons, Sept. 30, 1861, enclosed in Lyons to Russell, Oct. 8, 1861, *BPP: Civil War*, 16:626–27; Russell to Lyons, Oct. 26, 1861, ibid., 627; Bunch to Lyons, Oct. 31, 1861, enclosed in Lyons to Russell, Nov. 14, 1861, ibid., 633–34; Gladstone to Lewis, Sept. 21, 1861, Gladstone Papers, Brit. Lib., Add. Mss., 44,236, vol. 151.

17. Lyons to Russell, Sept. 24, 1861, Russell Papers, PRO 30/22/35.

18. Seward to CFA, Oct. 22, 1861, no. 108, *FRUS 1861*, 163; Seward to CFA, Oct. 23, 1861, no. 109, ibid., 165–66. Russell had learned of the revocation of the exequatur before Charles Francis Adams, resulting in his having to admit to Russell, when asked, that he did not know about it (CFA Diary, Nov. 12, 1861). Bunch did not leave Charleston until February 1863 (Case and Spencer, *U.S. and France*, 117).

19. CFA to Russell, Nov. 29, 1861, enclosed in CFA to Seward, Nov. 29, 1861, no. 81, and CFA to Russell, Nov. 21, 1861, enclosed in CFA to Seward, Nov. 22, 1861, no. 74, all in *FRUS 1861*, 3–5; Russell to CFA, Nov. 26,

1861, enclosed in CFA to Seward, Nov. 29, 1861, no. 81, ibid., 6–9.

20. Case and Spencer, *U.S. and France*, 115. The *Baltimore Sun* declared that "the Confederate Congress has accepted by resolution the Clauses II, III, and IV of the Declaration of Paris" (Aug 16, 1861, quoted in Lyons to Russell, Aug. 16, 1861, *BFSP 1864–1865*, 55:579). The *Charleston Mercury* reported the adoption (cited in Lyons to Russell, Aug. 23, 1861, ibid., 579–80).

21. CFA to Russell, Aug. 23, 1861, *BFSP 1864–1865*, 55:571–76; CFA to Seward, Aug. 30, 1861, no. 34, *FRUS 1861*, 135, 138–39.

22. Seward to CFA, Sept. 7, 1861, no. 83, *FRUS 1861*, 141–42; Russell to CFA, Aug. 28, 1861, *BFSP 1864–1865*, 55:576–79, also enclosed in CFA to Seward, Sept. 7, 1861, no. 39, *FRUS 1861*, 145–46.

23. See, for example, Vattel, *Law of Nations*, bk. 3, chap. 7, sects. 103–5; Wheaton, *Elements of International Law* (1836 ed.), pt. 4, sect. 414.

24. CFA to Russell, Aug. 15, 1861, *BFSP 1860–1861*, 51:229–30; CFA to Russell, Oct. 1, 1861, ibid., 237; Ferris, *Desperate Diplomacy*, 172–73. For Hotze's mission, see Secretary of State Robert Hunter to Hotze, Nov. 14, 1861, in Richardson, ed., *Messages and Papers of Confederacy*, 2:115–16, and James Mason (Confederate minister to London) to Hotze, Jan. 16, 1863, *ORN*, 2d ser., 3:659. The full title of Hotze's journal was the *Index: A Weekly Journal of Politics, Literature, and News*. See Eaton, *History of Confederacy*, 72–73, and Emory Thomas, *Confederate Nation*, 177–78. For a study that attempts to establish Hotze's impact on British leaders, see Cullop, *Confederate Propaganda in Europe*. Lyons's protests against the Union's arbitrary arrests of British subjects and the suspension of habeas corpus drew only Seward's reply that the president was defending the Constitution against treason and could take whatever measures he deemed necessary to protect the "public safety" (Lyons to Seward, Oct. 14, 1861, *BFSP 1860–1861*, 51:241–42; Seward to Lyons, Oct. 14, 1861, ibid., 243–47).

25. Reference to Russell's letter to Everett of July 12, 1861, found in Everett's reply to Russell, Aug. 19, 1861, Russell Papers, PRO 30/22/39. For characterizations of Russell, see miscellaneous draft in unidentified hand and undated, Russell Papers, PRO 30/22/118A, and Tilby, *Russell*, 50. For his hatred of slavery, see ibid., 197, and Russell to Cowley, Apr. 15, 1865, Russell Papers, PRO 30/22/106.

26. Everett to Russell, Aug. 19, 1861, Russell Papers, PRO 30/22/39.

27. Ibid.

28. Argyll to Russell, Sept. 11, 1861, ibid., PRO 30/22/25; Forster to Austen Henry Layard (under secretary), Sept. 11, 1861, Layard Papers, Brit. Lib., Add. Mss., 39,101, vol. 171; Reid, *Forster*, 1:289–92, 337–39; Ferris, *Desperate Diplomacy*, 41. Argyll was George John Douglas Campbell.

29. Russell to Cowley, Sept. 24, 1861, Russell Papers, PRO 30/22/104; Bourne, *Foreign Policy of Victorian England*, 96.

30. Berwanger, ed., Russell, *Diary*, 290 (Aug. 2, 3, 1861), 292 (Aug. 6); Lyons to Russell, Oct. 4, 1861, Russell Papers, PRO 30/22/35. For a sum-

mation of the tour, see Carroll, *Mercier and Civil War*, 86–90.

31. Mercier's views summarized in Lyons to Russell, Oct. 4, 1861, Russell Papers, PRO 30/22/35.

32. Ibid. Lyons was unable to determine British needs at the time, but he had discerned great alarm in England. On the contrary, British attention seemed to have turned to alternative sources of cotton. It was wise to endure the problem as temporary so as to become less dependent on only one country (ibid.). For the cotton interests of England and France, see Duberman, *CFA*, 277; Case and Spencer, *U.S. and France*, 127, 374–75; Blumenthal, *Reappraisal of Franco-American Relations*, 154–55.

33. Lyons to Russell, Oct. 4, 1861, Russell Papers, PRO 30/22/35.

34. Ibid. Lyons also feared for personal freedoms. "The progress towards Despotism and Anarchy," he argued, "is already frightfully rapid." According to Lyons, the Union commander in Missouri, John C. Frémont, was a potential military despot (Lyons to Russell, Sept. 6, Oct. 4, 1861, Russell Papers, PRO 30/22/35). Lyons later said that Mercier's recommendations were "too high" for Lyons to deal with. "They depend upon the extent of the need for cotton in England, on the relations between England and France, on public opinion in the two countries, and other matters which lie out of the range of my information" (Lyons to Russell, Oct. 28, 1861, ibid.).

35. Palmerston to Russell, Oct. 18, 1861, GC/RU/1139/1–2, Palmerston Papers; Palmerston to Russell, Oct. 6, 1861, Russell Papers, PRO 30/22/21.

36. Palmerston to Russell, Oct. 18, 1861, GC/RU/1139/1–2, Palmerston Papers; Palmerston to Layard, Oct. 20, 1861, Layard Papers, Brit. Lib., Add. Mss., 38,987, vol. 57.

37. Hanna and Hanna, *Napoleon III and Mexico*, 38–39; Schoonover, *Dollars over Dominion*, 56–58; Blumenthal, *Reappraisal of Franco-American Relations*, 152–53; Ferris, *Desperate Diplomacy*, 162; CFA Diary, Sept. 12, 1861; CFA to Seward, Sept. 28, 1861, CFA Letterbook. The U.S. Senate later rejected the loan proposal.

38. Russell to Queen Victoria, Sept. 27, 1861, in Gooch, ed., *Later Correspondence of John Russell*, 2:320–21. See also Russell to Cowley, Sept. 27, 1861, *BFSP 1861–1862*, 52:329–30; Lewis to Gladstone, Oct. 5, 1861, Gladstone Papers, Brit. Lib., Add. Mss., 44,236, vol. 151; Clarendon to Lewis, Oct. 4, 1861, in Maxwell, *Clarendon*, 2:240; Blumenthal, *Reappraisal of Franco-American Relations*, 167.

39. Quote from three European governments in Ferris, *Desperate Diplomacy*, 167. See also ibid., 154–70; Hanna and Hanna, *Napoleon III and Mexico*, 39–40; Schoonover, *Dollars over Dominion*, 145–46; Blumenthal, *Reappraisal of Franco-American Relations*, 169; Van Deusen, *William H. Seward*, 365–70. For an exhaustive treatment, see Bock, *Prelude to Tragedy*.

40. CFA to CFA, Jr., Sept. 20, 1861, in Ford, ed., *Adams Letters*, 1:48; Henry Adams to CFA, Jr., Oct. 25, 1861, ibid., 61–62; Henry Adams to CFA, Jr., Nov. 7, 1861, in Levenson et al., eds., *Letters of Henry Adams*, 1:262.

41. Russell to Lyons, Nov. 2, 1861, Russell Papers, PRO 30/22/96; Bel-

lows, "British Conservative Reaction to Civil War," 512–13, 522. Cecil thought that an independent South would come under world pressure to end slavery. See Lorimer, "Role of Anti-Slavery Sentiment in English Reactions to Civil War," 409. See also ibid., 407, 420.

CHAPTER FOUR

1. Among many accounts of the *Trent* affair, see Warren, *Fountain of Discontent*; Ferris, *Trent Affair*; Crook, *North, South, and Powers*, 99–170; Bourne, *Britain and Balance of Power*, 218–47; and Rawley, *Turning Points of Civil War*, 71–95. See also Mason's account in Mason, *James Mason*, 209–46. For Mason's instructions, see Secretary of State Robert Hunter to Mason, Sept. 23, 1861, *ORN*, 2d ser., 3:257–64. For Slidell's, see Hunter to Slidell, Sept. 23, 1861, ibid., 265–73. Wilkes, sixty-two years of age, had served the navy for forty years as explorer and scientist with what he considered poorly recognized distinction. Having been turned down for battle service in the Mexican War, he intended to exploit this second chance for military glory. See Long, "Glory-Hunting off Havana," 133.

2. Warren, *Fountain of Discontent*, 26–35; CFA, Jr., *Autobiography*, 128; CFA, Jr., "Crisis of Foreign Intervention," 3–5; Berwanger, ed., Russell, *Diary*, 164–65 (May 24, 1861); William H. Russell quoted in *Times* (London), Dec. 10, 1861, p. 9. The Kansas-Nebraska Act of 1854 had heightened the American arguments over slavery by introducing the principle of popular sovereignty into an area that had been closed to slavery by the Missouri Compromise of 1820. The new law allowed the people in the area to determine the question.

3. CFA, Jr., *Autobiography*, 127; CFA, Jr., to CFA, Nov. 19, 1861, in Ford, ed., *Adams Letters*, 1:71; Mason, *James Mason*, 216–17; Long, "Glory-Hunting off Havana," 138; Warren, *Fountain of Discontent*, 14–15.

4. American quoted in E. D. Adams, *GB and Civil War*, 1:217; CFA to Seward, Nov. 29, 1861, no. 81, *FRUS 1862*, 6–7; Wallace and Gillespie, eds., *Journal of Moran*, 2:914 (Nov. 27, 1861), 915 (Nov. 28, 1861); CFA Diary, Nov. 29, 30, 1861; Henry Adams to CFA, Jr., Nov. 30, 1861, in Levenson et al., eds., *Letters of Henry Adams*, 1:263–64; CFA, Jr., to CFA, Nov. 10, 1861, in Ford, ed., *Adams Letters*, 1:70.

5. Palmerston to Queen Victoria, Nov. 29, 1861, in Benson and Esher, eds., *Letters of Victoria*, 3:469; Palmerston to Russell, Nov. 29, 1861 (2 letters), Russell Papers, PRO 30/22/21; Westbury to Russell, Nov. 30, 1861, ibid., PRO 30/22/25; Russell, *Recollections and Suggestions*, 275; Argyll to Gladstone, Nov. 29, 1861, Gladstone Papers, Brit. Lib., Add. Mss., 44,099, vol. 14; Crook, *North, South, and Powers*, 125. Clarendon used the same words as had Palmerston—"deliberate and premeditated insult"—in writing the British ambassador in Paris, Lord Cowley, about the *Trent*. See Clarendon to Cowley, Nov. [?], 1861, in Wellesley, ed., *Secrets of Second Empire*, 223.

Russell later thanked Clarendon for his support in the crisis. See Russell to Clarendon, Dec. 6, 1861, in Gooch, ed., *Later Correspondence of John Russell*, 2:321.

6. Palmerston (in cabinet meeting) quoted in Warren, *Fountain of Discontent*, 109; ibid., 112–14, 116–17, 123; Crook, *North, South, and Powers*, 133; Jenkins, *Britain and War for Union*, 1:211; Russell to Lyons, Nov. 30, 1861 (no. 2), *BPP: Civil War*, 16:646–47; Russell to Lyons, Nov. 30, 1861 (no. 4), ibid., 647; Palmerston to Russell, Dec. 6, 1861, Russell Papers, PRO 30/22/21; Russell to Lyons, Dec. 7, 1861, ibid., PRO 30/22/96; "British Proclamation, prohibiting the Export of Gunpowder, Saltpetre, Nitrate of Soda, and Brimstone," Nov. 29, 1861, *BFSP 1860–1861*, 51:170; Ferris, *Trent Affair*, 62; Bell, *Palmerston*, 2:294–95. If Palmerston's declaration was "probably apocryphal," as Kenneth Bourne maintains, the atmosphere in London was tense enough to foster such a comment. See Bourne, "British Preparations for War with North," 606.

7. Hunter to Yancey, Rost, and Mann, Nov. 20, 1861, *ORN*, 2d ser., 3:297; Yancey, Rost, and Mann to Hunter, Dec. 2, 1861, ibid., 306; Mann to Hunter, Dec. 2, 1861, ibid., 307; Yancey, Rost, and Mann to Russell, Nov. 27, 1861, enclosed in Russell to Lyons, Dec. 7, 1861, FO 115/250, PRO.

8. Palmerston to Earl de Grey (under secretary for war), Nov. 11, 1861, Ripon Papers (Grey, or George Frederick Samuel Robinson), Brit. Lib., Add. Mss., 43,512, vol. 22; Lindsay to Layard, Dec. 10, 1861, ibid.; *Bee-Hive*, Nov. 23, Dec. 7, 1861, quoted in Foner, *British Labor and Civil War*, 29; Bourne, "British Preparations for War with North," 600–632. The editor of the *Bee-Hive* was George Troup, who, like many Englishmen, called for peaceful separation of the South. The journal was the official spokesman of the London Trades Council, although it did not necessarily reflect the views of all workers. Since most of the journal's supporters were outside Lancashire's mill districts, they were not economically involved in the American conflict and could look at it in a more detached way. They wanted the war to end, no matter which side won, so the cotton flow could resume. In January 1863 the *Bee-Hive*'s board of directors replaced Troup with Robert Hartwell, who was more attuned to the workers. From then on, the paper was pro-North. See Kevin Logan, "*Bee-Hive* Newspaper and British Working Class Attitudes toward Civil War." Lindsay worked with Napoleon in planning the French Compagnie Generale Transatlantique to connect France with either Norfolk, Virginia, or New Orleans. See Mason to Secretary of State Judah P. Benjamin, Nov. 4, 1862, *ORN*, 2d ser., 3:591–93; enclosure: Lindsay to Mason, Nov. 3, 1862, ibid., 593–95.

9. Lyons to Russell, Nov. 24, 1861, Russell Papers, PRO 30/22/36; Lyons to Russell, Nov. 29, 1861, ibid., PRO 30/22/14C; Newton, *Lyons*, 1:59. For Russian ties with the Union, see Saul, *Distant Friends*, 320–26.

10. Cowley to Russell, Dec. 3, 1861, FO 115/250, PRO; Lyons to Russell, Dec. 23, 1861, Russell Papers, PRO 30/22/14C; Russell to Cowley, Dec. 4, 7, 1861, ibid., PRO 30/22/104.

11. Crook, *North, South, and Powers*, 128–29; Warren, *Fountain of Discontent*, 154–55; Case and Spencer, *U.S. and France*, 199–201; Carroll, *Mercier and Civil War*, 105–18; Bourne, "British Preparations for War with North," 631.

12. Doyle to Cowley, Dec. 3, 1861, enclosed in Cowley to Russell, Dec. 3, 1861, FO 115/250, PRO; Russell to Cowley, Dec. 5, 9, 11, 16, 1861, Russell Papers, PRO 30/22/104; Russell to Gladstone, Oct. 13 [Dec.], 1861, Gladstone Papers, Brit. Lib., Add. Mss., 44,292, vol. 207; Russell to Clarendon, Dec. 9, 1861, in Gooch, ed., *Later Correspondence of John Russell*, 2:321. See also Ferris, *Trent Affair*, 83. Scott was the veteran military leader of the American war with Mexico in 1848 and the formulator of the Union's military strategy in the Civil War.

13. Pease and Randall, eds., *Diary of Browning*, 1:515 (Dec. 15, 1861); *Congressional Globe*, 37th Cong., 2d sess., 101 (House, Dec. 16, 1861), 119–22 (House, Dec. 17, 1861); Berwanger, ed., Russell, *Diary*, 331 (Dec. 16, 1861); Warren, *Fountain of Discontent*, 174–75.

14. CFA, Jr., to Henry Adams, Dec. 10, 1861, in Ford, ed., *Adams Letters*, 1:79, 81; Henry Adams to CFA, Jr., Dec. 13, 1861, in Levenson et al., eds., *Letters of Henry Adams*, 1:265–66; CFA to Seward, Dec. 11, 1861, no. 85, CFA Letterbook; Duberman, *CFA*, 280–81. In his dispatch to Seward of December 11, Adams reminded Seward that he had also been slow to send information regarding the Bunch affair, thereby giving the Palmerston ministry an advantage in the discussions.

15. CFA to Seward, Dec. 12, 1861, no. 88, CFA Letterbook; CFA to CFA, Jr., Dec. 20, 1861, in Ford, ed., *Adams Letters*, 1:88; Duberman, *CFA*, 281. See Seward to CFA, Nov. 30, 1861, no. 136, Disp., GB (NA).

16. CFA to CFA, Jr., Dec. 20, 1861, in Ford, ed., *Adams Letters*, 1:88–89. Russell had been an earl since July 1861.

17. Silver, ed., "Henry Adams' 'Diary of Visit to Manchester'"; Rost to Davis, Dec. 24, 1861, *ORN*, 2d ser., 3:311–12; Mann to Davis, Jan. 18, 1862, ibid., 318; Cobden to Bright, Dec. 7, 18, 1861, Cobden Papers, Brit. Lib., Add. Mss., 43,651, vol. 5; Bright to Cobden, Nov. 16, 1861, Jan. 10, 1862, Bright Papers, Brit. Lib., Add. Mss., 43,384, vol. 2; J. M. Mackay (businessman) to Layard, Dec. 9, 1861, Layard Papers, Brit. Lib., Add. Mss., 39,102, vol. 172; Jenkins, *Britain and War for Union*, 1:205; Carroll, *Mercier and Civil War*, 134–35.

18. Lyons to Russell, Nov. 29, 1861, *BPP: Civil War*, 16:155; Russell to Lyons, Dec. 20, 1861, ibid., 156; Lyons to Russell, Jan. 14, 1862, ibid., 179–80. For the legality of the stone fleet, see Wheaton, *Elements of International Law* (1866 ed.), Dana's notes, 360–61 n. 166.

19. Pease and Randall, eds., *Diary of Browning*, 1:516 (Dec. 21, 1861); Lyons to Russell, Dec. 23, 1861, Russell Papers, PRO 30/22/14C; Parish, *Civil War*, 412.

20. Warren, *Fountain of Discontent*, 148, 151–63, 167, 179, 181–82; Lincoln quote on "white elephants," ibid., 38; Cohen, "Sumner and *Trent* Affair";

Ferris, *Trent Affair*, 76, 78–79; Parish, *Civil War*, 412; Sumner to Bright, Dec. 23, 1861, in Palmer, ed., *Letters of Sumner*, 2:85–87; Sumner to Francis Lieber (lawyer and friend), Dec. 24, 1861, ibid., 88–89; Sumner to Seward, ca. Dec. 24, 1861, ibid., 90; Sumner to Bright, Dec. 27, 1861, ibid., 91; Sumner to Cobden, Dec. 31, 1861, ibid., 92–94; ibid., 87 n. 2, 90 n. l; Pease and Randall, eds., *Diary of Browning*, 1:518–19 (Dec. 25, 1861); Lincoln quote to Seward in William H. Seward, *Autobiography*, 3:26.

21. William H. Seward, *Autobiography*, 1:52, and 2:586; Seward to Lyons, Dec. 26, 1861, NTFL, GB (NA); Lyons to Seward, Dec. 27, 1861, NFBL (NA); Pease and Randall, eds., *Diary of Browning*, 1:519 (Dec. 27, 1861); E. D. Adams, *GB and Civil War*, 1:232–33; Warren, *Fountain of Discontent*, 183–84; Crook, *North, South, and Powers*, 161.

22. Moran Diary, Jan. 3, 1862; CFA to Seward, Dec. 27, 1861, no. 95, *FRUS 1862*, 12–13; CFA to CFA, Jr., Dec. 27, 1861, in Ford, ed., *Adams Letters*, 1:91–92; Memorials from Canada, Nova Scotia, and New Brunswick to Newcastle, Dec. 2, 1861, *BPP: Papers Relating to Canada, 1861–63*, 24:293–307; Warren, *Fountain of Discontent*, 123; Ferris, *Trent Affair*, 65.

23. CFA to Seward, Dec. 27, 1861, no. 95, *FRUS 1862*, 13–14; Henry Adams to CFA, Jr., Dec. 28, 1861, in Levenson et al., eds., *Letters of Henry Adams*, 1:267.

24. Argyll to Gladstone, Dec. 30, 1861, Jan. 1, 1862, Gladstone Papers, Brit. Lib., Add. Mss., 44,099, vol. 14; Lewis to Grey, Jan. [?] 1862, Ripon Papers, Brit. Lib., Add. Mss., 43,533, vol. 43; Russell to Cowley, Jan. 1, 2, 1862, Russell Papers, PRO 30/22/105.

25. Cobden to Bright, Jan. 1, 7, 10, 14, 29, 1862, Cobden Papers, Brit. Lib., Add. Mss., 43,652, 6; Merli, *GB and Confederate Navy*, 23; Eaton, *History of Confederacy*, 78. See also Burn, *Age of Equipoise*.

26. Bright to Cobden, Jan. 6, 9, 13, 1862, Bright Papers, Brit. Lib., Add. Mss., 43,384, vol. 2; Cobden to Bright, Jan. 8, 1862, Cobden Papers, Brit. Lib., Add. Mss., 43,652, vol. 6; Jenkins, *Britain and War for Union*, 1:243.

27. Cobden to Bright, Jan. 23, 1862, Cobden Papers, Brit. Lib., Add. Mss., 43,652, vol. 6; Bernath, *Squall Across Atlantic*, 11; Merli, "American Way with Blockades"; Crook, "Portents of War," 175.

28. CFA to Seward, Jan. 17, 1862, no. 102, *FRUS 1862*, 14–15; Moran Diary, Jan. 16, 1862; Henry Adams to CFA, Jr., Jan. 22, 1862, in Levenson et al., eds., *Letters of Henry Adams*, 1:271; Lewis to Grey, Jan. 22, 1862, Ripon Papers, Brit. Lib., Add. Mss., 43,533, vol. 43; Lyons to Russell, Jan. 3, 1862, Russell Papers, PRO 30/22/36; Russell to Lyons, Jan. 11, 1862, ibid., PRO 30/22/96; Russell to Lyons, Jan. 10, 1862, *BPP: Civil War*, 16:671–72; Palmerston to Gladstone, Jan. 9, 1862, Gladstone Papers, Brit. Lib., Add. Mss., 44,272, vol. 187; Russell to Gladstone, Jan. 26, 1862, ibid., 44,292, vol. 207; Lady John Russell to Lady Dunfermline, Jan. 13, 1862, in MacCarthy and Russell, eds., *Lady John Russell*, 195; Russell to Lyons, Jan. 23, 1862, NFBL (NA). Russell cited Vattel's *Law of Nations*, bk. 3, chap. 7, sect.

118, and Wheaton's *Elements of International Law* (1836 ed.), pt. 4, chap. 3, sect. 22 (ibid.).

29. CFA to Seward, Jan. 17, 1862, no. 103, *FRUS 1862*, 16–17; Henry Adams to Raymond, Jan. 24, 1862, in Levenson et al., eds., *Letters of Henry Adams*, 1:272; Henry Adams to Sumner, Jan. 30, 1862, ibid., 276; workers' assembly reported in *London Daily News*, Jan. 28, 1862, quoted in Foner, *British Labor and Civil War*, 11.

30. Henry Adams to CFA, Jr., Jan. 31, 1862, in Levenson et al., eds., *Letters of Henry Adams*, 1:278. See also ibid., 275–76 n. 2. Adams appeared correct about the blockade issue. Unknown to him, someone in London (not named in memo) had sent a confidential memorandum to the Confederate government, noting that the British Foreign Office had recently asked France and Russia two questions: Was the sinking of the stone fleet in Charleston's harbor contrary to law and civilization? Was the blockade effective and binding on neutrals? France called the destruction of harbors a violation of international law because the action, the Paris government argued, was irreparable. On the other issue, the French pronounced the blockade ineffective and declared that neutrals owed it no respect. Russia, though an open supporter of the Union, likewise declared the blockade ineffective and in violation of the Declaration of Paris (Confidential memo from London to State Department in Richmond, Jan. 31, 1862, Mason Papers; Mann to Davis, Feb. 1, 1862, *ORN*, 2d ser., 3:324–25).

31. CFA to Seward, Jan. 31, 1862, no. 109, *FRUS 1862*, 19–20. For a convincing refutation of the charge that the Conservatives favored the South, see Wilbur D. Jones, "British Conservatives and Civil War."

32. Berwanger, ed., Russell, *Diary*, 334 (Dec. 28, 1861); Mason to Hunter, Feb. 7, 1862, *ORN*, 2d ser., 3:331; Warren, *Fountain of Discontent*, 212; Jenkins, *Britain and War for Union*, 1:228–29; Pease and Randall, eds., *Diary of Browning*, 1:526 (Jan. 18, 1862); Lyons to Russell, Jan. 20, 1862, quoted in E. D. Adams, *GB and Civil War*, 2:80; Russell to Gladstone, Jan. 26, 1862, Gladstone Papers, Brit. Lib., Add. Mss., 44,292, vol. 207.

33. CFA to Seward, Jan. 10, no. 99, Jan. 24, 1862, no. 106 (on threat of intervention), CFA Letterbook; CFA to Richard Henry Dana, Jr. (the acquaintance), Feb. 6, 1862, ibid.; CFA to Everett, Feb. 21, 1862, ibid.; CFA to Seward, Feb. 13, 1862, no. 114, *FRUS 1862*, 26; Hotze to Hunter, Mar. 11, 1862, *ORN*, 2d ser., 3:361–62. See also Parish, *Civil War*, 413.

CHAPTER FIVE

1. Seward to CFA, Feb. 4, 1862, no. 178, *FRUS 1862*, 21; Lewis to William Vernon Harcourt (stepson-in-law), Feb. 4, 1862, Harcourt Papers, Box 12; Russell to Lyons, Feb. 1, 1862, enclosure: Russell to Lords Commissioners of the Admiralty, Jan. 31, 1862, *BPP: Civil War*, 16:181–82. For

the argument that the workers' distress was localized and had little impact on British policy, see Bourne, *Foreign Policy of Victorian England*, 91. Robert H. Jones points out that the workers had no members in Parliament and therefore exercised little influence on British policy ("Anglo-American Relations," 40).

2. CFA to Seward, Feb. 7, no. 112, *FRUS 1862*, 22; *Parl. Debates*, 165:43–46 (Lords, Feb. 6, 1862); Moran Diary, Feb. 7, 8, 10, 1862.

3. Russell to Confederate commissioners, Dec. 7, 1861, Mason Papers. The emissary to the foreign secretary was William Gregory, a pro-South member of Parliament who explained to Mason that since the Confederacy was "not as yet recognized," his proper course was to ask for an "unofficial interview" (Gregory to Mason, Feb. 7, 1862, ibid.). See also Russell to Lyons, Feb. 8, 1862, Russell Papers, PRO 39/22/96.

4. Mason to Secretary of State Robert M. Hunter, Feb. 22, 1862, plus enclosures: Mason to Russell, Feb. 8, 1862, and Russell to Mason, Feb. 8, 1862, Mason Papers, (Disp.). For the argument that the South was a victim of self-delusion, see Blumenthal, "Confederate Diplomacy." See also his *Reappraisal of Franco-American Relations*, 158–59.

5. Mason to Hunter, Feb. 22, 1862, plus enclosures: Mason to Russell, Feb. 8, 1862, and Russell to Mason, Feb. 8, 1862, Mason Papers (Disp.).

6. Lyons to Russell, Feb. 11, 1862, Russell Papers, PRO 30/22/36; Russell to Lyons, Mar. 1, 1862, ibid., PRO 30/22/96; Lewis to Harcourt, Feb. 19, 21, 1862, Harcourt Papers, Box 12; Case and Spencer, *U.S. and France*, 257, 260.

7. Lyons to Russell, Feb. 11, 28, 1862, Russell Papers, PRO 30/22/36; Lyons to Russell, Mar. 3, 1862, FO 146/1023, Cowley Papers.

8. *New York Tribune* (n.d.), quoted in McPherson, *Battle Cry of Freedom*, 396–404; Moran Diary, Feb. 20, Mar. 6, 1862; CFA Diary, Mar. 5, 1862; Mason, *James Mason*, 266; Brigg, ed., *Journals of Lancashire Weaver*, 134 (Mar. 4, 1862).

9. E. D. Adams, *GB and Civil War*, 2:7–9, 12; Jenkins, *Britain and War for Union*, 2:74–75; Ashmore, ed., "Diary of James Garnett," 1:77–78 (editor's remarks), and 2:112–14 (Sept. 5, 1861); Jeremiah Garnett (other mill owner mentioned in text) cited ibid., 114; Brigg, ed., *Journals of a Lancashire Weaver*, 130 (Nov. 16, 1861), 131 (Dec. 31, 1861), 132 (Jan. 1, 1862).

10. E. D. Adams, *GB and Civil War*, 1:267, 268 n. 2, 271; Forster to Ellis Yarnall, May 10, 1861, in Reid, *Forster*, 1:334; *Parl. Debates*, 165:1158–1230 (Commons, Mar. 7, 1862), 1233–43 (Lords, Mar. 10, 1862); Henry Adams to CFA, Jr., Mar. 15, 1862, in Ford, ed., *Adams Letters*, 1:119–20.

11. Moran Diary, Mar. 8, 1862; A. S. Green of Brit. FO, "Memorandum relative to Blockades" (for cabinet use and based on Wheaton and other international legal theorists), Mar. 3, 1862, Gladstone Papers, Brit. Lib., Add. Mss., 44,594, vol. 509. For the argument about the South's misuse of the blockade issue, see Blumenthal, "Confederate Diplomacy," 157, and his *Reappraisal of Franco-American Relations*, 159. The South's first secretary of

state, Robert Toombs, had urged the mortgaging of cotton, but his argument lost out to those who advocated "King Cotton diplomacy," which called for withdrawal of the good to assure recognition. The three Southern commissioners had likewise denied interest in material assistance and called for a renunciation of the blockade for the "general interests of mankind." See note from commissioners to Russell, Nov. 30, 1861, enclosed in Russell to Lyons, Dec. 7, 1861, FO 115/250, PRO. Russell had been promoted to the Lords on July 30, 1861.

12. E. D. Adams, *GB and Civil War*, 1:271–72, 272 n. 1. Russell's warning of a race war perhaps reminded his listeners of the rebellion in Haiti of the 1790s, the disappointing effect of emancipation on the West Indian colonies, the Sepoy rebellion in India of 1857, and England's ongoing problems in Ireland. For the sources of England's racial fears, see Crook, *North, South, and Powers*, 237–38, and McPherson, *Battle Cry of Freedom*, 558.

13. Mason, *James Mason*, 264, 266; Slidell to Hunter, Mar. 26, 1862, in Richardson, ed., *Messages and Papers of the Confederacy*, 2:207; Slidell to Hunter, Mar. 26, 1862, *ORN*, 2d ser., 3:372; Slidell to Mason, Mar. 28, 1862, Mason Papers; Mason to secretary of state, Mar. 11, 1862, ibid. (Disp.)

14. Hotze to Hunter, Mar. 11, 1862, *ORN*, 2d ser., 3:360–62; Addendum to above letter, Mar. 18, 1862, ibid., 363; Mason to Hotze, Jan. 16, 1863, ibid., 659.

15. CFA Diary, Mar. 8, 1862; CFA to Seward, Mar. 13, 1862, no. 131, *FRUS 1862*, 47–48; CFA to Seward, Mar. 20, 1862, no. 132, ibid., 51; CFA to Seward, Mar. 27, 1862, no. 135, ibid., 53–54.

16. CFA to Seward, Feb. 21, 1862, no. 119, CFA Letterbook; Seward to CFA, Mar. 10, 1862, no. 203, *FRUS 1862*, 46; Seward to CFA, Apr. 1, 1862, no. 218, ibid., 60; Crook, "Portents of War," 175. Lincoln did not tell Seward (and Welles) about his decision for emancipation until mid-July 1862. See below, Chapter 6.

17. Moran Diary, Mar. 20, 1862; CFA to Seward, Feb. 27, 1862, no. 123, enclosures: CFA to Russell, Feb. 18, 1862, Russell to CFA, Feb. 26, 1862, CFA to Russell, Feb. 27, 1862 (enclosure: report of British Commissioners of Customs, Feb. 22, 1862), all in *FRUS 1862*, 39–40; Russell to Lyons, Mar. 15, 1862, Russell Papers, PRO 30/22/96; E. D. Adams, *GB and Civil War*, 2:118.

18. Russell to Lyons, Mar. 22, 1862, Russell Papers, PRO 30/22/96; Moran Diary, Mar. 25, 26, Apr. 5, 1862; Brigg, ed., *Journals of a Lancashire Weaver*, 135 (Mar. 28, 1862).

19. Moran Diary, Apr. 10, 1862; CFA to Seward, Apr. 3, 1862, no. 140, *FRUS 1862*, 62; CFA Diary, Mar. 29, 1862; Memorials from Canadian bankers and merchants to Lords Commissioners of Her Majesty's Treasury (regarding concern for railroad), Feb. 1862, *BPP: Papers Relating to Canada, 1861–63*, 24:277–87; Duke of Newcastle to Governor General of Canada, and to Lt. Governors of New Brunswick and Nova Scotia, Apr. 12, 1862,

ibid., 314–15; Gladstone, "Memorandum on Intercolonial Railway, British North America," Apr. 5, 1862, Gladstone Papers, Brit. Lib., Add. Mss., 44,594, vol. 509; Bourne, *Foreign Policy of Victorian England*, 96.

20. Benjamin to Mason, Apr. 12, 1862, Mason Papers.

21. Seward to CFA, Apr. 14, 1862, no. 228, *FRUS 1862*, 67–70; Moran Diary, Apr. 17, 1862; Van Deusen, *William H. Seward*, 320–21.

22. Parish, *Civil War*, 398–99; Emory Thomas, *Confederate Nation*, 174–75. See also Owsley, *King Cotton Diplomacy*, 43.

23. Parish, *Civil War*, 398–400; Russell to Cowley, Apr. 19, 1862, Russell Papers, PRO 30/22/105; Hammond to Layard, Apr. 24, 1862, Layard Papers, Brit. Lib., Add. Mss., 38,951, vol. 21. The Confederate deal negotiated in 1863 secured a loan of $14.5 million from the French-owned Emile Erlanger and Company (Emory Thomas, *Confederate Nation*, 187). See also Gentry, "Confederate Success in Europe," and Lester, *Confederate Finance and Purchasing in GB*, chap. 2. Douglas B. Ball questions the success of the Erlanger loan because it rested on the bondholder's ability to convert his bonds into cotton certificates and then transport the product to Europe. By this time in the war, he argues, Confederate hopes for victory had diminished, partly because of the problem of sending cotton through a steadily tightening Union blockade (*Financial Failure and Confederate Defeat*, 75–79).

24. CFA to Seward, Apr. 16, 1862, no. 144, *FRUS 1862*, 70–73; CFA to Seward, Apr. 25, 1862, no. 148, ibid., 77; CFA to Seward, May 8, 1862, no. 156, ibid., 83–84; CFA Diary, Apr. 7, 15, May 3, 1862; Moran Diary, Apr. 17, 1862, LC; Palmerston to Gladstone, Apr. 29, 1862, Gladstone Papers, Brit. Lib., Add. Mss., 44, 272, VOL. 187.

25. Palmerston to Russell, Jan. 19, 1862, Russell Papers, PRO 30/22/22; Jenkins, *Britain and War for Union*, 1:177; Bourne, *Foreign Policy of Victorian England*, 89.

26. CFA to Seward, Jan. 24, 1862, no. 106; CFA Letterbook; Lyons to Russell, Mar. 3, 1862, FO 146/1024, Cowley Papers; Russell to Cowley, Mar. 8, 1862, FO 146/1022, ibid. The demand referred to by Russell was for $15 million of bonds in return for what he called a "fraudulent loan" of $750,000 to a "falling and bankrupt government" (Russell to Cowley, Mar. 11, 1862, FO 146/1023, ibid.). Russell was convinced that the British army was barely large enough to defend England and its colonies and could not be used in Mexico (Russell to John Crampton [minister to Madrid], Apr. 19, 1862, FO 146/1027, ibid.). See also Hanna and Hanna, *Napoleon III and Mexico*, 42–44; Bock, *Prelude to Tragedy*, 447; Jenkins, *Britain and War for Union*, 1:176–77; Crook, *North, South, and Powers*, 183–84; E. D. Adams, *GB and Civil War*, 1:259–60. If the French continued their course, the British government wanted the convention suspended and its minister in Mexico relocated to Bermuda to await instructions. The British supported continued occupation of Vera Cruz until French motives and events became clear (Russell to Cowley, Apr. 29, 1862, FO 146/1029, Cowley Papers). The French withdrew from Mexico in 1867.

27. Case and Spencer, *U.S. and France*, 275–78; Blumenthal, *Reappraisal of Franco-American Relations*, 141; Saul, *Distant Friends*, 334; John B. Jones, *Rebel War Clerk's Diary*, 78.

28. Case and Spencer, *U.S. and France*, 279–82; Blumenthal, *Reappraisal of Franco-American Relations*, 142; Evans, *Benjamin*, 174–75; Benjamin to Slidell, July 19, 1862, *ORN*, 2d ser., 3:463–64. Seward knew that the Paris government had no knowledge of Mercier's mission to Richmond. See folder 6293: DS Business 1861–62, dated Sept. 1862, but probably in error, in Seward Papers.

29. CFA to Seward, Apr. 25, no. 148, *FRUS 1862*, 77; CFA to Seward, May 2, 1862, no. 150, ibid., 79; Benjamin to Mason, Apr. 14, 1862, *ORN*, 2d ser., 3:391. For Shiloh, see McPherson, *Battle Cry of Freedom*, 405–15.

30. CFA to Seward, May 8, 1862, no. 156, *FRUS 1862*, 84; Moran Diary, May 8, 9, 1862.

31. McPherson, *Battle Cry of Freedom*, 353; CFA Diary, Mar. 19, 1862; Russell to Lyons, Mar. 22, 1862, Russell Papers, PRO 30/22/96; E. D. Adams, *GB and Civil War*, 2:82–83.

32. Lyons to Russell, Mar. 31, Apr. 8, 1862, Russell Papers, PRO 30/22/36; Seward to CFA, Apr. 8, 1862, no. 226, *FRUS 1862*, 65; text of treaty in *BPP: Papers Relating to Slave Trade, 1861–74*, 91:161–70. Ephraim D. Adams disputes Lyons's view and argues that even though reconstruction was important, so was antislavery. Seward recognized the treaty's impact on Civil War diplomacy (E. D. Adams, *GB and Civil War*, 1:275, and 2:10, 90). The British regarded the Lyons-Seward Treaty as a feeble effort to win their support and an admission of the limitations of the Union's antislavery sentiment. Two writers agree that Lincoln hoped, among other considerations, to attract British sentiment in the war by negotiating the treaty. See Milne, "Lyons-Seward Treaty of 1862," 511, and Henderson, "Anglo-American Treaty of 1862," 314.

33. E. D. Adams, *GB and Civil War*, 2:83–84; Thomas and Hyman, *Stanton*, 232–33; Lincoln to Congress, Apr. 16, 1862, *CWL*, 5:192; ibid., 370–71 n. 1.

34. References to Schurz and to Lincoln quote in E. D. Adams, *GB and Civil War*, 2:91–92; Moran Diary, Apr. 16, 1862.

35. Seward to CFA, Apr. 28, 1862, no. 240, *FRUS 1862*, 78; CFA to Seward, May 15, 1862, no. 160, ibid., 91; Williams, ed., *Diary from Dixie*, 215 (Apr. 27, 1862), 216 (Apr. 29); Woodward, ed., *Mary Chesnut's Civil War*, 326–27, 330, 333, 339; Moran Diary, May 12, 1862; Ashmore, ed., "Diary of James Garnett," 2:115 (May 12, 1862); McPherson, *Battle Cry of Freedom*, 418–20; Duberman, *CFA*, 287.

36. Memorandum enclosed in Slidell to Benjamin, Apr. 14, 1862, *ORN*, 2d ser., 3:393–95; Slidell to Benjamin, Apr. 18, 1862, ibid., 395–96; Mason to Benjamin, Apr. 21, 1862, ibid., 397–99; Case and Spencer, *U.S. and France*, 269–75. The following two paragraphs are based on these sources.

37. Presidential proclamation, May 12, 1862, enclosed in Seward to CFA,

May 12, 1862, no. 250, *FRUS 1862*, 88–89; Slidell to Benjamin, May 15, 1862, *ORN*, 2d ser., 3:419–20; Case and Spencer, *U.S. and France*, 282–85; Blumenthal, *Reappraisal of Franco-American Relations*, 142.

CHAPTER SIX

1. Henry Adams to CFA, Jr., May 16, 1862, in Levenson et al., eds., *Letters of Henry Adams*, 1:297–98; CFA to Seward, Dec. 20, 1861, no. 93, CFA Letterbook; CFA to Seward, May 22, 1862, no. 164, *FRUS 1862*, 98–99; Russell to CFA, May 17, 1862, enclosed ibid., 99; CFA to Seward, May 23, 1862, no. 165, ibid., 100. William H. Russell warned Englishmen that the Union might turn on England next (Atkins, *Life of William Howard Russell*, 1:vii; 2:3).

2. CFA Diary, May 3, 1862.

3. Lyons to Russell, May 16, 26, 1862, Russell Papers, PRO 30/22/36; Russell to Lyons, May 17, 1862, ibid., PRO 30/22/96. Russell also mentioned the Union's military successes in Yorktown, Virginia, and Corinth, Mississippi.

4. Lyons to Russell, May 23, June 9, 1862, ibid., PRO 30/22/36.

5. Lyons to Russell, May 16, 1862, *BFSP 1864–1865*, 55:514–18. For the South's destruction of cotton, see Owsley, *King Cotton Diplomacy*, 43–50.

6. Seward to CFA, May 28, 1862, no. 260, Disp., GB (NA). Moran thought Seward's note a "wholesome threat" (Moran Diary, June 16, 1862).

7. For the extensive correspondence on this matter, see Palmerston to CFA, June 11, 1862, PM/J/1, Palmerston Letterbook, Palmerston Papers; CFA to Palmerston, June 12, 16, 20, 1862, CFA Letterbook; CFA to Seward, June 13, 1862 (2 notes), ibid.; Palmerston to CFA, June 15, 1862, ibid.; CFA Diary, June 12, 13, 19, 20, 29, 1862; Palmerston to Russell, June 14, 1862, in Gooch, ed., *Later Correspondence of John Russell*, 2:325–26; Seward to CFA, June 28, 1862, no. 283, Disp., GB (NA). Seward later expressed regret for failing to see the danger in the "woman order" (Seward to CFA, July 5, 1862, no. 287, *FRUS 1862*, 124; Seward to CFA, July 9, 1862, no. 295, ibid., 127; Seward to CFA, Sept. 8, 1862, no. 336, ibid., 188. See also Henry Adams, *Education of Henry Adams*, 137, and Duberman, *CFA*, 288–91.

8. CFA Diary, June 13, 19, 20, 1862; Moran Diary, June 13, 24, 1862; Graebner, "Northern Diplomacy and European Neutrality," 66–67; Mason to State Department in Richmond, June 13, 1862, Mason Papers; Palmerston to Russell, June 13, 1862, Russell Papers, PRO 30/22/22. Moran thought that most of the British press had been calling for "the mediation to be all on one side, and that of the South" (Moran Diary, June 12, 1862). For a convincing refutation of the charge that the *Times* of London was biased toward the South, see Crawford, *Anglo-American Crisis*.

9. Graebner, "Northern Diplomacy and European Neutrality," 66; Henry Adams and Lyons quoted ibid., 67, 68; Moran Diary, June 14, 1862.

10. Graebner, "Northern Diplomacy and European Neutrality," 73–74.

11. Lindsay to Mason, June 18, 1862, Mason Papers.

12. Palmerston to Layard, June 19, 1862, Layard Papers, Brit. Lib., Add. Mss., 38,988, vol. 57; CFA to Seward, June 20, 1862, no. 176, *FRUS 1862*, 115.

13. CFA to Seward, June 20, 1862, no. 176, *FRUS 1862*, 115.

14. CFA Diary, June 29, 1862; CFA to Seward, July 3, 1862, no. 182, *FRUS 1862*, 122–23; Seward to CFA, July 18, 1862, no. 303, ibid., 142–44.

15. CFA Diary, July 1, 1862; Seward to CFA, June 24, 1862, no. 277, *FRUS 1862*, 116–17; CFA to Seward, June 26, 1862, no. 180, ibid., 118–19; Moran Diary June 21, 1862; Seward to Mercier in Graebner, "Northern Diplomacy and European Neutrality," 73.

16. Henry Adams to CFA, Jr., July 4, 1862, in Levenson et al., eds., *Letters of Henry Adams*, 1:305–6; Owsley, *King Cotton Diplomacy*, 136–37, 140–42.

17. Mason to Russell, July 7, 1862, *BFSP 1864–1865*, 55:724–27 (Mason's underlining in note). See also Benjamin to Mason, Apr. 8, 1862, *ORN*, 2d ser., 3:379–83, and Owsley, *King Cotton Diplomacy*, 45–46.

18. Monaghan, *Diplomat in Carpet Slippers*, 183, 226; "Appeal to Border State Representatives to Favor Compensated Emancipation," July 12, 1862, in *CWL*, 5:317–19; McPherson, *Battle Cry of Freedom*, 503–4; Current, *Lincoln Nobody Knows*, 221–22; Thomas and Hyman, *Stanton*, 238; Beale, ed., *Diary of Welles*, 1:70–71 (July 13, 1862). For an extended treatment of Lincoln's views, see Cox, *Lincoln and Black Freedom*. Cox does not view Lincoln as merely following Congress in making emancipation policy. The president, she argues, led the way (ibid., 14–15).

19. Cobden to Bright, July 12, 1862, Cobden Papers, Brit. Lib., Add. Mss., 43,652, vol. 6; Palmerston to Queen Victoria, July 14, 1862, quoted in Bell, *Palmerston*, 2:327; Mason to State Department in Richmond, July 15, 1862, Mason Papers, and Slidell to Mason, July 16, 1862, ibid.; Stuart to Russell, July 15, 1862, Russell Papers, PRO 30/22/36; Johnson to Lincoln, July 16, 1862, in *CWL*, 5:343 n. 1. Johnson was in New Orleans to inquire into charges of undisciplined behavior by the Union occupation force. See also Louis M. Sears, "Confederate Diplomat at Court of Napoleon III," 262–63. Stuart headed the British legation until Lyons returned from England in early November.

20. CFA to Seward, July 17, 1862, no. 186, *FRUS 1862*, 136–37; CFA Diary, July 15, 1862; Jenkins, *Britain and War for Union*, 2:94.

21. CFA Diary, July 14, 17, 1862; CFA to Seward, July 17, 1862, no. 189, *FRUS 1862*, 139–40; Mason to Russell, July 17, 1862, *BFSP 1864–1865*, 55:728–29.

22. *Parl. Debates*, 168:569–73 (Commons, July 18, 1862); Matthew, ed., *Gladstone Diaries*, 6:136 (July 18, 1862); Mason to Slidell, July 11, 13, 1862, Mason Papers.

23. Mason to Slidell, July 18, 1862, Mason Papers, and Benjamin to Mason, July 19, 1862, ibid.; Henry Adams to CFA, Jr., July 19, 1862, in

Levenson et al., eds., *Letters of Henry Adams*, 1:307–8; Hammond to Layard, July 18, 1862, Layard Papers, Brit. Lib., Add. Mss., 38,951, vol. 21; CFA to CFA, Jr., July 18, 1862, in Ford, ed., *Adams Letters*, 1:166; CFA Diary, July 18, 1862. See also Blumenthal, "Confederate Diplomacy."

24. Moran Diary, July 19, 1862; Henry Adams to CFA, Jr., July 19, 1862, in Levenson et al., eds., *Letters of Henry Adams*, 1:308; CFA Diary, July 18, 1862; Graebner, "Northern Diplomacy and European Neutrality," 67.

25. Moran Diary, July 19, 1862; Wallace and Gillespie, eds., *Journal of Moran*, 2:1041 n. 13; *Parl. Debates*, 168:511–22 (Lindsay, Commons, July 18, 1862), 522–27 (Taylor, Commons, July 18), 527–34 (Vane-Tempest, Commons, July 18), 534–38 (Forster, Commons, July 18); E. D. Adams, *GB and Civil War*, 2:22.

26. *Parl. Debates*, 168:569–73 (Commons, July 18, 1862).

27. Moran Diary, July 19, 1862; Graebner, "Northern Diplomacy and European Neutrality," 67.

28. CFA Diary, July 19, 1862; CFA to Seward, July 10, 1862, CFA Letterbook; CFA to Seward, July 31, 1862, no. 197, *FRUS 1862*, 159–60; Henry Adams to CFA, Jr., July 19, 1862, in Levenson et al., eds., *Letters of Henry Adams*, 1:308.

29. Charles Francis Adams warned the Union government that England needed grain from abroad—and mainly from the United States. See CFA to Seward, July 24, 1862, no. 193, Disp., GB (NA). For British interest in grain as a counterbalance to their need for cotton, see Schmidt, "Influence of Wheat and Cotton on Anglo-American Relations during Civil War," 431, 437, 439, and Khasigian, "Economic Factors and British Neutrality." British need for wheat, however, was never high enough to have an important impact on the intervention issue. See Ginzberg, "Economics of British Neutrality," 151, 155; Robert H. Jones, "Long Live the King?," 167–69; and E. D. Adams, *GB and Civil War*, 2:13–14 n. 2.

CHAPTER SEVEN

1. Russell to Stuart, July 19, 1862, Russell Papers, PRO 30/22/96; Stuart to Russell, July 21, 1862, ibid., PRO 30/22/36; Slidell to Mason, July 20, 1862, Mason Papers; Slidell memorandum, July 25, 1862, enclosed in Slidell to Benjamin, July 25, 1862, *ORN*, 2d ser., 3:481–87; Bourne, *Foreign Policy of Victorian England*, 91.

2. Seward to CFA, July 28, 1862, no. 308, *FRUS 1862*, 157; Stuart to Russell, July 21, 29, Aug. 4, 1862, Russell Papers, PRO 30/22/36; Russell to Stuart, July 25, 1862, ibid., PRO 30/22/96; Stuart to Russell, July 21, 1862, *BFSP 1864–1865*, 55:519; Russell to Stuart, Aug. 7, 1862, *BPP: Civil War*, 17:29. See also Brauer, "Slavery Problem," 450. Stuart thought Russell's dispatch of July 28 important enough to read it to Seward on August 16. Two weeks later, Stuart gave Seward a copy of the dispatch. See Stuart to Seward,

Aug. 30, 1862, with enclosure: Russell to Stuart, July 28, 1862, NFBL (NA).

3. Seward to CFA, July 28, 1862, no. 308, *FRUS 1862*, 156–58.

4. Beale, ed., *Diary of Welles*, 1:70–71 (July 13, 1862); "Emancipation Proclamation—First Draft," July 22, 1862, in *CWL*, 5:336–37; Thomas and Hyman, *Stanton*, 238–40.

5. Blair to Lincoln, July 23, 1862, in *CWL*, 5:337 n. 1; Donald, ed., *Inside Lincoln's Cabinet*, 99–100. On Lincoln's fear of alienating the border states, see his "Remarks to Deputation of Western Gentlemen," Aug. 4, 1862, in *CWL*, 5:357; William H. Seward, *Autobiography*, 3:74; Brauer, "Slavery Problem," 452; McPherson, *Battle Cry of Freedom*, 505; Van Deusen, *William H. Seward*, 328–29.

6. Lincoln to Reverdy Johnson, July 26, 1862, in *CWL*, 5:343; Lincoln to Belmont, July 31, 1862, ibid., 350; Belmont to Lincoln, Aug. 10, 1862, ibid., 351 n. 1; Lincoln to Cuthbert Bullitt, July 28, 1862, ibid., 344–45; Randall, *Constitutional Problems under Lincoln*, 377–78.

7. Pease and Randall, eds., *Diary of Browning*, 1:562 (July 24, 1862); E. D. Adams, *GB and Civil War*, 2:87.

8. Donald, ed., *Inside Lincoln's Cabinet*, 105–6 (Aug. 3, 1862); Grant and Grenville Dodge (officer) quoted in McPherson, *Battle Cry of Freedom*, 502.

9. Gasparin to Lincoln, July 18, 1862, in *CWL*, 5:355 n. 1; Lincoln to Gasparin, Aug. 4, 1862, ibid., 355–56 n. 1.

10. McPherson, *Battle Cry of Freedom*, 505–8; Cox, *Lincoln and Black Freedom*, 5, 14; Fehrenbacher, "Only His Stepchildren"; Fredrickson, "Man but Not Brother," 53; Oates, *With Malice toward None*, 41; Oates, "'Man of Our Redemption,'" 15–16, 19–20; Randall, *Constitutional Problems under Lincoln*, 370. For Lincoln's longtime aversion to slavery, see, among numerous examples, Lincoln's protest in the Illinois legislature on slavery, Mar. 3, 1837, in *CWL*, 1:75; Lincoln to Williamson Durley, Oct. 3, 1845, ibid., 348; Lincoln's speech at Bloomington, Illinois, Sept. 26, 1854, ibid., 2:239. In the 1854 speech he called slavery "a moral, social and political evil."

11. Russell to Mason, July 24, 31, 1862, Mason Papers (Disp.); Mason to Russell, July 24, 1862, *BFSP 1864–1865*, 55:729–31.

12. Mason to Russell, Aug. 1, 1862, *BFSP 1864–1865*, 55:731–33.

13. Russell to Mason, Aug. 2, 1862, Mason Papers (Disp.).

14. Mason to Benjamin, Aug. 4, 1862, ibid.

15. Mason to Mrs. Mason, July 20, 1862, quoted in McPherson, *Battle Cry of Freedom*, 555; Slidell to Davis, July 25, 1862, Richardson, ed., *Messages and Papers of the Confederacy*, 2:272; Gladstone to Col. [?] Neville, July 26, 1862, quoted in E. D. Adams, *GB and Civil War*, 2:26; Gladstone to wife, July 29, 1862, quoted in Morley, *Gladstone*, 2:75; Randall and Donald, *Civil War and Reconstruction*, 507.

16. Hammond to Layard, July 20, 28, 1862, Layard Papers, Brit. Lib., Add. Mss., 38,951, vol. 21; Lyons to Stuart, July 29, 1862, quoted in E. D. Adams, *GB and Civil War*, 2:26.

17. Seward to CFA, July 12, 1862, no. 299, *FRUS 1862*, 135; CFA to

Seward, July 31, 1862, no. 199, ibid., 162; CFA to Seward, Aug. 1, 1862, no. 201, ibid., 163; CFA Diary, July 31, 1862; Ridley, *Palmerston*, 557; Duberman, *CFA*, 293–94; E. D. Adams, *GB and Civil War*, 2:35, 118–22. See reference to British Foreign Enlistment Act of 1819 in "British Proclamation for the Observance of Neutrality in the contest between the United States and the Confederate States of America, May 13, 1861," *BFSP 1860–1861*, 51:165, 167. For Confederate shipbuilding activities in England, see Merli, *GB and Confederate Navy*, and Spencer, *Confederate Navy in Europe*.

18. Stuart to Russell, Aug. 16, 1862, *BFSP 1864–1865*, 55:520–21; Dudley quoted in McPherson, *Battle Cry of Freedom*, 555; Layard to [?] Horsfall, July 5, 1862, enclosed in Russell to CFA, Aug. 4, 1862, enclosed in CFA to Seward, Aug. 7, 1862, no. 205, *FRUS 1862*, 171; Russell, *Recollections and Suggestions*, 235.

19. Seward to CFA, Aug. 2, 1862, Disp., GB (NA). This section of Seward's note, not surprisingly, was deleted from the correspondence he turned over to Congress for publication.

20. E. D. Adams, *GB and Civil War*, 2:154; Matthew, ed., *Gladstone Diaries*, 6:139 (July 31, 1862); ibid., 142 (Aug. 12, 1862), 142 n. 2, 154 n. 10; Gladstone memorandum (on "Southern Gentleman"), July 31, 1862, in Guedalla, ed., *Gladstone and Palmerston*, 230–31; Gladstone to Russell, Oct. 17, 1862, ibid. See also Reid, ed., "Gladstone's 'Insincere Neutrality' during Civil War." According to one writer, Gladstone's primary motivations in life were religion and morality, which would help to substantiate his humanitarian concerns regarding the American war. See Butler, *Gladstone*, 122. Spence dreamed of establishing a steamship line between England and a Southern port and a railroad from the South to Matamoros, Mexico, both of which would facilitate evasion of the blockade. See Spence to Mason, Apr. 28, 1862, enclosed in Mason to Benjamin, May 2, 1862, *ORN*, 2d ser., 3:401–4. By the Compromise of 1850, the principle of popular sovereignty determined whether slavery would exist in New Mexico territory.

21. Gladstone to Argyll, Aug. 3, 1862, in Argyll, ed., *Argyll, Autobiography and Memoirs*, 2:191; Morley, *Gladstone*, 2:81; Magnus, *Gladstone*, 153.

22. *London Morning Post*, Aug. [?], 1862, quoted in CFA, Jr., *Before and After Treaty of Washington*, 43–44.

23. Palmerston to Queen Victoria, Aug. 6, 1862, quoted in Bell, *Palmerston*, 2:327. The queen offered no objection to an October intervention, although she wished that Austria, Prussia, and Russia would be consulted first. Perhaps the greatest influence on Victoria was King Leopold of Belgium, who urged Napoleon to persuade England to recognize the Confederacy or take some other step toward ending the American conflict. See CFA, Jr., "Crisis of Foreign Intervention," 13–14; Russell to Palmerston, Aug. 6, 1862, GC/RU/721, Palmerston Papers; Russell to Stuart, Aug. 7, 1862, *BFSP 1864–1865*, 55:519; Russell to Stuart, Aug. 8, 1862, Russell Papers, PRO 30/22/96.

24. Granville to Lord Stanley, Oct. 1, 1862, in Fitzmaurice, *Granville*, 1:442.

25. CFA, Jr., "Crisis of Foreign Intervention," 12; Argyll to Gladstone, Aug. 6, 1862, Gladstone Papers, Brit. Lib., Add. Mss., 44,099, vol. 14; Bright to Cobden, Aug. 6, 1862, Bright Papers, Brit. Lib., Add. Mss., 43,384, vol. 2; Cobden to Bright, Aug. 7, 1862, Cobden Papers, Brit. Lib., Add. Mss., 43,652, vol. 6. Cobden's argument for joint intervention is summarized in CFA Diary, June 29, 1862.

26. CFA Diary, Aug. 7, 1862; Stuart to Russell, Aug. 8, 1862, Russell Papers, PRO 30/22/36; Parish, *Civil War*, 393; Eaton, *History of the Confederacy*, 84; Crook, *North, South, and Powers*, 226–27; Golder, "Civil War through Eyes of Russian Diplomat," 454, 456–57; Adamov, "Russia and U.S. at Time of Civil War," 596–97; Saul, *Distant Friends*, 321–23, 331; Woldman, *Lincoln and Russians*, viii, 125, 127–30.

27. *Times* (London), Aug. 15, 1862, p. 6; Hammond to Layard, Aug. 17, 1862, Layard Papers, Brit. Lib., Add. Mss., 38,951, vol. 21; Stuart to Russell, Aug. 18, 1862, Russell Papers, PRO 30/22/36; Lewis to Grey, Aug. 27, 1862, Ripon Papers, Brit. Lib., Add. Mss., 43,533, vol. 43; Seward to CFA, Aug. 18, 1862, circular no. 20, *FRUS 1862*, 179; Moran Diary, Aug. 18, 1862. Moran referred to Seward's dispatch of August 2. See n. 19 above.

28. Greeley to Lincoln, Aug. 19, 1862, in *CWL*, 5:389 n. 1; Lincoln to Greeley, Aug. 22, 1862, ibid., 388; Stuart to Russell, Aug. 22, 1862, Russell Papers, PRO 30/22/36; Argyll to Gladstone, Aug. 26, 1862, Gladstone Papers, Brit. Lib., Add. Mss., 44,099, vol. 14; Argyll to Palmerston, Sept. 2, 1862, GC/AR/25/1, Palmerston Papers.

29. Slidell to State Department in Richmond, Aug. 24, 1862, in Graebner, "Northern Diplomacy and European Neutrality," 69–70; Stuart to Russell, Aug. 26, 1862, Russell Papers, PRO 30/22/36; Hammond to Layard, Aug. 28, 1862, Layard Papers, Brit. Lib., Add. Mss., 38,951, vol. 21.

30. Cobden to Bright, Aug. 28, 1862, Cobden Papers, Brit. Lib., Add. Mss., 43,652, vol. 6; Bright to Cobden, Aug. 30, 1862, Bright Papers, Brit. Lib., Add. Mss., 43,884, vol. 2; Gladstone to Argyll, Aug. 29, 1862, Gladstone Papers, Letter-Book, 1862–63, Brit. Lib., Add. Mss., 44,533, vol. 448; Gladstone to Russell, Aug. 30, 1862, ibid.; Zorn, "Bright and British Attitude to Civil War," 145.

31. For British industrial figures, see Mitchell, comp., *European Historical Statistics*, 355. For British shipping, see ibid., 618. Henry Adams to CFA, Jr., May 8, 1862, in Ford, ed., *Adams Letters*, 1:139; Lyons to Stuart, July 29, 1862, quoted in E. D. Adams, *GB and Civil War*, 2:26; Owsley, *King Cotton Diplomacy*, 137, 140; McPherson, *Battle Cry of Freedom*, 548–51; Hotze to Benjamin, Dec. 20, 1862, *ORN*, 2d ser., 3:632–33; Hotze quoted in Eaton, *History of the Confederacy*, 75–76. Cotton imports from India grew from 1861 until in 1864 it provided 67 percent of Britain's supplies. During the American war, 55 percent of Britain's cotton came from India. See Frenise Logan,

"India—Britain's Substitute for American Cotton," 475–76. England eventually found India's cotton inferior to that of the South and turned to Egypt for a product that matched the South's in quality, except for the Sea Island variety. See Earle, "Egyptian Cotton and Civil War," 527.

32. Jenkins, *Britain and War for Union*, 1:214; Lincoln, "Message to Congress in Special Session," July 4, 1861, in *CWL*, 4:438; Marx quoted in McPherson, *Battle Cry of Freedom*, 550. The British workers' sentiment regarding the Civil War was too complicated for one to conclude that they were either for or against the North or South. See ibid., 550–51. See also Marx and Engels, *Civil War*. For the claim that British workers favored the North because they believed it spoke for political and economic freedom, see Park, "English Workingmen and Civil War," and Greenleaf, "British Labor against American Slavery." For the argument that the textile workers favored the South, see Ellison, *Support for Secession*. Ellison's argument is not convincing, for she documents little evidence of workers' sentiment. Instead, she relies on the local press, which was not owned by workers, and on petitions calling for recognition of the South that she does not demonstrate to be signed by workers and that she admits were ignored by the British government. See Merli's critical review of her book in *Civil War Times Illustrated* 13 (Feb. 1975):49–50. For another argument similar to Ellison's, see Brook, "Confederate Sympathies in North-East Lancashire." Royden Harrison once emphasized pro-Confederacy feeling among workers, but he later reversed his stand, as shown in his article cited below. For his earlier argument, see his article "British Labour and Confederacy." Like Ellison, Harrison here focused on nonworking elements of the Lancashire district in attempting to determine workers' sentiment. For a study of English sympathy toward the South based on the "glittering illusion" of Southern gentility and military prowess, see Vanauken, *Glittering Illusion*. The publication date is misleading, for this book, except for an added epilogue, is an unrevised version of the author's B.Litt. thesis at Oxford University, completed in 1957 and entitled "English Sympathy for the South: The Glittering Illusion." For convincing refutations of this argument for pro-Southern sympathy, see Foner, *British Labor and Civil War*; Harrison, "British Labor and American Slavery"; Wright, "Bradford and Civil War"; Lorimer, "Role of Anti-Slavery Sentiment"; and Kevin Logan, "*Bee-Hive* Newspaper and British Working Class Attitudes toward Civil War."

33. Mitchell, comp., *European Historical Statistics*, 355, 618; Thouvenel quoted in Case and Spencer, *U.S. and France*, 289–90; Stuart to Russell, Sept. 1, 1862, Russell Papers, PRO 30/22/36.

34. Stuart to Russell, Sept. 9, 1862, Russell Papers, PRO 30/33/36.

35. Henry Adams to CFA, Jr., Feb. 13, 1863, in Ford, ed., *Adams Letters*, 1:253; Argyll to Gladstone, Sept. 2, 1862, Gladstone Papers, Brit. Lib., Add. Mss., 44,099, vol. 14.

36. F. O. Mitchell to Layard, Sept. 3, 1862, Layard Papers, Dipl. Ser., Brit. Lib., Add. Mss., 39,104, vol. 174; Stuart to Russell, Sept. 5, 1862, Russell

Papers, PRO 30/22/36; Bright to Cobden, Sept. 6, 1862, Bright Papers, Brit. Lib., Add. Mss., 43,384, vol. 2; Gladstone to Argyll, Sept. 8, 1862, Gladstone Papers, Letter-Book, 1862–63, Brit. Lib., Add. Mss., 44,533, vol. 448.

37. Henry Adams to CFA, Jr., Sept. 5, 1862, in Levenson et al., eds., *Letters of Henry Adams*, 1:309–10.

38. CFA Diary, Sept. 14, 1862; Bates quoted in *CWL*, 5:404 n. 1 (top); ibid., 486 n. 1 (top); Russell to Cowley, Sept. 13, 1862, Russell Papers, PRO 30/22/105; Palmerston to Russell, Sept. 14, 1862, ibid., PRO 30/22/14; Russell to Palmerston, Sept. 17, 1862, ibid.; Walpole, *John Russell*, 2:349; Duberman, *CFA*, 294; McPherson, *Battle Cry of Freedom*, 555–56; Lincoln quoted ibid., 533; Brauer, "British Mediation and Civil War," 57; E.D. Adams, *GB and Civil War*, 2:38, 41.

39. Thouvenel cited in McPherson, *Battle Cry of Freedom*, 554.

40. CFA Diary, Sept. 21, 1862; Seward quote in Mercier to Thouvenel, Sept. 9, 1862, quoted in Owsley, *King Cotton Diplomacy*, 330; Seward to Dayton, Sept. 8, 1862, quoted ibid., 330–31.

CHAPTER EIGHT

1. *Times* (London), Sept. 16, 1862, p. 6; *Morning Post* and *Morning Herald*, both dated Sept. 16, 1862, and quoted in Jenkins, *Britain and War for Union*, 2:151; ibid., 167; Palmerston to Russell, Sept. 14, 1862, Russell Papers, PRO 30/22/14D; Russell to Palmerston, Sept. 17, 1862, GC/RU/728, Palmerston Papers. Lewis agreed that the North had suffered a great defeat and saw no need to worry about a Northern invasion of Canada that winter of 1862 (Lewis to Grey, Sept. 18, 1862, Ripon Papers, Brit. Lib., Add. Mss., 43,533, vol. 43).

2. Palmerston to Russell, Sept. 22, 1862, Russell Papers, PRO 30/22/14D; Russell to Palmerston, Sept. 22, 1862, GC/RU/729, Palmerston Papers. Stuart's letter was dated September 9, 1862.

3. Palmerston to Russell, Sept. 23, 1862, Russell Papers, PRO 30/22/14D. One author insists, erroneously, that by mid-September Palmerston was still not aware of Russia's opposition to intervention or of Seward's dependence on Russia for assistance (Benjamin Thomas, *Russo-American Relations*, chap. 8).

4. Palmerston to Russell, Sept. 23, 1862, Russell Papers, PRO 30/22/14D.

5. Palmerston to Gladstone, Sept. 24, 1862, in Morley, *Gladstone*, 2:76; Russell to Gladstone, Sept. 26, 1862, Gladstone Papers, Brit. Lib., Add. Mss., 44,292, vol. 207; Russell to Cowley, Sept. 26, 1862, Russell Papers, PRO 30/22/105.

6. Gladstone to Palmerston, Sept. 25, 1862, Gladstone Papers, Brit. Lib., Add. Mss., 44,272, vol. 187.

7. McPherson, *Battle Cry of Freedom*, 545. See also Murfin, *Gleam of Bayonets*, and Stephen W. Sears, *Landscape Turned Red*.

8. Charles Francis Adams, Jr., claims that news of Antietam reached England on September 26 ("Crisis of Foreign Intervention," 32). Lynn M. Case and Warren F. Spencer show that the first stories of Antietam appeared in the Paris *Moniteur* on September 27 and 30, 1862 (*U.S. and France*, 339–40). In England, Moran first referred to the Union victory in his diary entry of September 30 (Moran Diary, Sept. 30, 1862). For the Shaftesbury episode, see Slidell to Benjamin, Sept. 29, 1862, *ORN*, 2d ser., 3:546, and Slidell to Benjamin, Oct. 9, 1862, ibid., 551. For Adams's assessment of Shaftesbury, see CFA to Everett, May 2, 1862, CFA Letterbook. Brauer argues that Antietam exemplified the war's futility and thereby explains the British move toward mediation ("British Mediation and Civil War," 50–51).

9. Benjamin to Mason, Sept. 26, 1862, Mason Papers; Lewis to Grey, Sept. 27, 1862, Ripon Papers, Brit. Lib., Add. Mss., 43,533, vol. 43; Hammond to Layard, Oct. 6, 1862, Layard Papers, Brit. Lib., Add. Mss., 38,951, vol. 21; Moran Diary, Sept. 27, 1862; Gladstone to James Hudson, Sept. 27, 1862, Gladstone Papers, Brit. Lib., Add. Mss., 44,533, vol. 448; Gladstone to Argyll, Sept. 29, 1862, ibid.

10 Stuart to Russell, Sept. 29, 1862, Russell Papers, PRO 30/22/36; Palmerston to Russell, Sept. 30, 1862, ibid., PRO 30/22/14D.

11. Stuart to Russell, Sept. 23, 1862, ibid., PRO 30/22/36; Case and Spencer, *U.S. and France*, 326–28, 338.

12. Argyll to Gladstone, Sept. 23, 1862, Gladstone Papers, Brit. Lib., Add. Mss., 44,099, vol. 14; Granville to Russell, Sept. 27, 1862, in Fitzmaurice, *Granville*, 1:443–44; Granville to Russell, Sept. 29, 1862, Russell Papers, PRO 30/22/25. Granville sent Russell two letters from correspondents who argued that the North would not approve mediation and that England had missed opportunities to ask the Russian tsar to propose the good offices of England, France, and Russia (J. Winslow to Lord Henry Brougham, Aug. 30, 1862, and Joseph Parkes to Brougham, Sept. 11, 1862, both enclosed in Granville to Russell, Sept. 30, 1862, ibid.). See also Crook, *North, South, and Powers*, 225.

13. Jenkins, *Britain and War for Union*, 2:63, 68; Clarendon to Lewis, Sept. 29, 1862, Clarendon Papers; CFA to Seward, no. 221, Sept. 12, 1862, *FRUS 1862*, 189–90.

14. Brady, "Reconsideration of Lancashire 'Cotton Famine,'" 156–58, suggests that there was no actual cotton famine because there was no shortage of cotton. Rather, the manufacturers had an overabundance of cotton and had held back production to drive up prices of finished goods. See also Ashmore, ed., "Diary of James Garnett," 2:115 (May 14, 19, July–Aug., Sept. 23, 1862), 126. Garnett served as mayor of Clitheroe from November 1863 to November 1865 (ibid., 131). For the introduction of improved equipment and techniques, see Blaug, "Productivity of Capital in Lancashire Cotton Industry," 360. Owsley does not date the beginning of the cotton famine until

late 1862 (*King Cotton Diplomacy*, 136). Mill owners, observers in London, and mill workers confirmed the hard times in Lancashire during the winter of 1862–63. Garnett recorded in his diary that the cotton famine reached its worst time then in Low Moor. He made many references throughout October 1862 to relief for the distressed. Clitheroe and other cotton towns had local relief committees that collected subscriptions and supplemental aid from poor law officials. The previous month the Garnetts furnished their own relief at first (Ashmore, ed. "Diary of James Garnett, 2:115–19, 131). See also Foner, *British Labor and Civil War*, 5; Ellison, *Support for Secession*, 95; and Henderson, *Lancashire Cotton Famine*, 127. Cobden wrote Bright that all England was "thriving" except Lancashire (Cobden to Bright, Sept. 19, 1862, Cobden Papers, Brit. Lib., Add. Mss., 43,652, vol. 6). The emphasis on distress continued through the last entry on October 9, 1864, by mill worker John O'Neil, when he noted that many mills had stopped in Lancashire (Brigg, ed., *Journals of a Lancashire Weaver*, 138 [Apr. 10, 1864], 144 [Oct. 9, 1864].

15. CFA to Seward, no. 229, Oct. 3, 1862, *FRUS 1862*, 205; Seward to CFA, no. 372, Oct. 18, 1862, ibid., 212–13.

16. Lincoln, "Reply to Emancipation Memorial Presented by Chicago Christians of All Denominations," Sept. 13, 1862, in *CWL*, 5:422–23.

17. Ibid., 419–21, 423; *Chicago Tribune*, Sept 23, 1862, and *Washington National Intelligencer*, Sept. 26, 1862, both cited ibid., 419 n. 1.

18. Seward to CFA, no. 336, Sept. 8, 1862, *FRUS 1862*, 188; Seward to CFA, circular, Sept. 22, 1862, ibid., 195; Donald, ed., *Inside Lincoln's Cabinet*, 149–51 (Sept. 22, 1862); "Preliminary Emancipation Proclamation," Sept. 22, 1862, in *CWL*, 5:434.

19. Jenkins, *Britain and War for Union*, 2:153; Franklin, *Emancipation Proclamation*, 129–40; McPherson, *Battle Cry of Freedom*, 510, 557–58; Oates, "'Man of Our Redemption,'" 17, 19–20; McPherson, *Lincoln and Second American Revolution*, 34–35.

20. McClellan to Mary Ellen (wife), Sept. 25, 1862, in Stephen W. Sears, ed., *Civil War Papers of McClellan*, 481.

21. Lincoln quoted in T.J. Barnett to Samuel L.M. Barlow, Sept. 25, 1862, quoted in McPherson, *Battle Cry of Freedom*, 558.

22. Brauer, "Slavery Problem," 467; Van Deusen, *William H. Seward*, 333; McConnell, "From Preliminary to Final Emancipation Proclamation," 275; Dennett, ed., *Diaries and Letters of Hay*, 50 (Sept. 26, 1862); George S. Denison (collector of internal revenue for Louisiana after Lincoln lifted the blockade) to Chase, Oct. 8, 1862, American Historical Association, *Annual Report of American Historical Association for Year 1902*, 2: *Diary and Correspondence of Chase*, 319.

23. Stuart also told Lyons of the Confederate retreat from Maryland and of the announcement of the preliminary emancipation proclamation (Stuart to Lyons, Sept. 23, 1862, Russell Papers, PRO 30/22/36; Stuart to Russell, Sept. 23, 26, 1862, ibid.). The Russian minister to the United States, Baron

Edouard de Stoeckl, believed that Lincoln used the proclamation as a military tool against the South and not as a means for promoting freedom. See Stoeckl to Russian foreign minister, Prince Alexander Gorchakov, Sept. 25, 1862, in Brauer, "Slavery Problem," 463.

24. Stuart to Russell, Oct. 7, 1862, Russell Papers, PRO 30/22/36; Hammond to Layard, Oct. 6, 1862, Layard Papers, Brit. Lib., Add. Mss., 38,951, vol. 21; Cobden to Bright, Oct. 6, 1862, Cobden Papers, Brit. Lib., Add. Mss., 43,652, vol. 6; E. D. Adams, *GB and Civil War*, 2:103 n. 5. A few days later, Stuart wrote Russell that the proclamation of emancipation seemed to be causing many in the Union armies and the border states to desert to the South (Stuart to Russell, Oct. 10, 1862, Russell Papers, PRO 30/22/36).

25. Heckman, "British Press Reaction to Emancipation Proclamation"; *Times* (London), Oct. 7, 1862, p. 8, Oct. 21, 1862, p. 9; *Spectator* (London, n.d.), quoted in Whitridge, "British Liberals and Civil War," 694; *Bee-Hive* (London), Oct. 11, 1862, quoted in Kevin Logan, "*Bee-Hive* Newspaper and British Working Class Attitudes toward Civil War," 341; "The Crisis of the American War," *Blackwood's Edinburgh Magazine* 92 (Nov. 1862): 636–46 (quote on 636).

26. Palmerston to Russell, Oct. 2, 3, 1862, Russell Papers, PRO 30/22/14D.

27. Palmerston to Russell, Oct. 2, 3, 1862, Russell Papers, PRO 30/22/14D; Jenkins, *Britain and War for Union*, 2:170. Merli points out Palmerston's reluctance to consider mediation after the battle of Antietam (*GB and Confederate Navy*, 118, 257, 259).

28. Russell to Palmerston, Oct. 2, 4, 6, 1862, GC/RU/731–33, Palmerston Papers. The Russian ambassador in London, Baron Philip Brunow, was struck by the Palmerston ministry's insistence upon "doing something" before Parliament reconvened after the first of the year. Gorchakov had already informed Stoeckl that Russia would not jeopardize its friendship with the United States (Brunow quoted and Gorchakov cited in E. D. Adams, *GB and Civil War*, 2:45 n. 2).

29. *Times* (London), Oct. 7, 1862, p. 8.

30. Seward to CFA, no. 359, Sept. 26, 1862, *FRUS 1862*, 202. McPherson argues that the battle of Antietam "frustrated Confederate hopes for British recognition and precipitated the Emancipation Proclamation. The slaughter at Sharpsburg therefore proved to have been one of the war's great turning points. . . . Thus ended the South's best chance for European intervention. . . . By enabling Lincoln to issue the Emancipation Proclamation the battle . . . ensured that Britain would think twice about intervening against a government fighting for freedom as well as Union" (*Battle Cry of Freedom*, 545, 556–57). Stephen W. Sears largely agrees: "If Antietam abruptly halted the movement toward foreign intervention, the proclamation on emancipation put the seal on the matter." He admits that the latter impact "was not immediately apparent" because of the venomous reaction in England to the

belief that Lincoln was trying to stir up slave revolts. Sears then claims that Lincoln's proclamation "made it virtually impossible for any civilized power to enter the conflict on the side of the South" (*Landscape Turned Red*, 334). Owsley declares that Antietam marked "the death-blow of Confederate recognition," for Palmerston "turned against present mediation when the news of Confederate military failure arrived" (*King Cotton Diplomacy*, 347). For the counterargument that the proclamation of emancipation had no major impact on British public opinion, see Hernon, "British Sympathies in Civil War."

CHAPTER NINE

1. See CFA, Jr., "Crisis of Foreign Intervention," 24; Jenkins, *Britain and War for Union*, 2:33, 63–64, 71; Brauer, "British Mediation and Civil War"; Graebner, "European Interventionism and Crisis of 1862."

2. Matthew, ed., *Gladstone Diaries*, 6:152 n. 6; *Times* (London), Oct. 8, 1862, p. 7, Oct. 9, 1862, pp. 7–8; Ridley, *Palmerston*, 558; Mann to Benjamin, Oct. 7, 1862, *ORN*, 2d ser., 3:551; Lawley to Gladstone, Dec. 23, 1862, Gladstone Papers, Brit. Lib., Add. Mss., 44,399, vol. 314. Lawley had been a member of Parliament and a private secretary to Gladstone but left England because of financial problems caused by gambling. See also CFA, Jr., "Crisis of Foreign Intervention," 32–33; CFA Diary, Oct. 8, 9, 12, 1862; CFA to Seward, Oct. 10, 1862, no. 237, *FRUS 1862*, 209; Crawford, *Anglo-American Crisis*, 132, 172 n. 8; Jenkins, "Lawley and Confederacy"; Jenkins, *Britain and War for Union*, 2:47–50. Two writers have found no evidence for the charge that Gladstone's speech was a "trial balloon" by the cabinet to gauge popular feeling. It seems likely that Gladstone was out of touch with the cabinet. See Merli and Wilson, "British Cabinet and Confederacy." See also Merli, *GB and Confederate Navy*, 100, 107–8, and Matthew, *Gladstone*, 133.

3. Cobden to Bright, Oct. 7, 1862;, Cobden Papers, Brit. Lib., Add. Mss., 43,652, vol. 6; Bright to Cobden, Oct. 8, 1862, Bright Papers, Brit. Lib., Add. Mss., 43,384, vol. 2; Magnus, *Gladstone*, 2, 18–19.

4. Argyll to Russell, Oct. 11, 1862, Russell Papers, PRO 30/22/25.

5. Clarendon to Lewis, Oct. 13, 1862, Clarendon Papers; Clarendon to Palmerston, Oct. 16, 1862, GC/CL/1207, Palmerston Papers; Crook, *North, South, and Powers*, 241.

6. Gladstone to Russell, Oct. 17, 1862, Gladstone Papers, Brit. Lib., Add. Mss., 44,292, vol. 207. See also Reid, ed., "Gladstone's 'Insincere Neutrality.'"

7. Palmerston to Russell, Oct. 12, 1862, Russell Papers, PRO 30/22/22; Palmerston to Russell, Oct. 17, Dec. 17, 1862, ibid., PRO 30/22/14D; CFA, Jr., "Crisis of Foreign Intervention," 32; Matthew, *Gladstone*, 133–34, 186; Gladstone to Arthur Gordon (the correspondent), Sept. 22, 1862, ibid.,

134; Jenkins, *Britain and War for Union*, 2:22–23. Palmerston expressed to Clarendon the same reservations about Gladstone's speech. See Palmerston to Clarendon, Oct. 20, 1862, in Maxwell, *Clarendon*, 2:267.

8. Hammond to Layard, Oct. 12, 18, 26, 27, 1862, Layard Papers, Brit. Lib., Add. Mss., 38,951, vol. 21.

9. Russell to Gladstone, Oct. 20, 26, 1862, Gladstone Papers, Brit. Lib., Add. Mss., 44,292, vol. 207.

10. CFA Diary, Oct. 8, 9, 23, 1862; Morley, *Gladstone*, 2:80; Moran Diary, Oct. 9, 24, 1862; CFA to Seward, Oct. 24, 1862, no. 248, *FRUS 1862*, 224.

11. Palmerston to Russell, Oct. 8, 1862, Russell Papers, PRO 30/22/14D.

12. Russell to Cowley, Oct. 11, 1862, ibid., PRO 30/22/105. Cowley was Henry Richard Charles Wellesley, First Earl Cowley.

13. Russell, "Memorandum" for FO, Oct. 13, 1862, Gladstone Papers, Brit. Lib., Add. Mss., 44,595, vol. 510; E. D. Adams, *GB and Civil War*, 2:49–50.

14. Argyll to Russell, Oct. 15, 1862, Russell Papers, PRO 30/22/25.

15. Lewis, ed., *Letters of George Cornewall Lewis*, vi, viii–ix, xi; Earl of Aberdeen to Lewis, Nov. 6, 1858, ibid., 352; Lewis to E. Twisleton (first friend), Jan. 21, 1861, ibid., 391–92; Lewis to Sir Edmund Head, governor of Canada (second friend), Mar. 10, 1861, ibid., 393; Lewis to Head, May 13, Sept. 8, 1861, ibid., 395, 402; Head to Twisleton, Nov. 30, 1861, ibid., 405–6; characterization of Lewis by Argyll in Argyll, ed., *Argyll, Autobiography and Memoirs*, 1:540.

16. Lewis at Hereford in CFA, Jr., "Crisis of Foreign Intervention," 37; Clarendon to Lewis, Oct. 13, 1862, Clarendon Papers; Palmerston to Clarendon, Oct. 20, 1862, in Maxwell, *Clarendon*, 2:267; Clarendon to Palmerston, Oct. 16, 1862, GC/CL/1207/1–3, Palmerston Papers; Lewis, "Memorandum on the American Question," Oct. 17, 1862, Gladstone Papers, Brit. Lib., Add. Mss., 44,595, vol. 510; Morley, *Gladstone*, 2:80; Merli, *GB and Confederate Navy*, 107–9. It was rumored that Palmerston had arranged for Lewis to deliver the speech at Hereford. Such rumors now seem unfounded. See E. D. Adams, *GB and Civil War*, 2:50, 50 n. 1; Crook, *North, South, and Powers*, 233.

17. Regarding Lewis's mention of the proclamation of emancipation, Gladstone inserted a marginal comment on the memo: "May have about played their last very *great* card" (Lewis, "Memorandum on the American Question," Oct. 17, 1862, Gladstone Papers, Brit. Lib., Add. Mss., 44,595, vol. 510).

18. Ibid. Lewis's quote was a loose rendition of Hamlet's words in William Shakespeare's play *The Tragedy of Hamlet, Prince of Denmark*, act 3, scene 1.

19. Russell to Stuart, Oct. 18 [?], 1862, Russell Papers, PRO 30/22/96; Russell to Cowley, Oct. 18, 1862, ibid., PRO 30/22/105; Russell to Palmerston, Oct. 18, 20, 1862, GC/RU/734–35, Palmerston Papers.

20. Palmerston to Russell, Oct. 20, 21, 22, 1862, Russell Papers, PRO 30/22/14D.

21. Russell claimed that Palmerston had decided against a cabinet meeting and only told Russell the day before (Russell to Grey, Oct. 28, 1862, in Gooch, ed., *Later Correspondence of John Russell*, 2:331–32). See also Lewis to Grey, Oct. 23, 1862, Ripon Papers, Brit. Lib., Add. Mss., 43,533, vol. 43; CFA Diary, Oct. 23, 1862; CFA to Seward, Oct. 24, 1862, no. 248, *FRUS 1862*, 224; E. D. Adams, *GB and Civil War*, 2:55; Clarendon to Lewis, Oct. 24, 1862, in Maxwell, *Clarendon*, 2:265.

22. Anderson to Stuart, Oct. 1, 1862, enclosed in Stuart to Russell, Oct. 7, 1862, Gladstone Papers, Brit. Lib., Add. Mss., 44,595, vol. 510.

23. Russell, Memo for FO, Oct. 23, 1862, ibid.

24. Palmerston to Russell, Oct. 23, 24, 1862, Russell Papers, PRO 30/22/14D.

25. Clarendon to Lewis, Oct. 24, 1862, in Maxwell, *Clarendon*, 2:265–66.

26. Russell to Palmerston, Oct. 24, 1862, GC/RU/736, Palmerston Papers.

27. Gladstone, "The War in America," Oct. 24, 1862, Gladstone Papers, Brit. Lib., Add. Mss., 44,595, vol. 510.

28. Lewis to Russell, Oct. 25, 1862, Russell Papers, PRO 30/22/25; Russell to Lewis, Oct. 26, 1862, ibid., PRO 30/22/14D; Jenkins, *Britain and War for Union*, 2:177.

29. Grey to Russell, Oct. 27, 1862, Russell Papers, PRO 30/22/25; Russell to Grey, Oct. 28, 1862, in Gooch, ed., *Later Correspondence of John Russell*, 2:332.

30. Granville to Lord Stanley, Oct. 1, 1862, in Fitzmaurice, *Granville*, 1:442; Palmerston to Russell, Oct. 26, 1862, Russell Papers, PRO 30/22/14D.

CHAPTER TEN

1. Crook, *North, South, and Powers*, 248; E. D. Adams, *GB and Civil War*, 2:60; Owsley, *King Cotton Diplomacy*, 335; Carroll, *Mercier and Civil War*, 239–40; Case and Spencer, *U.S. and France*, 356–61. Case and Spencer claim that Napoleon "apparently" based his plan on Russell's objectives of September (ibid., 356).

2. Stuart to Russell, Oct. 17, 24, 26, 1862, Russell Papers, PRO 30/22/36. Stuart repeated his support for intervention in a letter to George Elliot (Stuart to Elliott, Oct. 24, 1862, ibid., PRO 30/22/36). For Mercier's pro-separatist feelings, see Case and Spencer, *U.S. and France*, 353. For Stuart's pro-South sympathies, see any number of his dispatches to Russell while Lyons was in London from June through early November 1862.

3. Cowley to Russell, Oct. 27, 1862, Russell Papers, PRO 30/22/14D; Cowley's memorandum of his conversation with Drouyn, Oct. 28, 1862, FO 27/1446, PRO. The new French foreign minister, Edouard Drouyn de Lhuys, later assured Cowley that the emperor's only purpose was to end the

war. Drouyn preferred waiting a while. Besides, he explained to Cowley, if the North spurned the proposal Russia would doubtless refuse to join England and France in extending recognition to the South (ibid.).

4. Memo of Slidell interview with Napoleon on Oct. 28, 1862, enclosure B in Slidell to Benjamin, Oct. 28, 1862, *ORN*, 2d ser., 3:574–77. See also Case and Spencer, *U.S. and France*, 356–57, and Owsley, *King Cotton Diplomacy*, 333–36. Drouyn wrote Mercier that the government in Paris would not try to force the North into compliance (Drouyn to Mercier, Oct. 30, 1862, cited ibid., 336).

5. Memo of Slidell interview with Napoleon; Slidell to Mason, Oct. 29, 1862, Mason Papers. Although Slidell's note of October 29 did not arrive in Richmond until December 31, he wrote Mason on the same day—October 29—about the interview. Mason presumably informed Benjamin soon afterward (and long before December 31) because on December 11 Benjamin wrote Mason of the Confederacy's support for a six-month armistice (ibid.). See also Case and Spencer, *U.S. and France*, 356–57, 364.

6. Bulloch, *Secret Service of Confederate States in Europe*, 2:23–24; Benjamin to Mason, Dec. 11, 1862, Mason Papers; Benjamin to Mason, Jan. 15, 1863, *ORN*, 2d ser., 3:656; Mason to Benjamin, Nov. 6, 1862, in Richardson, ed., *Messages and Papers of the Confederacy*, 2:359.

7. Benjamin to Mason, Oct. 28, 31, 1862, Mason Papers.

8. Cowley to Russell, Oct. 31, 1862, FO 27/1446/1236, PRO; Russell to Lyons, Nov. 1, 1862, Russell Papers, PRO 30/22/96; Russell to Cowley, Nov. 1, 1862, ibid., PRO 30/22/105.

9. Case and Spencer, *U.S. and France*, 361. Ephraim D. Adams argues that Napoleon never offered a mediation, although it was implied (*GB and Civil War*, 2:60 n. 2).

10. Russell to Palmerston, GC/RU/739, Nov. 3, 1862, Palmerston Papers.

11. King (Leopold) of Belgium to Palmerston, Oct. 30–Nov. 3, 1862, Russell Papers, PRO 30/22/14D; Leopold to Russell, Oct. 31, 1862, in Gooch, ed., *Later Correspondence of John Russell*, 2:332; Palmerston to Russell, Nov. 2, 1862, Russell Papers, PRO 30/22/14D. Palmerston focused on Greek problems in his November 2 letter and in others through December (Palmerston to Russell, Nov. 2, 1862, and after, ibid.).

12. Stuart to Russell, Nov. 4, 1862, Russell Papers, PRO 30/22/36.

13. Stuart to Russell, Nov. 7, 1862, ibid.; Russell to Grey, Oct. 28, 1862, in Gooch, ed., *Later Correspondence of John Russell*, 2:332; McPherson, *Battle Cry of Freedom*, 561–62; Graebner, "Northern Diplomacy and European Neutrality"; Brauer, "British Mediation and Civil War."

14. Lyons to Russell, Nov. 11, 1862, Russell Papers, PRO 30/22/36.

15. Lyons to Russell, Nov. 14, 1862, ibid.

16. Ibid.; Lyons to Russell, Nov. 17, 1862, *BFSP 1864–1865*, 55:534–39. Russell showed his lack of understanding of the American political system when he had to ask Lyons if the election of the next president would be in autumn 1864 (Russell to Lyons, Nov. 8, 1862, Russell Papers, PRO 30/22/

96). Lyons's biographer remarks in vague terms that while the minister was home in London, he was in "constant communication with the cabinet" and that the ministers opposed interference in the American war but thought it "might be forced upon them." See Newton, *Lyons*, 1:89–90.

17. Lyons to Russell, Nov. 18, 24, 1862, Russell Papers, PRO 30/22/36; Lyons to Russell, Nov. 18, 1862 (confidential), no. 438, FO 5/838, PRO.

18. Gardiner, *Harcourt*, 1:125, 127, 132–37; Jenkins, *Britain and War for Union*, 2:179–80; Crook, *North, South, and Powers*, 241; Merli, *GB and Confederate Navy*, 114–15.

19. Historicus letter dated Nov. 4, 1862, in *Times* (London), Nov. 7, 1862, pp. 6–7; letter reprinted in *Letters by Historicus*, 3–15 (quotes ibid., 8, 9–10); Historicus, "Neutrality or Intervention," ibid., 41–51 (quotes ibid., 42, 43, 46, 47, 48, 49–50, 51) (letter in *Times* [London], Nov. 17, 1862, p. 9). Historicus argued that Palmerston had been wrong in October in defining "Lewis's Doctrine" as an argument for England to wait on granting recognition until the Union did so; Lewis had called instead for "*de facto* independence" (letter dated Nov. 8, 1862, in *Letters by Historicus*, 8). See also E. D. Adams, *GB and Civil War*, 2:63; Crook, *North, South, and Powers*, 251; CFA, Jr., "Crisis of Foreign Intervention," 40–41. Hotze wrote Benjamin that the *Times*'s refusal to print his rebuttal to Historicus showed favor to the Palmerston ministry (Hotze to Benjamin, Nov. 22, 1862, *ORN*, 2d ser., 3:611–12).

20. Lewis, "Recognition of the Independence of the Southern States of the North American Union," Nov. 7, 1862, Gladstone Papers, Brit. Lib., Add. Mss., 44,595, vol. 510. The original draft (though incomplete) is in the National Library of Wales in Aberystwyth. See Lewis Papers, War Office and India, 3509, 3510, and 3514. The assistant keeper of the Department of Manuscripts and Records, Gwyn Jenkins, has assured me that there are no other references to this aspect of the Civil War in Lewis's papers.

21. Lewis, "Recognition of Independence."

22. Ibid.

23. When Lewis wrote that recognition of independence by a foreign government was "recognition of a fact," Gladstone responded in the margin: "in what sense?" Lewis showed a precedent for caution. The United States itself sent a secret agent to Hungary in 1850 to determine how far the revolt had progressed before deciding whether to extend recognition. Austria complained in a formal diplomatic manner, discouraging the government in Washington from making such a decision (ibid.).

24. Lewis cited Austin, *Province of Jurisprudence Determined*, 214, in support of his argument pertaining to recognition. (The quote, however, is on 206–7.) Austin was the first professor of jurisprudence (philosophy of law) at the University of London when it was founded in 1826. Two years later, Lewis was among a number of Benthamites who attended Austin's lectures on the subject of jurisprudence. In 1836 Austin joined Lewis as commissioners to offer advice on constitutional and legal reforms in Malta. See "Introduction," viii, ibid., by H. L. A. Hart. Lewis's other historical examples were the

Netherlands, Portugal, Greece, Belgium, the South American colonies and Spain, and the South American colonies and Portugal (Lewis, "Recognition of Independence").

25. Lewis, ibid., cited Vattel, *Law of Nations*, bk. 3, sect. 295.

26. Lewis, ibid., cited Wheaton, *Elements of International Law* (1836 ed.), pt. 1, sect. 26.

27. Lewis's reference to recognition was to Mason's letter, which appeared in the *Times* of London on October 22, 1862, p. 8. On the question of what recognition could have done for the South, Gladstone wrote in the margin of Lewis's memo that the action would "accelerate the issue" of independence (Lewis, "Recognition of Independence").

28. Ibid.

29. Ibid.; Lewis to Harcourt, Nov. 21, 1862, Harcourt Papers, Box 12. Lewis cited Vattel, *Law of Nations*, bk. 3, sect. 295. See also ibid., sect. 296. The law of nature is, of course, the basis of international law.

30. Lewis, "Recognition of Independence."

31. Ibid.

32. Lord Napier (British ambassador in St. Petersburg) to Russell, Nov. 8, 1862, cited in E. D. Adams, *GB and Civil War*, 2:63, 66; Lewis to Clarendon, Nov. 11, 1862, in Maxwell, *Clarendon*, 2:268; Jenkins, *Britain and War for Union*, 2:180. Russell, the reader will recall, had first learned of the French proposal on an unofficial basis on November 1.

33. Lewis to Clarendon, Nov. 11, 1862, Clarendon Papers; Gladstone to wife, Nov. 12, 13, 1862, in Morley, *Gladstone*, 2:85.

34. Lewis to Clarendon, Nov. 11, 1862, Clarendon Papers. On November 13 an article appeared in the *Times* of London, Lewis noted, "throwing cold water on the invitation." He assumed that someone had informed the editor, John Delane, of the cabinet's decision. See *Times*, Nov. 13, 1862, p. 8. Palmerston, one might note, maintained close ties with Delane. See Crawford, *Anglo-American Crisis*, 18.

35. Russell to Cowley, Nov. 13, 1862, Cowley Papers, FO 146/1046; Cowley to Russell, Nov. 18, 1862, cited in Case and Spencer, *U.S. and France*, 363.

36. Gladstone to wife, Nov. 12, 1862, in Morley, *Gladstone*, 2:85; Lyons to Russell, Nov. 28, 1862, Russell Papers, PRO 30/22/36.

37. Moran Diary, Nov. 11, 12, 13, 1862; *Times* (London), Nov. 13, 1862, p. 8; CFA Diary, Nov. 15, 1862; Russian letter in *Journal of St. Petersburg*, Nov. 15, 1862, published in *Times* (London), Nov. 17, 1862, p. 12, and enclosed in CFA to Seward, Nov. 15, 1862, no. 261, *FRUS 1863*, 3; CFA to Seward, Nov. 13, 1862, no. 259, ibid., 1. (Adams was referring to the *Journal of St. Petersburg*.) See also Saul, *Distant Friends*, 334–35, and Woldman, *Lincoln and Russians*, 133–35. On November 15 word arrived in London from the American legation in Paris that Drouyn had declared that if England and Russia declined, the proposal would die. "I hope so," Moran tersely remarked (Moran Diary, Nov. 15, 1862).

38. Lyons to Russell, Dec. 2, 1862, *BFSP 1864–1865*, 55:539–40; Seward to Dayton, Nov. 30, 1862, ibid., 435–36; Seward to CFA, Dec. 8, 1862, no. 418, *FRUS 1863*, 12–13; Seward to Bayard Taylor, Dec. 7, 1862, no. 9, U.S., DS, Diplomatic Instructions of DS, 1801–1906, Russia, NA. Taylor had sent dispatches dated Nov. 11, 12, and 15, all assuring President Lincoln of the tsar's friendly policy.

39. Lawley to Gladstone, Dec. 23, 1862, Gladstone Papers, Brit. Lib., Add. Mss., 44,399, vol. 314; *Index*, Nov. 20, 1862, p. 56, quoted in E. D. Adams, *GB and Civil War*, 2:68.

40. E. D. Adams, *GB and Civil War*, 2:69; CFA Diary, Nov. 15, 1862, May 3, 1868; Seward to CFA, Aug. 2, 1862, no. 314, *FRUS 1862*, 165–66; Duberman, *CFA*, 297–98; *Richmond Whig* quoted in *Index*, Jan. 15, 1863, p. 191, quoted in E. D. Adams, *GB and Civil War*, 2:68. In Charles Francis Adams's "Reminiscences of his mission to Great Britain, 1861–1862," which he began in September 1867, he called Russell a man of "unquestioned integrity" and remarked, "It was fortunate I had just such a person to deal with during my difficult times" (CFA, Miscellany, Adams Family Papers, reel 296).

41. Slidell in late November 1862, quoted in CFA, Jr., "Crisis of Foreign Intervention," 51; Harcourt to Lewis [1863?], Harcourt Papers, Box 12.

42. CFA to Seward, Dec. 4, 1862, no. 268, *FRUS 1863*, 11; Palmerston to Russell, Dec. 17, 1862, Russell Papers, PRO 30/22/14D; Grote to Lewis, Dec. 27, 1862, ibid. (J.S.G.? [illegible] to Russell and written five months after the *Alabama*'s escape from Liverpool in July 1862); Gladstone to Field, Nov. 27, 1862, Gladstone Papers, Brit. Lib., Add. Mss., 44,399, vol. 314. Field was involved in developing the transatlantic cable. Palmerston told the king of Belgium that England would have accepted the French proposal for a joint communication to North and South if it had had a chance for success. Intervention in two to three months might work. See Palmerston to king of Belgium, Nov. 18, 1862, PM/J/1, Palmerston Letterbook, Palmerston Papers.

CONCLUSION

1. For writers who have shown Lewis's participation in the interventionist debates, see n. 8 of Introduction, above. Two of those cited, Frank J. Merli and Theodore A. Wilson, attribute nonintervention primarily to Palmerston. See their article "British Cabinet and Confederacy," 261–62. The final decision, of course, rested with Palmerston, but it was Lewis who provided convincing historical and legal evidence supporting the prime minister's inclination to stay out of the war.

2. Bright to Cobden, Dec. 24, 1862, Bright Papers, Brit. Lib., Add. Mss., 43,384, vol. 2; Henry Adams to CFA, Jr., Jan. 27, 1863, in Ford, ed., *Adams Letters*, 1:243–45; CFA Diary, Jan. 2, 13, 16, 17, Feb. 27, 1863; CFA to

Seward, Jan. 2, 1863, no. 289, Disp., GB (NA). See also Jordan and Pratt, *Europe and Civil War*, 145–63.

3. Even Stoeckl thought the Emancipation Proclamation "impolitic and impractical" and intended to stir up slave rebellions in the South (Saul, *Distant Friends*, 335).

4. For intervention as the real threat to Anglo-American relations but coming to an end in November 1862, see Beloff, "Historical Revision no. CXVIII," 47. For Napoleon's unilateral mediation offer, see Case and Spencer, *U.S. and France*, chap. 11. For the Roebuck-Lindsay affair, see ibid., chap. 12; Owsley, *King Cotton Diplomacy*, chap. 13; Crook, *North, South, and Powers*, 309–12, 314–15; E. D. Adams, *GB and Civil War*, 2:164–78; Jenkins, *Britain and War for Union*, 2:309–13. After praising Southerners as English gentlemen, Roebuck denounced Northerners as "the scum of Europe." See *Parl. Debates*, 171:1826 (Commons, June 30, 1863). Roebuck had earlier told Palmerston: "The North will never be our friends. Of the South you can make friends. They are Englishmen. They are not the scum and refuse of Europe." See Roebuck to Palmerston, Aug. 1862, in Leader, *Roebuck*, 296. One member of Parliament, Sir John Trelawny, considered Roebuck's speech "clever" and "amusing" but did not believe he had aroused much support for recognition. See Jenkins, ed., *Parliamentary Diaries of Trelawny*, 260 (June 30, 1863). See also ibid., 261, 265. For the argument that commercial concerns helped maintain Anglo-American ties, see Claussen, "Peace Factors in Anglo-American Relations." For Mason's instructions to leave England, see Benjamin to Mason, Aug. 4, 1863, Mason Papers. Mason departed on September 21, a week after Benjamin's directive arrived in London (Mason to Russell, Sept. 21, 1863, ibid. [Disp.]). Mason remained as Southern commissioner on the Continent but did not give up on recognition. He returned to England twice to talk unofficially with Palmerston about the matter—on July 14, 1864, and March 14, 1865. By the time of the second meeting, the Davis administration had become so desperate that it sent Congressman Duncan F. Kenner of Louisiana to Europe to instruct Slidell and Mason to offer emancipation in exchange for French and British recognition. Napoleon would not move without England, and Palmerston showed no interest in Mason's implied offer. Indeed, the prime minister emphasized that slavery was not the reason for nonintervention and that the South had simply not proved its claim to independence. Lee surrendered to Grant less than a month later. See Mason to Benjamin, June 1, Aug. 4, Nov. 10, 1864, ibid.; Mason to Benjamin, Mar. 31, 1865, ibid. For the Kenner mission and the South's thoughts on emancipation, see Crook, *North, South, and Powers*, 356–59; Bauer, "Last Effort." Mason thought England had refused recognition because of its fear of war with the United States and its belief that a long war would hurt North and South while benefiting England (ibid.). For England's wartime profits, see Parish, *Civil War*, 400. For the end of the so-called cotton famine, see ibid. and Owsley, *King Cotton Diplomacy*, 137–38. In January 1863 an unofficial French mediation effort developed that involved Horace

Greeley, editor of the *New York Tribune*, William C. Jewett, a private American citizen known for adventurist activities, and Mercier. Nothing came of the attempt. See Spencer, "Jewett-Greeley Affair."

5. Seward to John Bigelow, Dec. 2, 1862, in Bigelow, *Retrospections*, 1:579. Others pronounced intervention dead. See E. D. Adams, *GB and Civil War*, 2:73–74; McPherson, *Battle Cry of Freedom*, 556; Parish, *Civil War*, 182; Bass, "Fall of Crisis." For Palmerston's concerns about Europe and Canada, see Beloff, "Historical Revision no. CXVIII," 42, and Robert H. Jones, "Anglo-American Relations," 39. Problems in Poland and Schleswig-Holstein particularly drew England's attention.

6. Seward to CFA, Aug. 27, 1866, folder 6302: DS Printed Material, Seward Papers; Report to Lord Stanley on Seward's letter respecting *Alabama* claims, Feb. 14, 1867, Law Officer's Reports, America, 1866–68, FO 83/2225, PRO. See also Cook, *Alabama Claims*.

7. For a thought-provoking prognostication on what would have happened to Anglo-American relations had England intervened in the Civil War, see Nevins, *War for Union*, 2:242.

BIBLIOGRAPHY

PRIMARY MATERIALS

Manuscript Sources

Adams, Charles Francis. Diary. Adams Family Papers. Massachusetts Historical Society, Boston, Massachusetts.

―――. Letterbook. Adams Family Papers. Massachusetts Historical Society, Boston, Massachusetts.

―――. Miscellany. Adams Family Papers. Massachusetts Historical Society, Boston, Massachusetts.

Bright, John. Papers. British Library, London, England.

Clarendon, Fourth Earl of (George William Frederick Villiers). Papers. Bodleian Library, Oxford University, Oxford, England.

Cobden, Richard. Papers. British Library, London, England.

Cowley, Lord (Henry Richard Charles Wellesley, First Earl Cowley). Papers. FO 146. Public Record Office, Kew, England.

Gladstone, William E. Papers. British Library, London, England.

Great Britain. Foreign Office. FO 5 (ser. 2), America, United States, Public Record Office, Kew, England.

―――. FO 27, France, General Correspondence, Public Record Office, Kew, England.

―――. FO 83, Great Britain and General, Law Officer's Reports, America, 1866–68, Public Record Office, Kew, England.

―――. FO 115, Embassy and Consular Archives, America, United States. Public Record Office, Kew, England.

―――. FO 146, Embassy and Consular Archives, France, Public Record Office, Kew, England.

Harcourt, William Vernon. Papers. Stanton-Harcourt Collection, Bodleian Library, Oxford University, Oxford, England.

Layard, Sir Austen Henry. Papers. British Library, London, England.

Lewis, George Cornewall. Papers. National Library of Wales, Aberystwyth, Wales.

Mason, James M. Papers. Manuscript Division, Library of Congress, Washington, D.C.

Moran, Benjamin. Diary. Manuscript Division, Library of Congress, Washington, D.C.

Palmerston, Lord (Henry John Temple). Papers. University of Southampton, Southampton, England.

Ripon, First Marquis of (Earl de Grey, George Frederick Samuel Robinson). Papers. British Library, London, England.

Russell, Lord John (First Earl Russell). Papers. Public Record Office, Kew, England.

Seward, William H. Papers. Rush Rhees Library, University of Rochester, Rochester, New York.

United States. Department of State. Dispatches from United States Ministers to Great Britain, 1792–1870, National Archives, Washington, D.C.

———. Diplomatic Instructions of the Department of State, 1801–1906, Great Britain, National Archives, Washington, D.C.

———. Diplomatic Instructions of the Department of State, 1801–1906, Russia, National Archives, Washington, D.C.

———. Notes from the British Legation in the United States to the Department of State, 1791–1906. National Archives, Washington, D.C.

———. Notes to Foreign Legations in the United States from the Department of State, 1834–1906, Great Britain. National Archives, Washington, D.C.

Published Sources

Adams, Charles Francis, Jr. *Before and After the Treaty of Washington: The American Civil War and the War in the Transvaal*. New York: New York Historical Society, 1902.

———. Charles Francis, Jr. *1835–1915: An Autobiography*. Boston: Houghton Mifflin, 1916.

Adams, Henry. *The Education of Henry Adams: An Autobiography*. Boston and New York: Houghton Mifflin, 1918.

American Historical Association. *Annual Report of the American Historical Association for the Year 1902*. 2 vols. Vol. 2: *Sixth Report of Historical Manuscripts Commission: With Diary and Correspondence of Salmon P. Chase*. Washington, D.C.: U.S. Government Printing Office, 1903.

Argyll, Duchess of, ed. *George Douglas, Eighth Duke of Argyll (1823–1900) Autobiography and Memoirs*. 2 vols. London: John Murray, 1906.

Ashmore, Owen, ed. "The Diary of James Garnett of Low Moor, Clitheroe, 1858–65." Vol. 1: "Years of Prosperity, 1858–60." In *Transactions of the Historic Society of Lancashire and Cheshire for the Year 1969* 121:77–98. Liverpool: Printed for Society, 1970. Vol. 2: "The American Civil War and the Cotton Famine, 1861–65." In *Transactions of the Historic Society of Lancashire and Cheshire for the Year 1971* 123:105–43. Liverpool: Printed for Society, 1972.

Austin, John. *The Province of Jurisprudence Determined*. London: Weidenfeld and Nicolson, 1832.

Basler, Roy P., ed. *The Collected Works of Abraham Lincoln*. 8 vols. and Index. New Brunswick: Rutgers University Press, 1953–55.

Baxter, James P., ed. "Papers Relating to Belligerent and Neutral Rights." *American Historical Review* 34 (October 1928): 77–91.

Beale, Howard K., ed. *The Diary of Edward Bates, 1859–1866*. Washington, D.C.: U.S. Government Printing Office, 1933.

———. *Diary of Gideon Welles: Secretary of the Navy under Lincoln and Johnson*. 3 vols. New York: Norton, 1960.

Benson, Arthur C., and Viscount Esher, eds. *The Letters of Queen Victoria, 1837–1861*. 3 vols. London: John Murray, 1908.

Bernard, Mountague. *A Historical Account of the Neutrality of Great Britain during the American Civil War*. London: Longmans, Green, Reader, and Dyer, 1870.

Berwanger, Eugene H., ed. William Howard Russell. *My Diary North and South*. Philadelphia: Temple University Press, 1988.

Bigelow, John. *Retrospections of an Active Life*. 5 vols. New York: Baker and Taylor, 1909–13.

Bourne, Kenneth, and D. Cameron Watt, eds. *British Documents on Foreign Affairs: Reports and Papers from the Foreign Office Confidential Print*. Pt. 1, ser. C: *North America, 1837–1914*, vols. 5 and 6; *The Civil War Years, 1859–1865*. Bethesda, Md.: University Publications of America, 1986.

Brigg, Mary, ed. *The Journals of a Lancashire Weaver, 1856–64, 1872–75*. In *The Record Society of Lancashire and Cheshire* 122. Liverpool: Printed for the Society, 1982.

Buckle, George E., ed. *The Letters of Queen Victoria, 1862–1878*. 2d ser., 2 vols. New York: Longmans, Green, 1926–28.

Bulloch, James D. *The Secret Service of the Confederate States in Europe*. 2 vols. 1883. Reprint. New York: Thomas Yoseloff, 1959.

Connell, Brian, ed. *Regina vs. Palmerston: The Correspondence between Queen Victoria and Her Foreign and Prime Minister, 1837–1865*. Garden City, N.Y.: Doubleday, 1961.

Davis, Jefferson. *The Rise and Fall of the Confederate Government*. 2 vols. New York: D. Appleton, 1881.

Dennett, Tyler, ed. *Lincoln and the Civil War in the Diaries and Letters of John Hay*. New York: Dodd, Mead, 1939.

Donald, David, ed. *Inside Lincoln's Cabinet: The Civil War Diaries of Salmon P. Chase*. New York: Longmans, Green, 1954.

Ford, Worthington C., ed. *A Cycle of Adams Letters, 1861–1865*. 2 vols. Boston: Houghton Mifflin, 1920.

Gooch, G. P., ed. *The Later Correspondence of Lord John Russell, 1840–1878*. 2 vols. London: Longmans, Green, 1925.

Great Britain. *British Parliamentary Papers, 1801–1899*. 1,000 vols. Shannon: Irish University Press, date varies by volume.

———. Foreign Office. *British and Foreign State Papers*. 116 vols. London: William Ridgway, 1812–1925.

———. Parliament. *British Sessional Papers* (House of Commons and Lords). 1801–1900.

Guedalla, Philip, ed. *Gladstone and Palmerston: Being the Correspondence of*

Lord Palmerston with Mr. Gladstone, 1851–1865. Covent Garden: Victor Gollancz, 1928.

Hansard, Thomas C., ed. *Hansard's Parliamentary Debates*. 3d ser. 356 vols. London: Wyman, 1830–91.

Hoole, W. Stanley, ed. "Notes and Documents: William L. Yancey's European Diary, March–June, 1861." *Alabama Review* 25 (April 1972): 134–42.

Jenkins, T. A., ed. *The Parliamentary Diaries of Sir John Trelawny, 1858–1865*. London: Royal Historical Society, 1990.

Jones, John B. *A Rebel War Clerk's Diary*. 1866. Reprint edited by Earl S. Miers. New York: Sagamore Press, 1958.

Jones, Robert H. "The American Civil War in the British Sessional Papers: Catalogue and Commentary." *Proceedings of the American Philosophical Society* 107 (October 1963): 415–26.

Letters by Historicus on Some Questions of International Law. London: Macmillan, 1863.

Levenson, J. C., et al., eds. *The Letters of Henry Adams*. 6 vols. Cambridge, Mass.: Harvard University Press, 1982–88.

Lewis, Gilbert F., ed. *Letters of the Right Hon. Sir George Cornewall Lewis*. London: Longmans, Green, 1870.

MacCarthy, Desmond, and Agatha Russell, eds. *Lady John Russell: A Memoir with Selections from Her Diaries and Correspondence*. New York: John Lane, 1911.

Mason, Virginia. *The Public Life and Diplomatic Correspondence of James M. Mason*. Roanoke, Va.: Stone Printing & Manufacturing Co., 1903.

Matthew, H. C. G., ed. *The Gladstone Diaries*. 9 vols. Oxford: Clarendon, 1978.

Mitchell, Brian R., comp. *European Historical Statistics, 1750–1970*. New York: Columbia University Press, 1975.

Monroe, Haskell M., Jr., et al., eds. *The Papers of Jefferson Davis*. 5 vols. Baton Rouge: Louisiana State University Press, 1971–85.

Palmer, Beverly W., ed. *The Selected Letters of Charles Sumner*. 2 vols. Boston: Northeastern University Press, 1990.

Pease, Theodore C., and James G. Randall, eds. *The Diary of Orville Hickman Browning*. 2 vols. Springfield: Illinois State Historical Library, 1925.

Pratt, Fletcher, ed. William Howard Russell. *My Diary North and South*. New York: Harper, 1954.

Reid, Robert L., ed. "William E. Gladstone's 'Insincere Neutrality' during the Civil War." *Civil War History* 15 (December 1969): 293–307.

Richardson, James D., ed. *A Compilation of the Messages and Papers of the Confederacy, Including the Diplomatic Correspondence, 1861–1865*. 2 vols. Nashville: U.S. Publishing Co., 1905.

Russell, John Earl. *Recollections and Suggestions, 1813–1873*. Boston: Roberts Brothers, 1875.

Sears, Stephen W., ed. *The Civil War Papers of George B. McClellan: Selected Correspondence, 1860–1865*. New York: Ticknor and Fields, 1989.

Seward, Frederick W. *Reminiscences of a Wartime Statesman and Diplomat, 1830–1915.* New York: Putnam's, 1916.

Seward, William H. *Autobiography of William H. Seward from 1801 to 1834. With a Memoir of His Life, and Selections from His Letters from 1831 to 1846.* Edited by Frederick W. Seward. 3 vols. New York: D. Appleton, 1877.

Silver, A. W., ed. "Henry Adams' 'Diary of a Visit to Manchester.' " *American Historical Review* 51 (October 1945): 74–89.

United States. *Congressional Globe.*

————. Department of State. *Papers Relating to Foreign Affairs, Accompanying the Annual Message of the President to the Second Session of the Thirty-Seventh Congress, 1861.* Washington, D.C.: U.S. Government Printing Office, 1861.

————. *Papers Relating to Foreign Affairs Communicated to Congress, December 1, 1862.* Washington, D.C.: U.S. Government Printing Office, 1863.

————. *Papers Relating to Foreign Affairs, Accompanying the Annual Message of the President to the First Session of the Thirty-Eighth Congress.* Washington, D.C.: U.S. Government Printing Office, 1864.

————. Federal Courts. *The Federal Cases Comprising Cases Argued and Determined in the Circuit and District Courts of the United States.* St. Paul: West, 1896.

————. Naval War Records Office. *Official Records of the Union and Confederate Navies in the War of the Rebellion.* 2d ser. 3 vols. Washington, D.C.: U.S. Government Printing Office, 1894–1927.

————. Supreme Court. *U.S. Supreme Court Reports: Cases Argued and Decided in the Supreme Court of the United States,* 5, 6, 7, 8 Wheaton, *Lawyers' Edition.* Rochester, N.Y.: Lawyers' Co-operative Publishing Company, 1918.

Vattel, Emmerich de. *The Law of Nations, or, Principles of the Law of Nature Applied to the Conduct and Affairs of Nations and Sovereigns.* Philadelphia: Abraham Small, 1817.

Wallace, Sarah A., and Frances E. Gillespie, eds. *The Journal of Benjamin Moran, 1857–1865.* 2 vols. Chicago: University of Chicago Press, 1949.

Wellesley, F. A., ed. *Secrets of the Second Empire: Private Letters from the Paris Embassy, Selections from the Papers of Henry Richard Charles Wellesley, 1st Earl Cowley, Ambassador at Paris, 1852–1867.* New York: Harper, 1929.

Wheaton, Henry. *The Elements of International Law.* 1836. 8th ed., edited by Richard Henry Dana, Jr., Boston: Little, Brown, 1866.

Williams, Ben A., ed. *A Diary from Dixie by Mary Boykin Chesnut.* Boston: Houghton Mifflin, 1949.

Woodward, C. Vann, ed. *Mary Chesnut's Civil War.* New Haven: Yale University Press, 1981.

Newspapers, Magazines, and Contemporary Journals

Blackwood's Edinburgh Magazine (England).
Punch (London).
Times (London).

SECONDARY MATERIALS

Books

Adams, Ephraim D. *Great Britain and the American Civil War*. 2 vols. New York: Longmans, Green, 1925.
Atkins, John B. *The Life of Sir William Howard Russell: The First Special Correspondent*. 2 vols. New York: E. P. Dutton, 1911.
Ball, Douglas B. *Financial Failure and Confederate Defeat*. Urbana: University of Illinois Press, 1991.
Bell, Herbert C. F. *Lord Palmerston*. 2 vols. London: Longmans, Green, 1936.
Beringer, Richard E., Herman Hattaway, Archer Jones, and William N. Still, Jr. *Why the South Lost the Civil War*. Athens: University of Georgia Press, 1986.
Bernath, Stuart L. *Squall Across the Atlantic: American Civil War Prize Cases and Diplomacy*. Berkeley: University of California Press, 1970.
Blumenthal, Henry. *A Reappraisal of Franco-American Relations, 1830–1871*. Chapel Hill: University of North Carolina Press, 1959.
Bock, Carl H. *Prelude to Tragedy: The Negotiation and Breakdown of the Tripartite Convention of London, October 31, 1861*. Philadelphia: University of Pennsylvania Press, 1966.
Bourne, Kenneth. *Britain and the Balance of Power in North America, 1815–1908*. Berkeley: University of California Press, 1967.
———. *The Foreign Policy of Victorian England, 1830–1902*. Oxford: Clarendon, 1970.
Burn, W. L. *The Age of Equipoise: A Study of the Mid-Victorian Generation*. London: Allen & Unwin, 1964.
Butler, Perry. *Gladstone: Church, State and Tractarianism—A Study of His Religious Ideas and Attitudes, 1809–1859*. New York: Oxford University Press, 1982.
Callahan, James M. *Diplomatic History of the Southern Confederacy*. New York: Frederick Ungar, 1901.
Carroll, Daniel B. *Henri Mercier and the American Civil War*. Princeton: Princeton University Press, 1971.
Case, Lynn M., and Warren F. Spencer. *The United States and France: Civil War Diplomacy*. Philadelphia: University of Pennsylvania Press, 1970.
Catton, Bruce. *The Coming Fury*. Garden City, N.Y.: Doubleday, 1961.

Cook, Adrian. *The Alabama Claims: American Politics and Anglo-American Relations, 1865–1872*. Ithaca: Cornell University Press, 1975.

Coulter, E. Merton. *The Confederate States of America, 1861–1865*. Baton Rouge: Louisiana State University Press, 1950.

Cox, LaWanda. *Lincoln and Black Freedom: A Study in Presidential Leadership*. Columbia: University of South Carolina Press, 1981.

Crawford, Martin. *The Anglo-American Crisis of the Mid-Nineteenth Century: The Times and America, 1850–1862*. Athens: University of Georgia Press, 1987.

Crook, D. P. *Diplomacy during the American Civil War*. New York: Wiley, 1975.

———. *The North, the South, and the Powers, 1861–1865*. New York: Wiley, 1974.

Cullop, Charles P. *Confederate Propaganda in Europe, 1861–1865*. Coral Gables, Fla.: University of Miami Press, 1969.

Current, Richard N. *The Lincoln Nobody Knows*. New York: Hill and Wang, 1958.

Donald, David H. *Charles Sumner and the Rights of Man*. New York: Knopf, 1970.

Duberman, Martin. *Charles Francis Adams, 1807–1886*. Boston: Houghton Mifflin, 1961.

Eaton, Clement. *A History of the Southern Confederacy*. New York: Free Press, 1954.

Ellison, Mary. *Support for Secession: Lancashire and the American Civil War*. Chicago: University of Chicago Press, 1972.

Evans, Eli N. *Judah P. Benjamin: The Jewish Confederate*. New York: Free Press, 1988.

Ferris, Norman B. *Desperate Diplomacy: William H. Seward's Foreign Policy, 1861*. Knoxville: University of Tennessee Press, 1976.

———. *The Trent Affair: A Diplomatic Crisis*. Knoxville: University of Tennessee Press, 1977.

Fitzmaurice, Lord Edmond. *The Life of Granville George Leveson Gower, Second Earl Granville, 1815–1891*. 2 vols. London: Longmans, Green, 1905.

Fladeland, Betty. *Men and Brothers: Anglo-American Antislavery Cooperation*. Urbana: University of Illinois Press, 1972.

Foner, Philip S. *British Labor and the American Civil War*. New York: Holmes and Meier, 1981.

Franklin, John Hope. *The Emancipation Proclamation*. Garden City, N. Y.: Doubleday, 1963.

Gardiner, A. G. *The Life of Sir William Harcourt*. 2 vols. New York: George H. Doran, 1923.

Hanna, Alfred J., and Kathryn A. Hanna. *Napoleon III and Mexico: American Triumph over Monarchy*. Chapel Hill: University of North Carolina Press, 1971.

Henderson, William O. *The Lancashire Cotton Famine, 1861–1865*. 1934.

Reprint. New York: Augustus M. Kelley, 1969.

Hendrick, Burton J. *Statesmen of the Lost Cause: Jefferson Davis and His Cabinet*. New York: Literary Guild, 1939.

Hyman, Harold M., and William M. Wiecek. *Equal Justice under Law: Constitutional Development, 1835–1875*. New York: Harper, 1982.

Jenkins, Brian. *Britain and the War for the Union*. 2 vols. Montreal: McGill-Queen's University Press, 1974, 1980.

Jones, Howard. *To the Webster-Ashburton Treaty: A Study in Anglo-American Relations, 1783–1843*. Chapel Hill: University of North Carolina Press, 1977.

Jordan, Donaldson, and Edwin J. Pratt. *Europe and the American Civil War*. Boston: Houghton Mifflin, 1931.

Kelly, Alfred H., Winfred A. Harbison, and Herman Belz. *The American Constitution: Its Origins and Development*. 6th ed. New York: Norton, 1983.

Krein, David F. *The Last Palmerston Government*. Ames: Iowa State University Press, 1978.

Lauterpacht, Hersh. *Recognition in International Law*. Cambridge, England: Cambridge University Press, 1947.

Leader, Robert E. *Life and Letters of John Arthur Roebuck*. London: Edward Arnold, 1897.

Lester, Richard I. *Confederate Finance and Purchasing in Great Britain*. Charlottesville: University Press of Virginia, 1975.

McPherson, James M. *Abraham Lincoln and the Second American Revolution*. New York: Oxford University Press, 1990.

———. *Battle Cry of Freedom: The Civil War Era*. New York: Oxford University Press, 1988.

Magnus, Philip. *Gladstone: A Biography*. 1954. Reprint. New York: E. P. Dutton, 1964.

Marx, Karl, and Frederick Engels. *The Civil War in the United States*. New York: International Publishers, 1937.

Matthew, H. C. G. *Gladstone, 1809–1874*. New York: Oxford University Press, 1986.

Maxwell, Herbert. *The Life and Letters of George William Frederick, Fourth Earl of Clarendon*. 2 vols. London: Edward Arnold, 1913.

Merli, Frank J. *Great Britain and the Confederate Navy, 1861–1865*. Bloomington: Indiana University Press, 1970.

Monaghan, Jay. *Diplomat in Carpet Slippers: Abraham Lincoln Deals with Foreign Affairs*. Indianapolis: Bobbs-Merrill, 1945.

Morley, John. *The Life of William Ewart Gladstone*. 3 vols. London: Macmillan, 1903.

Murfin, James V. *The Gleam of Bayonets: The Battle of Antietam and the Maryland Campaign of 1862*. New York: Thomas Yoseloff, 1965.

Nevins, Allan. *The War for the Union*. 4 vols. New York: Charles Scribner's Sons, 1959–71.

Newton, Lord. *Lord Lyons: A Record of British Diplomacy*. 2 vols. London: Edward Arnold, 1913.

Oates, Stephen B. *With Malice toward None: The Life of Abraham Lincoln*. New York: Harper & Row, 1977.

Owsley, Frank L. *King Cotton Diplomacy: Foreign Relations of the Confederate States of America*. Rev. by Harriet C. Owsley, Chicago: University of Chicago Press, 1959.

Parish, Peter J. *The American Civil War*. New York: Holmes and Meier, 1975.

Randall, James G. *Constitutional Problems under Lincoln*. Rev. ed. Urbana: University of Illinois Press, 1951.

Randall, James G., and David H. Donald. *The Civil War and Reconstruction*. 2d ed. Lexington, Mass.: D. C. Heath, 1969.

Rawley, James A. *Turning Points of the Civil War*. Lincoln: University of Nebraska Press, 1966.

Reid, T. Wemyss. *Life of the Right Honourable William Edward Forster*. 2 vols. London: Chapman and Hall, 1888.

Ridley, Jasper. *Lord Palmerston*. New York: E. P. Dutton, 1971.

Saul, Norman E. *Distant Friends: The United States and Russia, 1763–1867*. Lawrence: University Press of Kansas, 1991.

Schoonover, Thomas D. *Dollars over Dominion: The Triumph of Liberalism in Mexican-United States Relations, 1861–1867*. Baton Rouge: Louisiana State University Press, 1978.

Sears, Louis M. *John Slidell*. Durham: Duke University Press, 1925.

Sears, Stephen W. *Landscape Turned Red: The Battle of Antietam*. New York: Ticknor and Fields, 1983.

Spencer, Warren F. *The Confederate Navy in Europe*. University, Ala.: University of Alabama Press, 1983.

Stevens, Kenneth R. *Border Diplomacy: The Caroline and McLeod Affairs in Anglo-American–Canadian Relations, 1837–1842*. Tuscaloosa: University of Alabama Press, 1989.

Thistlethwaite, Frank. *The Anglo-American Connection in the Early Nineteenth Century*. Philadelphia: University of Pennsylvania Press, 1959.

Thomas, Benjamin P. *Russo-American Relations, 1815–1867*. Baltimore: Johns Hopkins Press, 1930.

Thomas, Benjamin P., and Harold M. Hyman. *Stanton: The Life and Times of Lincoln's Secretary of War*. New York: Knopf, 1962.

Thomas, Emory M. *The Confederate Nation, 1861–1865*. New York: Harper & Row, 1979.

Tilby, A. Wyatt. *Lord John Russell: A Study in Civil and Religious Liberty*. London: Cassell, 1930.

Tyrner-Tyrnauer, A. R. *Lincoln and the Emperors*. New York: Harcourt, Brace, 1962.

Vanauken, Sheldon. *The Glittering Illusion: English Sympathy for the Southern Confederacy*. Worthing, England: Churchman, 1988.

Van Deusen, Glyndon G. *William Henry Seward*. New York: Oxford University Press, 1967.

Walpole, Spencer. *The Life of Lord John Russell*. 2 vols. London: Longmans, Green, 1889.

Ward, Sir A. W., and G. P. Gooch, eds. *The Cambridge History of British Foreign Policy, 1783–1919*. 3 vols. Vol. 2: *1815–1866*. New York: Macmillan, 1923.

Warren, Gordon H. *Fountain of Discontent: The Trent Affair and Freedom of the Seas*. Boston: Northeastern University Press, 1981.

Willson, Beckles. *John Slidell and the Confederates in Paris (1862–65)*. New York: Minton, Balch, 1932.

Wise, Stephen R. *Lifeline of the Confederacy: Blockade Running during the Civil War*. Columbia: University of South Carolina Press, 1988.

Woldman, Albert A. *Lincoln and the Russians*. Cleveland: World, 1952.

Articles and Essays

Adamov, E. A. "Russia and the United States at the Time of the Civil War." *Journal of Modern History* 2 (December 1930): 586–602.

Adams, Charles Francis, Jr. "The British Proclamation of May, 1861." *Massachusetts Historical Society Proceedings* 48 (1915): 190–241.

———. "The Crisis of Foreign Intervention in the War of Secession, September–November, 1862." *Massachusetts Historical Society Proceedings* 47 (1914): 372–424.

Adams, Henry. "Why Did Not England Recognize the Confederacy?" *Massachusetts Historical Society Proceedings* 66 (1942): 204–22.

Bauer, Craig A. "The Last Effort: The Secret Mission of the Confederate Diplomat, Duncan F. Kenner." *Louisiana History* 22 (Winter 1981): 67–95.

Baxter, James P. "The British Government and Neutral Rights, 1861–1865." *American Historical Review* 34 (October 1928): 9–29.

———. "Some British Opinions as to Neutral Rights, 1861–1865." *American Journal of International Law* 23 (July 1929): 517–37.

Bellows, Donald. "A Study of British Conservative Reaction to the American Civil War." *Journal of Southern History* 51 (November 1985): 505–26.

Beloff, Max. "Historical Revision No. CXVIII: Great Britain and the American Civil War." *History* 37 (February 1952): 40–48.

Blaug, Mark. "The Productivity of Capital in the Lancashire Cotton Industry during the Nineteenth Century." *Economic History Review* 2d ser., 13 (1961): 358–81.

Blumenthal, Henry. "Confederate Diplomacy: Popular Notions and International Realities." *Journal of Southern History* 32 (May 1966): 151–71.

Bourne, Kenneth. "British Preparations for War with the North, 1861–

1862." *English Historical Review* 76 (October 1961): 600–632.

Brady, Eugene A. "A Reconsideration of the Lancashire 'Cotton Famine.'" *Agricultural History* 37 (July 1963): 156–62.

Brauer, Kinley J. "British Mediation and the American Civil War: A Reconsideration." *Journal of Southern History* 38 (February 1972): 49–64.

———. "Seward's 'Foreign War Panacea': An Interpretation." *New York History* 55 (April 1974): 133–57.

———. "The Slavery Problem in the Diplomacy of the American Civil War." *Pacific Historical Review* 46 (August 1977): 439–69.

Brook, Michael. "Confederate Sympathies in North-East Lancashire, 1862–1864." *Lancashire and Cheshire Antiquarian Society* 75–76 (1977): 211–17.

Claussen, Martin P. "Peace Factors in Anglo-American Relations, 1861–1865." *Mississippi Valley Historical Review* 26 (March 1940): 511–22.

Cohen, Victor H. "Charles Sumner and the *Trent* Affair." *Journal of Southern History* 22 (May 1956): 205–19.

Crook, D. P. "Portents of War: English Opinion on Secession." *Journal of American Studies* 4 (1970): 163–79.

Earle, Edward M. "Egyptian Cotton and the American Civil War." *Political Science Quarterly* 41 (December 1926): 520–45.

Ellsworth, Edward W. "Anglo-American Affairs in October of 1862." *Lincoln Herald* 66 (Summer 1964): 89–96.

Fehrenbacher, Don E. "Only His Stepchildren: Lincoln and the Negro." *Civil War History* 20 (December 1974): 293–310.

Ferris, Norman B. "William H. Seward and the Faith of a Nation." In *Traditions and Values: American Diplomacy, 1790–1865*, edited by Norman A. Graebner, 153–77. Lanham, Md.: University Press of America, 1985.

Fredrickson, George M. "A Man but Not a Brother: Abraham Lincoln and Racial Equality." *Journal of Southern History* 41 (February 1975): 39–58.

Gentry, Judith F. "A Confederate Success in Europe: The Erlanger Loan." *Journal of Southern History* 36 (May 1970): 157–88.

Ginzberg, Eli. "The Economics of British Neutrality during the American Civil War." *Agricultural History* 10 (October 1936): 147–56.

Golder, Frank A. "The American Civil War through the Eyes of a Russian Diplomat." *American Historical Review* 26 (April 1921): 454–63.

Graebner, Norman A. "European Interventionism and the Crisis of 1862." *Journal of the Illinois State Historical Society* 69 (February 1976): 35–45.

———. "Northern Diplomacy and European Neutrality." In *Why the North Won the Civil War*, edited by David Donald, 55–78. 1960. Reprint. New York: Collier, 1962.

Greenleaf, Richard. "British Labor against American Slavery." *Science and Society* 17 (Winter 1953): 42–58.

Harrison, Royden. "British Labor and American Slavery." *Science and Society* 25 (December 1961): 291–319.

———. "British Labour and the Confederacy: A Note on the Southern Sympathies of Some British Working Class Journals and Leaders during the American Civil War." *International Review of Social History* 2 (1957): 78–105.

Heckman, Richard A. "British Press Reaction to the Emancipation Proclamation." *Lincoln Herald* 71 (Winter 1969): 150–53.

Henderson, Conway W. "The Anglo-American Treaty of 1862 in Civil War Diplomacy." *Civil War History* 15 (December 1969): 308–19.

Hernon, Joseph M., Jr. "British Sympathies in the American Civil War: A Reconsideration." *Journal of Southern History* 33 (August 1967): 356–67.

Jenkins, Brian. "Frank Lawley and the Confederacy." *Civil War History* 23 (June 1977): 144–60.

Johnson, Robert E. "Investment by Sea: The Civil War Blockade." *American Neptune* 32 (January 1972): 45–57.

Jones, Robert H. "Anglo-American Relations, 1861–1865, Reconsidered." *Mid-America* 45 (January 1963): 36–49.

———. "Long Live the King?" *Agricultural History* 37 (July 1963): 166–69.

Jones, Wilbur D. "The British Conservatives and the American Civil War." *American Historical Review* 58 (April 1953): 527–43.

Khasigian, Amos. "Economic Factors and British Neutrality, 1861–1865." *Historian* 25 (August 1963): 451–65.

Logan, Frenise A. "India—Britain's Substitute for American Cotton, 1861–1865." *Journal of Southern History* 24 (November 1958): 472–80.

Logan, Kevin J. "The *Bee-Hive* Newspaper and British Working Class Attitudes toward the American Civil War." *Civil War History* 22 (December 1976): 337–48.

Long, John S. "Glory-Hunting off Havana: Wilkes and the *Trent* Affair." *Civil War History* 9 (June 1963): 133–44.

Lorimer, Douglas A. "The Role of Anti-Slavery Sentiment in English Reactions to the American Civil War." *Historical Journal* 19 (June 1976): 405–20.

McConnell, Roland C. "From Preliminary to Final Emancipation Proclamation: The First Hundred Days." *Journal of Negro History* 48 (October 1963): 260–76.

Maurer, Oscar. " 'Punch' on Slavery and Civil War in America, 1841–1865." *Victorian Studies* 1 (September 1957): 5–28.

Merli, Frank J., and Theodore A. Wilson. "The British Cabinet and the Confederacy." *Maryland Historical Magazine* 65 (Fall 1970): 239–62.

Milne, A. Taylor. "The Lyons-Seward Treaty of 1862." *American Historical Review* 38 (April 1933): 511–25.

Oates, Stephen B. "Henry Hotze: Confederate Agent Abroad." *Historian* 27 (February 1965): 131–54.

———. " 'The Man of Our Redemption': Abraham Lincoln and the Emancipation of the Slaves." *Presidential Studies Quarterly* 9 (Winter 1979): 15–25.

Park, Joseph H. "The English Workingmen and the American Civil War."
Political Science Quarterly 39 (September 1924): 432–57.

St. Clair, Sadie D. "Slavery as a Diplomatic Factor in Anglo-American
Relations during the Civil War." *Journal of Negro History* 30 (July 1945):
260–75.

Scherer, Paul H. "Partner or Puppet? Lord John Russell at the Foreign
Office, 1859–1862." *Albion* 19 (Fall 1987): 347–71.

Schmidt, Louis B. "The Influence of Wheat and Cotton on Anglo-American
Relations during the Civil War." *Iowa Journal of History and Politics* 16
(July 1918): 400–439.

Sears, Louis M. "A Confederate Diplomat at the Court of Napoleon III."
American Historical Review 26 (January 1921): 255–81.

Spencer, Warren F. "The Jewett-Greeley Affair: A Private Scheme for
French Mediation in the American Civil War." *New York History* 51 (April
1970): 238–68.

Whitridge, Arnold. "British Liberals and the American Civil War." *History
Today* 12 (October 1962): 688–95.

Wright, D. G. "Bradford and the American Civil War." *Journal of British
Studies* 8 (May 1969): 69–85.

Zorn, Roman J. "John Bright and the British Attitude to the American Civil
War." *Mid-America* 38 (July 1956): 131–45.

Dissertations, Theses, and Unpublished Manuscripts

Bass, Patrick G. "Fall of Crisis: European Intervention and the American
Civil War, September–November, 1862." Ph.D. dissertation, Clare-
mont, 1986.

Bourne, Kenneth. "The Foreign Secretaryship of Lord Stanley, July 1866–
December 1868." Ph.D. dissertation, University of London, 1955.

Gallas, Stanley. "Lord Lyons and the Civil War, 1859–1864: A British
Perspective." Ph.D. dissertation, University of Illinois at Chicago
Circle, 1982.

Merli, Frank J. "The American Way with Blockades: Reflections on the
Union Blockade of the South." Paper delivered before the Tenth Naval
History Symposium, U.S. Naval Academy, Annapolis, Maryland, Sep-
tember 1991.

Vanauken, Sheldon. "English Sympathy for the South: The Glittering
Illusion." B.Litt. thesis, Oxford University, 1957.

INDEX

Abolition. *See* Slavery

Adams, Charles Francis (Union minister in London), 1, 7, 8, 15, 18, 23, 27, 32, 33, 42–66 passim, 70, 71, 76, 77, 84, 90–140 passim, 147, 151, 152, 153, 159, 168, 171, 182, 183, 185, 186, 192, 210, 220, 222, 223, 225, 229, 230, 237 (n. 44), 238 (n. 12), 241 (n. 8), 242 (n. 18), 247 (n. 14), 249 (n. 30), 271 (n. 40); described, 30–31; tempers Seward's dispatches, 31; first meeting with Lord John Russell, 34–35; believes war with England imminent over *Trent*, 89; instrumental in halting Union arms deals with British firms, 122–23; considers slavery the central issue in war, 123; supports Lincoln's move against slavery, 132; protests Confederate shipbuilding activities in England, 146

Adams, Charles Francis, Jr. (son of Union minister in England), 30, 83, 84, 88–89, 222–23

Adams, Henry (son and secretary of Union minister in England), 54–55, 59, 77–78, 84, 89, 90, 94, 96, 97–98, 105, 127, 130, 133, 134, 136, 155, 159

Adams, John, 30

Adams, John Quincy, 30

Alabama (ship), 68, 146–47, 149, 230

Albert, Prince: role in *Trent* affair, 85

Alexander II (Russian tsar), 152

American Colonization Society: supported by Lincoln, 131

American Union, The (Spence), 149, 258 (n. 20)

Anderson, H. Percy, 192–93

Antietam (Sharpsburg), battle of (1862), 8, 167–80 passim, 185, 225, 262 (n. 8), 264 (n. 27), 264–65 (n. 30)

Antislavery. *See* Slavery

Anti-Slavery Society (British), 119

Appomattox Courthouse: Confederate surrender (1865), 230

Argyll, Duke of (George John Douglas Campbell; British lord privy seal), 94, 149, 154, 168, 225; pro-Union, 71, 84; opposes intervention, 151, 157–58, 169–70, 181, 182, 183, 187, 189; considers slavery the central issue in war, 158

Armistice, 8, 10, 36, 116, 204, 210, 211, 218

Austin, John (British legal theorist), 38, 214, 224, 269 (n. 24)

Austria, 123, 145, 160, 164, 193, 194, 195, 216, 217, 269 (n. 23)

Balance of power: in North America, 11, 108

Bates, Edward (Union attorney general), 59, 159; fears race war in South, 17

Bee-Hive (London): favors Southern separation, 85–86, 246 (n. 8); opposes proclamation of emancipation, 176

Belgium, 217

Belligerent, 38, 44, 46, 49, 64, 67, 128. *See also* England

Belmont, August, 141, 142

Benjamin, Judah P. (Confederate attorney general; secretary of state), 33, 111, 112, 116, 133, 155, 168, 201, 202, 203, 227

Bermuda (ship), 68

Blackwood's Edinburgh Magazine: opposes proclamation of emancipation, 177

Blair, Montgomery (Union postmaster general), 141

Blockade, 39, 236 (n. 24); paper, 13, 47, 49, 53, 55, 60, 106, 130, 202. *See also* Lincoln, Abraham; Union

Border states, 16, 106, 117, 130, 131, 143, 144, 150, 174, 185

Boston Courier, 90

Brazil, 155

Bremen, 5

Bright, John (member of Parliament), 151, 158; pro-Union, 90, 96, 183, 225; opposes war over *Trent*, 91, 92, 94, 95; considers Southern separation a fait accompli, 96; favors neutrality, 154–55; opposes intervention, 183

Browning, Orville (U.S. senator from Illinois), 55, 88, 91, 98

Brunow, Baron Philip (Russian ambassador to London), 106, 220, 264 (n. 28)

Bulloch, James (Confederate agent in Europe), 202

Bull Run (Manassas), battle of: first (1861), 8, 56, 57–58, 59, 60, 62, 68, 73, 74, 77, 78, 83, 86, 96, 100, 132, 154, 160; second (1862), 159, 160, 162, 163, 164, 166, 168

Bunch, Robert (British consul in Charleston), 62–66, 67, 70, 71, 102, 242 (nn. 15, 18), 247 (n. 14)

Butler, Benjamin (Union general): issues "woman order" in New Orleans (1862), 126, 254 (n. 7)

Buxton, Thomas Fowell, 71–72

Canada, 3, 11, 20, 45, 46, 58, 60, 68, 75, 85, 93, 94, 95, 96, 97, 111, 177, 190, 223, 228, 261 (n. 1)

Canning, George (British foreign secretary), 46, 212, 214

Canning, Stratford, 151

Cecil, Lord Robert, 78, 245 (n. 41)

Central America, 26

Charleston Mercury, 50

Chase, Salmon P. (Union secretary of treasury), 141, 142, 159, 175

Chesnut, Mary Boykin, 119

Chicago Christians of All Denominations, 172

Chicago Tribune, 172

China, 155, 158

Civil War: dual status of, 2, 44

Clarendon, fourth earl of (George William Frederick Villiers), 77, 170–71; opposes intervention, 184, 189, 194

Cobden, Richard (member of Parliament), 129, 131–32, 154, 203, 225; pro-Union, 90, 183; opposes war over *Trent*, 91, 92, 94, 95; considers Southern separation a fait accompli, 96; favors joint intervention, 123, 151; fears slave uprising caused by emancipation, 176; opposes intervention, 183

Confederacy: secession, 3, 10, 20–37 passim, 43, 44, 55, 58, 70, 83, 108, 123, 145, 149, 185, 189, 216; denies slavery an issue in war, 4, 5, 37, 96, 108; shipbuilding in England, 29, 68, 110, 146–47, 226, 230; commissioners in Europe, 30, 32–33, 45, 51, 59, 62, 70, 71, 80, 86, 90, 101, 251 (n. 11); King Cotton diplomacy, 32, 113, 139, 251 (n. 11); restricts cotton exports, 45, 69, 119, 124, 125, 131, 136; shipbuilding in France, 201–2; offers

123, 144, 145, 146, 154, 166,
170, 182, 183, 186, 187, 192,
211, 215, 223, 225; does not
understand the war, 3–4, 36, 43,
55, 70–71, 108, 127; considers
Southern separation the solution,
3, 4, 126, 128, 138, 140, 162,
178, 212; humanitarian concerns
regarding the war, 4, 8, 9, 35,
70, 96, 98, 99, 100, 108, 137,
149, 161, 212, 228; interest in
intervention, 5, 8, 10–11, 35, 36,
74–75, 86, 126–39 passim, 144,
145, 146, 150–59 passim, 172;
lacks terms of settlement, 5, 24,
150, 177, 182, 190, 196, 217,
228, 230; considers Southern
separation a fait accompli, 7–8,
22, 54, 57, 68, 78, 99, 108; criti-
cizes Union for war of subjugation, 8; influence of mill workers
on government policy, 8, 9, 54,
69, 90–91, 95, 97, 104–5, 130,
132, 138, 155, 156, 167, 170–71,
184, 201, 246 (n. 8), 250 (n. 1),
260 (n. 32), 263 (n. 14); commercial concerns regarding the
war, 8, 13, 34, 42, 45, 50, 54, 85,
96, 98, 108, 123, 149, 161, 228;
fears slave insurrection in South,
8, 16, 35, 59, 72, 98, 99, 135,
140, 161, 174, 175, 179, 180,
226, 264–65 (n. 30); interest in
dismembered United States, 8,
48, 85, 107, 134; interest in
Southern cotton, 11, 16, 26, 32,
33, 35, 59, 72, 75, 78, 90, 91,
99, 104, 105, 106, 113, 129, 130,
136, 137, 139, 140, 146, 154,
155, 156, 158, 170, 178, 185,
212, 217, 225, 246 (n. 8); concert
with France, 13, 14, 15, 24, 32,
41, 45, 47, 49, 51, 52, 53, 72, 73,
86–87, 114, 116, 119, 124, 187,
191, 234 (n. 18); interest in

Northern wheat, 26, 137, 183,
256 (n. 29); queen's proclamation
of neutrality (1861), 27–30, 31–
32, 33, 34, 35, 42, 43, 44, 45,
51, 54, 147; believes conflict a
civil war, 28, 35–36, 43, 67;
prize issue, 28–29, 40, 42, 43,
49, 67, 83, 92, 240 (n. 24); cotton surplus, 45, 50, 54, 60, 69,
74, 95, 123, 171; intervention in
Mexico, 76–77, 114, 115, 204;
considers proclamation of emancipation an act of desperation,
154, 179, 225; cotton famine
(1862–63), 171, 226, 262–63
(n. 14); cabinet meeting regarding Napoleon's intervention
plan (1862), 217–20; workers
praise Emancipation Proclamation, 225
Erlanger loan (1863), 252 (n. 23)
Everett, Edward (former U.S. minister in London), 68, 70–71, 99;
urges mediation by England,
France, and Russia (1861), 5

Field, Cyrus, 223, 271 (n. 42)
Flahault, Count Charles de (French
ambassador to London), 120,
187, 191
Florida (ship), 68, 110, 111
Foreign Enlistment Act, British
(1819), 28, 110, 146
Forster, William E. (member of
Parliament): favors neutrality,
29, 71–72, 105; fears slave insurrection, 135; opposes intervention, 182
Fort Donelson: captured by Union
(1862), 104, 105, 107, 115, 143
Fort Henry: captured by Union
(1862), 104, 107, 115, 143
Fort Sumter, battle of (1861), 1, 3,
22, 24, 35, 71
Fort Warren, 81, 83

France, 10, 20; neutrality, 2, 3, 14, 27, 88; favors intervention, 5, 72–73, 74–75, 86, 138, 139, 145, 156, 157, 159, 160, 164, 169, 176, 199–210 passim, 218, 219, 220, 221, 222; interest in Southern cotton, 72, 73, 74, 114, 123, 155, 156, 170; intervention in Mexico, 76, 77, 114–15, 252 (n. 26); would withdraw belligerent rights from Confederacy, 114; fears slave uprising in South, 176; recognizes American independence (1778), 214, 215

Frank Leslie's Illustrated Newspaper, 228

Fredericksburg, battle of (1862), 226

Frémont, John C., 244 (n. 34)

Fugitive Slave Law (1850), 83, 86

Garnett, James (British mill owner), 104, 105, 119, 171, 263 (n. 14)

Gasparin, Count Agénor-Etienne de (French writer), 143

Geneva: arbitral commission (1871), 229–30

Germany, 94

Gerolt, Baron Frederick C. J. von (Prussian minister in Washington), 36

Gettysburg, battle of (1863), 227

Gladstone, William E. (British chancellor of exchequer), 64, 114, 148, 165, 266 (n. 17), 269 (n. 23), 270 (n. 27); considers Southern separation irrevocable, 4, 184; favors intervention, 7, 133, 139, 145, 149, 150–51, 155, 158–59, 166, 167, 168, 180, 181, 185, 194–95, 196, 218, 219, 222–23, 258 (n. 20); concerned about workers, 9; Newcastle speech (1862), 182–86, 191, 196,

265 (n. 2), 266 (n. 7); fears slave uprising in South, 195

Gorchakov, Prince Alexander (Russian foreign minister), 264 (n. 28)

Grant, Ulysses S., 104, 116, 143, 272 (n. 4)

Granville, Earl (cabinet member sitting in House of Lords), 196; opposes intervention, 151, 169, 170, 181–82

Great Britain. *See* England

Greeley, Horace, 153, 272–73 (n. 4)

Gregory, William (member of Parliament): pro-Confederacy, 22, 54, 136, 250 (n. 3); motion to renounce blockade, 105, 108

Grey, Sir George (cabinet member from Home Office), 206; opposes intervention, 182, 192, 195

Grier, Robert (U.S. Supreme Court justice), 238 (n. 11)

Grote, George, 223

Grotius, Hugo (Dutch legal theorist), 38

Haiti: recognized by Lincoln (1862), 131

Hammond, Edmund (British under secretary for foreign affairs), 133, 153, 168; favors intervention, 146; anti-Union, 154, 185; opposes proclamation of emancipation, 176; fears slave uprising in South, 185

Hammond, James H., 32

Hampton Roads: battle of ironclads (1862), 110

Harcourt, William Vernon ("Historicus"), 210–11, 216, 223, 269 (n. 19)

Hay, John (Lincoln's secretary): fears race war in South, 17

"Historicus." *See* Harcourt, William Vernon

with Confederate *Merrimack* (1862), 110
Moran, Benjamin (assistant secretary to Charles Francis Adams), 84, 93, 96, 101–19 passim, 127, 130, 133, 134, 135, 136, 153, 168, 186, 220, 254 (n. 8), 270 (n. 37)
Morning Herald (London): favors intervention, 162
Morning Post (London): favors intervention, 149–50, 162
Morocco, 158
Morrill Tariff (1861), 34, 68
Mure, Robert, 62, 63, 64

Naples, 22
Napoleon I (emperor of France), 72
Napoleon III (emperor of France), 20, 72, 73, 86, 94, 97, 107, 121, 139, 191, 200, 246 (n. 8), 258 (n. 23), 272 (n. 4); intervention in Mexico, 87, 91, 115, 170, 204; favors intervention in American war, 103, 119–20, 187, 198–205 passim, 210, 216, 218, 219, 221, 222, 226, 229; regrets granting belligerent rights to Confederacy, 114; skeptical about Union restoration, 129
Napoleon, Prince Jerome Bonaparte, 73
Napoleonic Wars (1793–1815), 28, 212
National Intelligencer (Washington), 125
Neutrality. *See* England; France
New Brunswick, 93
Newcastle, Duke of (cabinet member from Colonial Office), 93–94, 135; opposes intervention, 181, 192
New Orleans: captured by Union (1862), 119, 120–21, 122, 123, 125, 127, 136, 146, 213

New York Herald, 58
New York Tribune, 104, 153
North. *See* Union
Nova Scotia, 93

O'Neil, John (Lancashire mill worker), 104–5, 110, 171, 263 (n. 14)
Oregon: settlement (1846), 26

Palmerston, Henry John Temple, third viscount (British prime minister), 2, 3, 9, 26, 35–36, 38, 42–43, 45, 54, 57, 62, 63, 64, 66, 69, 73, 87–100 passim, 106, 111, 114, 120, 132, 133, 134, 147, 156, 159, 170, 176, 183, 184, 189, 192, 194, 201, 203, 228, 239 (n. 21), 242 (n. 15), 245 (n. 5), 266 (nn. 7, 16), 267 (n. 21), 269 (n. 19), 270 (n. 34); believes Southern separation irrevocable, 4, 22–23, 24, 128, 220, 222, 227; heads coalition cabinet, 8; opposes intervention, 8, 51, 75–76, 127, 128, 135–36, 272 (n. 4); described, 18–20; opposes African slave trade, 20; intervention in Mexico, 76, 77, 115; prepares for war over *Trent*, 84–85, 93; pragmatist, 108, 181; denounces Butler's "woman order," 126; favors intervention, 150–51, 154, 162–63, 164, 165, 166, 167, 168, 169, 196; hesitancy about intervention, 177–97 passim, 205, 218, 219, 222, 223, 224, 225, 229, 230, 264 (n. 27), 265 (n. 30), 271 (nn. 42, 1); opposes proclamation of emancipation, 191
Palmerston, Lady, 110, 126, 167
Parliament (British), 48, 96, 97, 98, 101, 107, 119, 151, 170, 226; balance between Liberals and Con-

America), 23–24, 25, 33, 50, 53, 55, 58, 73, 83, 88
Russia, 5, 145, 157, 164, 165, 166, 178, 187, 191, 193, 194, 199, 204, 205, 207, 208, 209, 216, 217; pro-Union, 86, 87, 151, 152, 195, 196, 201, 229, 249 (n. 30), 264 (n. 28); rejects Napoleon's interventionist plan, 218, 220

Sanford, Henry (Union minister in Brussels), 156
San Jacinto (ship), 80, 81
Santo Domingo, 15
Saratoga, battle of (1777), 214
Schurz, Carl (Union minister in Madrid), 118–19
Scott, Winfield (Union general), 88, 247 (n. 12)
Search, act of, 83, 93, 118
Seward, Frederick W. (assistant secretary of state and son of secretary), 52, 59
Seward, William H. (Union secretary of state), 1, 11, 23, 24, 28, 30, 31, 32, 33, 36, 38, 46, 47, 48–49, 54, 55, 60–73 passim, 83–123 passim, 129, 130, 131, 138, 143, 145, 153, 157, 160–61, 171, 175, 182, 206, 210, 215, 220, 221–22, 229, 230, 241 (n. 8), 242 (nn. 13, 15), 247 (n. 14), 253 (n. 28); warns that intervention means war with Union, 4, 6, 7, 12–13, 14, 15, 18, 27, 45, 53, 88, 89, 140, 147, 149, 151; opposes mediation, 5, 127–28; believes slavery the root cause of war, 7; calls for war with European nations intervening in Western Hemisphere, 15, 77; sees political dangers in war over slavery, 16; fears race war in South, 17; meeting with

Lyons and Mercier (1861), 51–52; note to Lyons regarding Trent, 92–93; treaty with Lyons outlawing African slave trade (1862), 118, 253 (n. 32); warns that intervention might spawn slave revolt, 125–26, 139, 203; urges postponement of proclamation of emancipation until Union victory on battlefield, 141; favors move against slavery, 142; opposes Russian intervention (1861), 231–32 (n. 3)
Seymour, Horatio, 199, 206
Shaftesbury, Earl of, 167–68
Sharpsburg. See Antietam, battle of
Shiloh (Pittsburg Landing), battle of (1862), 115, 116, 117, 143
Slavery, 23, 35, 48, 54, 60, 78, 86, 94–108 passim, 135, 136, 140, 142, 144, 149, 154, 156, 159, 161, 170, 182, 191, 206, 222, 225, 226, 272 (n. 4); as root cause of war, 7; abolition of, 15, 16, 55, 68, 71, 72, 107, 129, 139, 141, 143, 153, 158, 173, 183, 189, 190, 217; antislavery sentiment in Union, 16, 117–19, 131, 172, 179; inseparable from question of Union, 17, 55, 109; antislavery sentiment in England, 17, 59, 71, 137, 141, 151, 155, 158, 189; African slave trade, 20, 33, 118; compensation and colonization for slaves declared free in District of Columbia (1862), 118. See also Confederacy; Union
Slidell, John (Confederate minister in Paris), 107, 109, 120, 121, 132, 133, 139, 145, 154, 167, 168, 199, 201, 202, 203, 220, 222, 272 (n. 4); Trent, 80–98 passim
Smith, Caleb (Union secretary of interior), 159

Somerset, Duke of, 93
South. *See* Confederacy
South Carolina: secession (1860), 20
Spain, 15, 215; intervention in Mexico, 76, 77, 114, 115, 204
Spectator (London), 211; pro-Union but unhappy with proclamation of emancipation, 176
Spence, James (author of *The American Union*), 149, 258 (n. 20)
Stanton, Edwin M. (Union secretary of war), 141, 159
Stoeckl, Baron Edouard de (Russian minister in Washington), 5, 12, 14, 115, 152, 209, 220, 264 (n. 23); considers intervention, 199, 206, 231–32 (n. 3); believes proclamation of emancipation intended to cause slave uprising, 272 (n. 3)
Story, Joseph (U.S. Supreme Court justice), 46
Stowe, Harriet Beecher (author of *Uncle Tom's Cabin*), 72
Stuart, William (British chargé in Washington), 132, 147, 156, 158, 160, 164, 169, 178, 190, 203, 255 (n. 19); criticized, 8, 166, 206, 208; believes Union will instigate slave rebellion, 139, 175, 176; anti-Union, 152–53, 154; favors intervention, 157, 199, 206, 207
Sumner, Charles, 27, 32, 51, 91, 92, 94, 153, 154
Sutherland, Duchess of, 158

Taylor, P. A. (member of Parliament): pro-Union, 134–35
Thouvenel, Edouard (French foreign secretary), 41, 73, 115, 120, 154, 156, 157, 160, 191, 201; favors intervention, 121
Times (London), 23, 36, 58, 77, 96,

153, 182, 211, 222, 269 (n. 19); recommends Southern separation, 126; favors recognition of Confederacy, 162; fears slave uprising in South, 176; opposes proclamation of emancipation, 179–80; opposes Napoleon's intervention plan, 220, 270 (n. 34)
Toombs, Robert (Confederate secretary of state), 251 (n. 11)
Trent (ship): crisis (1861–62), 9, 80–99, 100, 101, 102, 105, 107, 113, 120, 133, 135, 219, 245 (n. 5)
Tropic Wind (U.S. admiralty court case in 1861), 46, 51, 239 (n. 18), 240 (n. 25)
Turner, Nat, 174

Union: calls South's resistance an insurrection, 1, 2, 29, 35, 38, 43, 46, 47, 53; blockade, 2, 3, 12, 26, 34, 45–69 passim, 74, 75, 76, 80, 86–113 passim, 120, 121, 123, 131, 136, 165, 170, 177, 189, 199–212 passim, 218, 226, 229–30, 239 (n. 19), 249 (n. 30), 251 (n. 11), 252 (n. 23), 258 (n. 20); calls South's resistance a rebellion, 2, 26, 44; denies slavery an issue in war, 4, 5, 15, 16, 22, 34, 37, 96, 108; mystical concept of, 4–5, 22; port closing issue, 49, 50, 55, 60, 61, 68, 103, 239 (n. 21); "stone fleet," 91, 103, 249 (n. 30). *See also* Lincoln, Abraham
U.S. Constitution. *See* Constitution, U.S.

Vane-Tempest, Lord Adolphus (member of Parliament): pro-Confederacy, 135
Vattel, Emmerich de (Swiss theorist